P9-CBL-421

Cultivating Coaching Mindsets

AN ACTION GUIDE FOR LITERACY LEADERS

Cultivating Coaching Mindsets

AN ACTION GUIDE FOR LITERACY LEADERS

RITA M. BEAN AND JACY IPPOLITO

Copyright © 2016 by Learning Sciences International

All rights reserved. Tables, forms, and sample documents may be reproduced or displayed only by educators, local school sites, or nonprofit entities who have purchased the book. Except for that usage, no part of this book may be reproduced, transmitted, or displayed in any form or by any means (photocopying, digital or electronic transmittal, electronic or mechanical display, or other means) without the prior written permission of the publisher.

1400 Centrepark Blvd, Suite 1000
West Palm Beach, FL 33401
717-845-6300

email: pub@learningsciences.com
learningsciences.com

Printed in the United States of America

21 20 19 18 17 16   1 2 3 4 5 6

Library of Congress Control Number: 2016935666

Publisher's Cataloging-in-Publication Data
provided by Five Rainbows Cataloging Services

Names: Bean, Rita M. | Ippolito, Jacy.

Title: Cultivating coaching mindsets : an action guide for literacy leaders / Rita M. Bean [and] Jacy Ippolito.

Description: West Palm Beach, FL : Learning Sciences, 2016.

Identifiers: ISBN 978-1-941112-33-5 (pbk.)

Subjects: LCSH: Literacy--Study and teaching. | Language arts teachers. | Education. | Reading. | BISAC: EDUCATION / Professional Development. | EDUCATION / Teaching Methods & Materials / Language Arts.

Classification: LCC LB1576 .B41 2016 (print) | LCC LB1576 (ebook) | DDC 372.6/044--dc23.

MIX
Paper from
responsible sources
FSC® C008955

Table of Contents

Acknowledgments xi

About the Authors xiii

Preface xv

CHAPTER 1

Remodeling Schools for Effective Literacy Learning: The Case for Coaching 1

Basic Beliefs About Coaching 2
Pathways Into Coaching 4
What Is Coaching and How Does It Support High-Quality Literacy Instruction? 5
Framework for Thinking and Working Like a Coach 6
Major Assumptions About Coaching 13
Summary 17
Activities 17

CHAPTER 2

Cultivating Coaching Mindsets: Ways of Thinking and Working Like a Coach 19

Frame 1: Thinking Like a Leader; Authentic Leadership and Leading Adult
    Learning 20
Frame 2: Thinking Like a Facilitator; Coaching Roles, Stances, and Positionality 26
Frame 3: Thinking Like a Designer; Considering Form and Function 29
Frame 4: Thinking Like an Advocate; Standing for Something 31

Summary 36

Activities 36

CHAPTER 3

Coaching for Student Success: What 21st Century Literacy Leaders Need to Know

Coaching for Student Success: What 21st Century
Literacy Leaders Need to Know 37

Standards as the Driver for Developing Curriculum That Meets High Expectations . 38

Major Shifts: How *Now* Is Different From *Then* 40

Marrying the Content and Processes of Effective Literacy Instruction 44

Technology as a Tool to Support Teacher and Student Learning 51

Thinking Ahead to School-Wide Literacy Programming 54

Summary 55

Activities 55

CHAPTER 4

Analyzing and Shaping School Culture: All Systems Go!

Analyzing and Shaping School Culture: All Systems Go! 57

School Culture: How Important Is It? 59

Creating Change at the Organizational Level: Improving Literacy Instruction 62

Diversity: Human Capital 64

The Principal and Coaching 67

Working With Other Specialized Professionals 71

Example of a School Change Initiative: The Importance of System-Wide Change . . . 72

Summary 73

Activities 73

CHAPTER 5

Overview: Ways of Working With Teachers

Overview: Ways of Working With Teachers 75

The Power of Language: Talking With Individuals and Groups of Teachers 76

The Power of Discussion-Based Protocols 79

Coaching Activities for Developing Relationships With Individuals and Groups
    of Teachers 83

Summary 90

Activities 90

CHAPTER 6

Working With Individual Teachers to Analyze and Transform Instructional Practices 91

Modeling 93
Co-Teaching 95
Observing 97
The Observation Cycle 99
Summary 111
Activities 111

CHAPTER 7

Working With Groups to Establish Schools as Places of Learning 113

Why Coaches Work With Groups 114
General Guidelines for Working With Groups of All Sizes 116
Small-Group Coaching 119
Other Strategies for Facilitating Small Groups 122
Large-Group Presentations 126
Ideas for Follow-Up 128
Group Activities That Support the Development of Professional Learning
    Communities 128
Summary 132
Activities 132

CHAPTER 8

Assessment as a Guide for Student Literacy Learning and School Improvement 135

Assessment of Student Learning: What and Why 136
Large-Scale, High-Stakes Measures: Potential and Pitfalls 138
Ideas for Literacy Leaders: Using Data to Improve Classroom Instruction 141
Teach Students to Self-Assess and Set Their Own Learning Goals 146
Using Data for School and District Improvement 147
Summary 151
Activities 151

CHAPTER 9

Developing, Implementing, and Sustaining School-Wide Literacy Programs 153

The Role of Literacy Leaders in Improving School-Wide Literacy 154

Establishing a Literacy Leadership Team 156

The Needs-Assessment Process 159

The Comprehensive Literacy Plan: Planning for Action 162

Implementation and Sustainability: Keys to Change 164

Developing or Selecting Materials for the Literacy Program 168

Maintaining the Dual Focus on Individuals and the System 170

Summary 171

Activities 172

CHAPTER 10

Working With Families and Communities 173

The Importance of Engaging Families and Community 174

Ideas for Developing a School Culture That Understands, Values, and Celebrates the Diversity of Its Communities 175

Build Two-Way Communication Channels to Enhance Family Understanding and Involvement 178

Capitalizing on Community Resources by Establishing Relationships 181

Summary 186

Activities 186

CHAPTER 11

The Literacy Leader as Lifelong Learner 187

A Quick Caveat About "Expertise" 188

Knowledge That Supports Literacy Leadership Work 190

Self-Assessments: Possibilities and Pitfalls 197

A Quick Reminder About the Many Pathways to Becoming an Effective Coach 203

A Final Note About Our Own Coaching Habits of Mind 204

Summary 204

Activities 204

CHAPTER 12

Coaching Cases: Stories of Coaches and Coaching

Coaching Cases: Stories of Coaches and Coaching 207
Case 1: The Evolution of a Coach. 208
Case 2: Learning, Leading Learning, and Enacting Disciplinary Literacy at
    Brookline High School 212
Case 3: Conducting a Needs Assessment: An Example of the CALS in Action 218
Case 4: Pennsylvania Institute for Instructional Coaching (PIIC) 220

Appendix A: Ways of Thinking and Working Like a Coach
Framework 225

Appendix B: For Further Study: Resources for Literacy Leaders 231

Appendix C: Note-Taking Organizer When Coach Is Modeling
Instruction 239

Appendix D: Observation Protocol for Content-Area Instruction. 241

Appendix E: Lesson Analysis Guide for the Post-Observation
Conversation 245

Appendix F: Developing a Comprehensive Assessment System. 247

Appendix G: Sample Assessment-Focused Professional Learning
Experiences 251
The Large-Group Meeting 251
Follow-Up Questions for the Grade-Level or Academic Team. 252
Implementation 252
Individual Support and Feedback 252

Appendix H: Developing a Comprehensive Reading Plan:
Questions to Consider 253
Curriculum Questions 253
Instruction Questions 254
Assessment Questions 254
Process-for-Change Questions. 255

Appendix I: Action-Planning Guide 257

Appendix J: An Adapted Data-Driven Dialogue Protocol From
Hudson High School 261
Phase I: Predictions—5 Minutes—On Your Own 261
Phase II: Observations—15 Minutes—On Your Own 262
Phase III: Sharing Observations—15 Minutes—In Small Groups 262
Phase IV: Inferences Dialogue—15 Minutes—In Small Groups 262
Phase V: Whole-Team Inference Dialogue—20 Minutes—As a Whole Team 262

References 265

Index 281

Acknowledgments

Thank you to my family for your love and support: Erin Eichelberger, Derek and Barbie Eichelberger, and their children, Ethan, Ava, and Dylan (whose school adventures keep me grounded). Many, many thanks to Tony Eichelberger, my husband and best friend, for his encouragement and critical reading.

I also want to thank my literacy colleagues, especially Diane Kern, Ginny Goatley, Allison Swan Dagen, and Vicki Risko, as well as coaches in the field, especially Katy Carroll and Christina Steinbacher-Reed, for sharing their insights and perspectives about literacy coaching. A special thank-you to the committee members who worked on the national survey of specialized literacy professionals. Our interactions during the three years of the study influenced greatly my thinking about literacy coaching in schools.

—Rita M. Bean

Thank you to my family—Victoria, Milo, Emily, Jim, and Elaine Ippolito. You make everything possible and meaningful.

Also, thank you to Joanna Lieberman, Lisa Messina, Nancy King, Kevin Fahey, Gene Thompson-Grove, my friends at the School Reform Initiative, my colleagues at Salem State University, and the many other "coaches" who have shaped my own thinking about adult learning and facilitation.

—Jacy Ippolito

We also would like to acknowledge and thank the coaches and literacy leaders who contributed their voices and ideas to this book: Linda DiMartino, Ellen Eisenberg, Shauna Magee, Jenee Ramos, Kate Leslie, Astrid Allen, Christina Steinbacher-Reed, Marsha Turner, Annette Vietmeier, Tracy Toothman, Fran Hardisty, and Todd Wallingford.

Learning Sciences International would like to thank the following:

Tracie Hallissey
2013 Sanford Teacher of the Year
Willard School
Sanford, Maine

Andrea (Noonan) Fox
2013 North Dakota Teacher of the Year
Cheney Middle School
West Fargo, North Dakota

Diane E. Kern
Associate Professor
University of Rhode Island
School of Education
Kingston, Rhode Island

Joshua Lawrence
Asst. Professor
UC Irvine, School of Education
Irvine, California

About the Authors

Rita M. Bean is professor emerita, University of Pittsburgh, Department of Instruction and Learning. For over twenty-five years, she taught students preparing to be reading specialists and also served as director of the Reading Center. Prior to joining the university, she taught at the elementary level and served as reading coordinator (K–12), the role which stimulated her interest in coaching to support teacher professional learning. Dr. Bean has focused her research on the role and impact of reading specialists and literacy coaches in schools. She served as co-director of a large-scale evaluation study of a literacy initiative in Pennsylvania that included coaching as a major approach for professional learning. She has also participated in several national studies that have resulted in position statements about the role of reading specialists and literacy coaches (International Literacy Association). Results of her research have been published in many journals and books. Recent books include *The Reading Specialist: Leadership and Coaching for the Classroom, School, and Community* (2015) and a co-edited volume, *Best Practices of Literacy Leaders: Keys to School Improvement* (2011). She received her BS from Edinboro University of Pennsylvania and her master's degree and PhD from the University of Pittsburgh. Dr. Bean received the University of Pittsburgh's Distinguished Teacher Award and the Chancellor's Distinguished Service Award for her community and outreach efforts to improve literacy. In 2009, she was elected to the Reading Hall of Fame and is currently serving as its president.

Jacy Ippolito is an associate professor in the School of Education at Salem State University, Salem, Massachusetts. Jacy's research and teaching focus on the intersection of adolescent and disciplinary literacy, literacy coaching, teacher leadership, and school reform. Jacy is specifically interested in the roles that teacher leaders, principals, and literacy coaches play in helping institute and maintain instructional change at middle and high school levels. Jacy continues to conduct research on adolescent and disciplinary literacy, literacy coaching, teacher leadership, and school reform while also consulting in K–12 schools. Results of Jacy's research and consulting work can be found in a number of books and journals (including *The Journal of Adolescent & Adult Literacy*, *The Journal of Staff Development*, and *The Elementary School Journal*). Recent books include *Adolescent Literacy in the Era of the Common Core* (2013) and *Adolescent Literacy* (2012), both by Harvard Education Press. Jacy completed his undergraduate degrees in English and psychology in the University of Delaware's Honors Program, before completing his master's degree and doctorate in language and literacy at the Harvard Graduate School of Education. Prior to his work in higher education, Jacy taught in the Cambridge Public Schools, Cambridge, Massachusetts, as a middle school reading specialist, literacy coach, and drama teacher. Thus began his professional interest in the roles, responsibilities, and impact of literacy leaders and coaches.

Preface

We wrote *Cultivating Coaching Mindsets: An Action Guide for Literacy Leaders* for the many professionals in schools who have responsibility for improving literacy instruction for students. These educators work with colleagues to create environments in which instruction is challenging, rigorous, and at the same time motivational, fostering students' excitement about literacy learning. Empirical evidence suggests that "coaching," as a literacy leadership tool, can lead to promising and improved instructional practices and, as a result, can improve student literacy learning. However, we also believe that "coaching" is not the sole purview of those with the title "literacy coach." This is a book for *all* literacy leaders who engage in coaching. Some may hold formal leadership roles, such as literacy or instructional coaches, principals, supervisors, or others whose titles vary, given idiosyncrasies across districts or states. Others work more informally to facilitate effective instruction; these professionals include reading specialists, teacher leaders, or classroom teachers who assume leadership roles (e.g., working with student teachers, mentoring novice teachers). Regardless of title, all educators need the leadership and facilitation skills to guide, nurture, and motivate colleagues in ways that influence literacy instruction—increasing the ability of all educators in a school and district to advance students' reading, writing, and communication skills. Further, all educators need leadership skills to participate effectively in collaborative activities that spur and support change at school and district levels.

These beliefs, that many different educators coach, and that developing and sustaining effective literacy instruction requires action across all grades and subjects, led us to the title of this book: *Cultivating Coaching Mindsets: An Action Guide for Literacy Leaders*. Not all who coach hold the title of coach, but all those who coach to improve literacy learning, in its broadest sense, are "literacy leaders." Thus, this book is for all literacy leaders, formal and informal, each of whom can benefit from adopting particular ways of thinking and working when they engage in coaching work. Therefore, in this book we move back and forth between the terms "coach," "coaching," and the broader term "literacy leader," reflecting the wide range of responsibilities and titles that educators in schools hold.

Given the large number and variety of educators who find themselves coaching colleagues, we designed the book to be used in several different ways. It can be used as a resource by literacy leaders to inform everyday practices, for example, how to effectively plan and hold small-group meetings. Those who prepare literacy leaders will find it useful as a tool in their undergraduate and graduate programs. Likewise, those responsible for leading ongoing professional learning experiences for coaches, specialists, teachers, or other literacy leaders in school settings will also find the book useful as a reference resource. Consequently, depending on readers' professional roles and specific reading purposes, this book can be read sequentially, chapter by chapter as part of a course or study group, or in bits and pieces with specific chapters or sections chosen to address particular interests and needs (e.g., a literacy coach looking for ideas about providing feedback to teachers with whom he is working). We do recommend, however, that readers review the introductory chapters 1–4 in order, as they provide the underlying principles and frameworks that guide our thinking throughout the remainder of the book.

Whether reading sequentially or for specific information, this book includes several features that will guide readers in thinking carefully about the concepts and tools highlighted in each of the chapters. For example, we introduce Melinda, a literacy leader, in chapter 1, and then follow her journey throughout each chapter as a means of illustrating across the book how one educator attempts to meet the challenges of her new role. Additional features found in each chapter include:

- **Guiding questions.** At the beginning of each chapter, we provide a few guiding questions that highlight the key perspectives or content of the specific chapter. These are followed by a paragraph that introduces the purposes or overall goals of the chapter.

- **Icons to highlight or identify key information.** We recognize the need to help busy educators locate information efficiently. So, we use three different icons to highlight key information in each chapter. Three types of information are highlighted: Key Questions for Literacy Leaders to Consider (reflective questions to guide professional learning); Important Resources (tools and resources that are often immediately usable); and Ideas for Practice (coaching methods and techniques that might guide future work).

- **"Reflect" and "Put Into Practice" boxes.** Throughout the chapters, readers will also find boxes that identify specific issues for them to think about or reflect on. Likewise, where appropriate, we have inserted "Put Into Practice" boxes that describe activities readers can implement immediately, or that allow readers to "try out" specific recommendations discussed in that chapter. We hope these boxes provide readers with moments to stop and reflect about what they are reading or to go beyond reading about a specific notion by putting it into practice.

- **Vignettes.** Throughout the chapters, we provide quotes from various literacy leaders who coach to illustrate how a variety of educators think about the topics being addressed. In chapter 12, the final chapter, we include four longer cases in which literacy leaders share accounts of their own coaching work across different positions at varying grade levels. In one case, a literacy coach discusses her evolution from early school-based coaching in an elementary school to her current position as an "external" coach. In a second case, a trio of high school content-area teachers discuss their work as teacher leaders supporting colleagues as they collectively design and implement disciplinary literacy practices for secondary students. In the third case, a high school literacy leadership team shares how they conducted a literacy needs assessment with teachers and students in order to create more targeted professional development and instructional practices. Finally, a state-level leader describes a large-scale, state-wide coaching initiative and its evolution.

- **End-of-chapter activities.** At the end of each chapter, we identify specific activities that can be used to assist readers in digging deeper or expanding upon what they have learned. Ideas for specific follow-up readings or practical activities are included in this section. In almost every chapter, one of the activities is focused on asking readers to stop and think about their current practices and what they might be able to do in the future in their school settings—based on the framework for coaching that we describe in chapter 2. We provide readers with a template in the first appendix (appendix A) to facilitate this reflective work.

- **Appendices.** The appendices primarily provide tools or templates that can be printed and used by readers in their work. However, they also provide the opportunity for readers, interested in particular topics, to extend their learning and jumpstart school-based professional conversations. For example, in appendix B, we provide a number of resources and references that readers can explore if they are interested in additional readings on topics in specific chapters (perhaps as part of formal coursework, or in schools as part of study groups). We realize that we cannot pursue, in-depth, all the critical issues literacy leaders face in education today, and therefore we wanted to share with readers additional resources we have found useful in our work.

While some appendices (like appendix B) identify resources, other appendices provide guidance for literacy leaders engaging in particular professional learning activities, such as leading classroom observations or facilitating a needs assessment process. Each of the appendices is connected closely to a particular chapter's content, yet the appendices are also meant to stand alone and be used and referenced as literacy leaders might need.

Our goal was to write a book that was a blend of theory and practice—that would be reader friendly and provide ideas that those in the field could use in their daily work. Collaborating on the writing of this book created opportunities for us to think deeply about coaching, what it means, and how it can be operationalized so that it is an effective tool for improving instructional practices in various contexts and at the classroom, school, and district levels. Writing collaboratively created opportunities for us to challenge each other in ways that helped each to learn more about coaching across roles and contexts. Coaching, like many aspects of education, is a complex construct viewed in different ways by different educational professionals. We hope our perspectives about ways of thinking and working as a coach help readers consider (and reconsider!) their own views and practices.

Writing this book has been a tremendous learning experience for us. We have reflected, questioned, and had some difficult conversations about what we believe about literacy instruction (preK–grade 12) and coaching—and how our beliefs mesh with current research about adult learning and school change. We have several goals and expectations for this book and its readers: First, that reading the book will provide opportunities for learning, reflecting, and raising questions about the connections between your work and the ideas we present. Second, that all those who take responsibility for guiding and supporting the work of teachers see the value of improving their own learning and becoming better at leading efforts to improve teaching and learning in individual classrooms and across entire schools. Finally, we hope that this book will serve as an action guide, referred to again and again over time, to support educators' self- and school-improvement processes.

Whatever your coaching context, we hope this book supports you in supporting colleagues and continuing your own journey of continual learning!

—Rita M. Bean and Jacy Ippolito

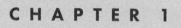

C H A P T E R   1

Remodeling Schools for Effective Literacy Learning: The Case for Coaching

GUIDING QUESTIONS

1. Why is coaching best viewed as a set of activities rather than as a role?

2. What are the four tenets of the Framework for Thinking and Working Like a Coach?

3. In what ways do basic assumptions about coaching affect the roles and responsibilities of literacy leaders?

When her principal asked Melinda, an experienced classroom teacher, to coach two new teachers in teaching literacy, Melinda began to search for resources that would help her better understand these new and exciting responsibilities. In many ways, this book presents both the research and resources that we would want to fall into Melinda's hands. While fictional, Melinda represents a compilation of the many literacy leaders with whom we have worked over the years. Having both personally walked in Melinda's shoes and mentored many new literacy leaders like Melinda, we have chosen to begin each of our chapters with a brief snapshot of the tasks that Melinda is taking on and the questions that she might be asking along the way. Each chapter then serves as a resource for helping literacy leaders who coach to answer questions similar to Melinda's. Consequently, the two main purposes of the book are (1) to provide those who coach with an understanding of how coaching requires particular *ways of thinking* about adult learners in schools and (2) to suggest numerous related *ways of working* with adult learners, including dozens of practical tools for those who coach to operationalize the ways of thinking.

In this introductory chapter, we present what we view as foundational knowledge for and key assumptions about effective coaching, providing professionals like Melinda and other literacy leaders with key information about coaching and its potential for improving classroom practices and student literacy learning.

Coaching, although a somewhat new phenomenon, has gained momentum during the past several decades. In business, there are executive coaches; in medicine, health coaches; and in education, instructional coaches. Educational coaches come with a variety of titles (e.g., academic, change, instructional, literacy, and so on) and a dizzying and diverse number of roles and responsibilities. However, all those who coach, whether in business, medicine, or education, share a fundamental similarity, a desire to support the work of colleagues while continually improving their own practice. Atul Gawande, a nationally known surgeon and writer, realizing that he had reached a plateau in his learning, worked with a coach to further develop his technical skills and his ability to work with other members of his team. Gawande makes several key points about coaching; specifically, "the allegiance of the coach is to the people they work with; their success depends on it. And the existence of a coach depends on the acknowledgement that even expert practitioners have significant room for improvement" (Gawande, 2011). In other words, coaches must establish a trusting relationship with those they coach. Most important, all of us can improve as professionals; that is, we can become better at what we do. Coaching can play a big part in that process.

Given the importance of quality instruction, especially literacy instruction, as a key to student learning, accompanied by 21st century workplace demands and higher expectations for students, there is a need for those responsible for literacy instruction to think differently about how and what they teach. Further, as Gawande indicates, effective coaching can facilitate the learning of adult educators and assist them in meeting the challenges of providing high-quality literacy instruction. Before exploring further what we mean by "effective coaching" through our Framework for Thinking and Working Like a Coach, we begin simply by sharing two basic beliefs about the enterprise of coaching, which have shaped our work in schools, our research, and most certainly this book.

Basic Beliefs About Coaching

One of our basic beliefs mentioned throughout this book is that many educators in schools take on coaching responsibilities, from those with the title of "coach" to others such as reading specialists, teacher leaders, cooperating and mentor teachers, facilitators, consultant teachers, assistant principals, and (at times) principals. In other words, we view coaching as an *activity* rather than as a *role*. All of these individuals, regardless of title, may assume coaching responsibilities, which run the gamut from serving as a resource or mentor to others, co-planning and co-teaching, to observing and providing feedback, and so on. The notion that many educators hold coaching responsibilities in schools is consistent with current research evidence that schools with a culture of shared leadership and collaboration are well positioned to increase student literacy learning (Bryk, Sebring, Allensworth, Luppescu, & Easton, 2010; Lewis-Spector & Jay, 2011; Louis, Leithwood, Wahlstrom, & Anderson, 2010). If we limit coaching responsibilities to only those who hold the formal title of "coach," then we risk losing or undermining the wealth of experience, knowledge, and savvy of capable teachers and leaders.

This brings us to our second basic belief: coaching can be critically important to improving literacy teaching and learning in schools, across *all* grades and *all* content areas. Certainly, coaching can be beneficial for those responsible for teaching reading in the elementary schools—for teachers working with the youngest learners who are just beginning to learn the basics of sound-symbol connections or mastering their first sight words, to those working in upper grades, where the focus might shift to vocabulary and comprehension instruction. Moreover, there is also much more emphasis on the importance of "disciplinary literacy" strategies across all grades as a means of improving students' content learning (Hynd-Shanahan, Holschuh, & Hubbard, 2004; Shanahan & Shanahan, 2008, 2012, 2014; Shanahan, Shanahan, & Misischia, 2011; Moje, 2015). Standards such as the Common Core State Standards (CCSS) (National Governors Association Center for Best Practices [NGA] & Council of Chief State School Officers [CCSSO], 2010) have emphasized the key role of literacy as a means of improving academic learning. In other words, coaching is key to helping teachers across all grades and subjects take on the challenge of merging content and literacy teaching and learning. But who are these educators identified as literacy leaders, and how did they acquire their coaching responsibilities? In the following section, we discuss briefly some of the common ways that educators become literacy leaders with coaching responsibilities.

VOICES FROM THE FIELD

In 2013–2014, the district made the decision to transition the specialists into coaches. Up until that time, the reading specialist's main role was intervention and direct service of students. When the transition was made, administration suggested a 60 percent coaching and 40 percent intervention balance; however, the coaching model has looked different at each school, and even from year to year based on budget/staffing cuts, administrative changes, etc. Currently, I spend about 50 percent of my day working with students and 50 percent coaching.

—Shauna Magee, literacy coach

Pathways Into Coaching

Some teachers are asked to serve as coaches because they have been identified as effective literacy teachers. Others, like Shauna in the preceding Voices From the Field, find themselves in a coaching role because of a shift in responsibilities (e.g., from instructing students to also coaching teachers). The diverse titles of those with coaching roles reflect the many different pathways of individuals who become and serve as literacy leaders. In a recent national survey of specialized literacy professionals (Bean, Kern, Goatley, Ortlieb, Shettel, Calo et al., 2015), respondents varied greatly, not just in the titles they held but in the ways in which they became coaches. Some held reading specialist certifications and were asked to coach either on a full- or part-time basis. Others were Reading Recovery teachers who taught half the day and worked with teachers during the other half. In middle and secondary schools, those who coached came from even more diverse backgrounds. Some had been reading specialists, perhaps at the elementary level, while others were teachers of the disciplines who had been selected for the position. Survey results also indicated that 75 percent of the respondents held master's degrees. At the same time, 53 percent were certified as reading specialists. Many respondents indicated the value of an advanced degree in literacy education, the importance of a supervised field experience (e.g., shadowing a coach), and coaching experiences in a school setting during their preparation programs.

Given the results of this survey and other research in the field, the International Literacy Association (2015) released a position statement titled *The Multiple Roles of School-Based Specialized Literacy Professionals*, accompanied by a research brief summarizing the rationale and evidence for three specialized literacy positions: the reading/literacy specialist, the literacy coach, and the literacy coordinator/supervisor. Although three distinct positions were identified, the documents make clear that those holding any of these positions must develop the leadership skills and abilities to work collaboratively with teachers and to support teacher professional learning and school-change efforts—that is, to coach. The position statements and research brief can be downloaded from the International Literacy Association's website (www. literacyworldwide.org).

Although reading specialist certification is one key pathway into coaching, and while we encourage all those serving as literacy leaders to enroll in such a certification program, we also recognize the existence of other pathways to becoming a coach. Some schools have asked experienced teachers to serve as teacher leaders responsible for supporting and facilitating professional learning activities for teachers. At secondary levels, where literacy leaders most frequently work with teachers of the disciplines who have different responsibilities and backgrounds from teachers at the elementary level, excellent content-area teachers have been identified as coaches and then provided with experiences that build their literacy knowledge and coaching expertise. Given that literacy is at the core of improving student learning in the academic disciplines, such initiatives make good sense. For descriptions of a high school disciplinary literacy initiative led by content-area teachers who coach, as well as a statewide coaching initiative providing professional learning experiences for coaches, see example cases in chapter 12.

What Is Coaching and How Does It Support High-Quality Literacy Instruction?

In the previous section, we highlighted the importance of coaching as a means of improving teaching and learning. Next, we define coaching more clearly and discuss the coaching framework that serves as the foundation for this book. We view coaching as a process of *facilitated* inquiry that enables teachers to make decisions, solve problems, and set and achieve both individual goals and the goals of the organization, specifically to improve classroom instructional practices and student literacy learning. Further, such *collaborative* inquiry contributes to cultural and organizational changes necessary for improving the learning of all students.

Effective coaching includes a set of coaching behaviors that support adult learning, collaboration, and design work, all in service of the continual improvement of literacy instruction in a school. As such, coaching can include any number of activities (e.g., holding conversations with teachers designed to increase awareness and reflectivity about instructional issues, modeling various interventions or strategies, observing, facilitating meetings about instruction or data, and so on) and can occur between individuals or in groups. It can provide valuable learning experiences for those directly responsible for teaching literacy as well as for those whose responsibility is teaching academic subjects (e.g., history, science, and so on). Although the stance of the coach, or how the coach approaches interactions with teachers, may differ depending upon teacher knowledge, experience, and desire to change, coaching must always be built upon a respect for the goals and beliefs of individual teachers about teaching, learning, and literacy. At the same time, the ultimate goal of coaching is to improve student learning, and as such, requires coaches to address issues that increase the capacity of teacher teams and the school as a whole to provide the very best educational experiences for all of its students. This brings us to a discussion of our Framework for Thinking and Working Like a Coach.

Framework for Thinking and Working Like a Coach

The four basic tenets in this framework hold true for all those who coach. They include: thinking about individuals and systems simultaneously, adopting coaching mindsets and roles, differentiating professional learning experiences, and developing a culture conducive to coaching (see figure 1.1).

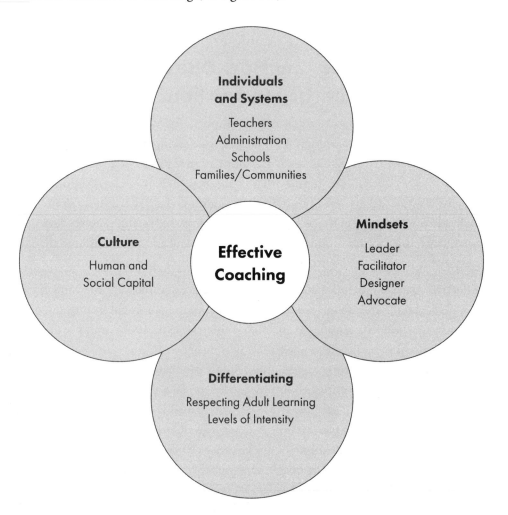

Figure 1.1: Framework for Thinking and Working Like a Coach.

*Visit **www.learningsciences.com/bookresources** to download a reproducible version of this figure.*

Tenet 1: Thinking About Individuals and Systems Simultaneously

When working as a literacy leader—as a formal reading specialist, literacy coach, literacy director, or as an informal teacher leader—one of the first and most important frames to adopt is a simultaneous concern for the needs of individuals and larger systems. All too often smart, talented literacy coaches and leaders exhaust themselves by exclusively attending to the needs of teachers one-on-one. Similarly, others fail to make inroads with teachers, because they tilt exclusively toward systems-level thinking, constantly planning for larger-group and whole-school initiatives, without attending to the individual differences and needs that arise among faculty. Others get caught up in management tasks—such as organizing assessment results, ordering and arranging materials, and so forth—that reduce the time and energy for coaching (Deussen, Coskie, Robinson, & Autio, 2007; Smith, 2007).

A recent study of four literacy coaches by Mangin and Dunsmore (2015) highlights what many in the field have guessed for some time: that while coaches and literacy leaders are often asked to support system-wide instructional change, coach preparation and support more often prepares them to work with individuals, "respond[ing] to teachers' individualized needs" (p. 187). Maintaining this dual focus requires clear communication with school and district leadership about the vision and theory of action for systems-level change. Questions that literacy leaders can ask themselves as they endeavor to adopt a dual focus on individuals and systems include:

▸ To what extent are the principal, literacy specialist/coach, and district-level leaders on the same page about the goals of literacy reform efforts?

▸ How clearly can each of these stakeholders articulate shared goals and action steps?

▸ How clearly have system-wide change efforts been communicated to (and solicited from / generated by!) teachers across grades and schools?

▸ To what degree must work with individual teachers fit within a larger framework for change versus simple support of individual teachers' interests and needs?

As Mangin and Dunsmore suggest in their study, without clearer alignment of focus at both the systems level and individual level, coaches may default to thinking that "the sum of individual changes across teachers [might be] equivalent to systemic reform" (p. 203), which we would argue is rarely the case, particularly in large, urban schools and districts where fragmentation is often the norm. By maintaining a dual focus on individuals and the larger system, literacy leaders act as organizational glue, building the collective capacity of teachers and leaders to move toward common, effective literacy instructional practices. (For more about working at the school or system level, see chapters 4 and 9.)

Tenet 2: Adopting Coaching Mindsets and Roles

How you *think* about the process of improving literacy teaching and learning matters a great deal as you strive to make changes in individual classrooms as well as in entire schools and districts. As scholars of organizational learning have written about extensively (see McDonald, 2014; Schön & Rein, 1994; Schein, 2010), the *mental models* or *frames* that we hold, and through which we view the world, matter enormously. Our mental models and frames shape how we think about our work and how we think about change processes.

Much of coaching work is about helping colleagues to become more reflective practitioners and shift their instruction in order to improve outcomes for students. However, if the work of coaching is viewed through a purely technical lens (Heifetz, Grashow, & Linsky, 2009) or as single-loop learning (Argyris & Schön, 1974, 1996)—in other words, learning that simply requires detection of a problem and implementation of a known solution—then this *frame* for coaching will likely not produce the deep, systemic changes that most literacy leadership work is meant to provoke. Instead, if coaching work is to result in deep changes in teachers' beliefs and instructional practices, then coaches must push toward adaptive (Heifetz et al., 2009) or double-loop learning (Argyris & Schön, 1974, 1996)—in other words, the kind of learning that results in a fundamental questioning of beliefs, assumptions, and practices as steps toward transforming teaching and learning (rather than simply tinkering around the edges). Adaptive learning processes involve the analysis not just of current dilemmas but the analysis and shifting of an organization's fundamental beliefs, assumptions, and ways of operating.

Consider this example of the differences between a technical and adaptive learning focus. After identifying third graders' poor homework performance, teachers use a technical focus and assign a modified homework packet rather than using an adaptive focus in which they and their colleagues take the time to deeply analyze what students are or aren't doing with homework, question the purpose of the homework assignments, and perhaps reconsider and reinvent which various homework experiences are best suited to increasing reading, writing, and communication skills. Such adaptive learning requires educators to analyze their own assumptions about teaching and learning as part of the problem-solving process. While literacy leaders may be eager to solve current teaching and learning dilemmas quickly, the work of Argyris, Schön, and Heifetz reminds us that it is just as important to learn about our own adult learning and work habits if we are ever going to solve not just today's dilemmas, but also respond more effectively to future dilemmas as well.

In chapter 2, "Cultivating Coaching Mindsets," we review four large frames, or mental models, that we have found effective, adaptive literacy leaders to hold over time. These include thinking like a leader, a facilitator, a designer, and an advocate. These mindsets, when applied consistently over time by dedicated coaches and informal leaders, produce the longest-lasting and biggest changes in teaching and learning. Most importantly, these frames are most successful when they align with coaching practices (the focus of the rest of this book). The alignment between espoused theory (i.e., what we *say* we do) and theories-in-use (i.e., what we *actually* do) (Argyris & Schön, 1974) is of utmost importance as literacy leaders talk the talk *and* walk the walk of organizational learning.

Tenet 3: Differentiating Professional Learning Experiences

Too often, professional learning for adult educators has tended to be generic (a "one size fits all" approach), short-term, and focused on transmitting technical information. Have you ever sat through a workshop that seemed only tangentially related to you and your professional needs? There is recognition in today's schools that professional learning is and should be more than simply providing teachers with information; instead, "it is at its heart the development of habits of learning" (Fullan, 2001, p. 253).

Effective professional learning takes into account what is known about adult learning: it must be authentic and meaningful, include interaction with others, and provide adults with control over their own learning, including opportunities to learn in different ways and at different rates (Bean, 2015). Effective coaching does just that! When working with individuals and groups of teachers, literacy leaders must take into consideration the type of learning experiences best suited for these individuals at that time. We introduce the Levels of Intensity (figure 1.2, page 10) as a helpful tool, a continuum to help literacy leaders consider how they might differentiate coaching activities for various individuals and groups of teachers.

At the first level, the work of the coach is one of building relationships of trust. Without trust, nothing more can happen. Without trust, the suggestions of a specific coach will most likely be ignored. Without trust, change will most likely be superficial rather than transformational. Without trust, teachers may be thinking, "Oh no. Here comes that coach again . . . " At this level, coaches must find the key that unlocks the door to trust. Activities may include holding conversations about specific students who are having difficulty, locating resources or helping teachers develop materials, or just being a good listener when a teacher is having a tough day. Coaches and teachers at this level can begin to solidify trusting relationships by developing norms for how to work together and by asking questions of each other to promote reflective thinking.

Level 1: Building Relationships (Informal/Less Intense)	Level 2: Analyzing Practice (Semi-Formal/Slightly More Intense)	Level 3: Transforming Practice & Making Teaching Public (Formal/Intense)
• Having conversations with colleagues (getting to know one another, identifying issues or needs, setting goals, problem solving) • Establishing schedules for meeting with groups of teachers and individuals • Establishing norms for collaboration and conversation • Developing and providing materials for or with colleagues • Developing curriculum with colleagues • Participating in professional development activities with colleagues (conferences, workshops) • Leading or participating in study groups • Assisting with assessment of students • Instructing students to learn about their strengths and needs	• Having conversations with individual colleagues about teaching, learning, and literacy (analyzing data, lessons) • Co-planning lessons • Revisiting norms for collaboration and making certain they facilitate group work • Introducing discussion-based protocols to assist in the analysis of student work, the holding of group conversations about student/teacher work, and so on, which require higher degrees of trust • Holding team meetings (grade level, data, department) • Analyzing student work to assist teachers in planning instruction • Analyzing and interpreting assessment data (helping teachers use results for instructional decision making)	• Having conversations focusing on co-planning, co-teaching, and teaching dilemmas • Modeling and discussing lessons • Co-teaching lessons • Expanding the range of discussion-based protocols used, including those that require higher degrees of risk/trust and surface assumptions related to issues of equity and social justice • Helping individuals and groups design their own discussion-based protocols and collaboration routines • Visiting classrooms and providing feedback to teachers as part of the planning/observation/debrief cycle • Conducting individual and group analysis of videotaped lessons of teachers

• Coaching on-the-fly (having unscheduled, brief meetings with teachers that provide opportunities for additional coaching)	• Making presentations at professional development meetings • Assisting with online professional development	• Engaging in lesson study with teachers • Participating in and leading professional learning communities • Providing support to teachers as a result of teacher performance evaluation outcomes • Involvement in efforts to improve school literacy programs • Facilitating school-community partnership work

Figure 1.2: Coaching activities (Levels of Intensity) of specialized literacy professionals.

Adapted from the following three sources: R. M. Bean, 2004; International Literacy Association, 2015; J. Ippolito, 2013.

At the second level, analyzing practice becomes more of a goal, with coaching activities focusing on how to improve literacy instructional practices. Coaches and teachers can collaborate by analyzing data, lessons, or student work, thinking together about how such data can inform instruction. They might co-plan lessons that address specific approaches to literacy and talk about which groupings might be best to convey concepts to students—whole class, small groups, or a combination. Coaches and teachers at this level can revisit group norms, reflect on how well a group functions, and revise ways of working in order to allow for deeper, more meaningful conversations.

At the third level, coaching becomes about changing or transforming practice. Coaches most likely can be found modeling, co-teaching, and observing. At the same time, they are participating with teachers in a level of discourse where they are questioning their own and others' practices, assumptions, and beliefs, going beyond what MacDonald (2011) calls, "a culture of nice" (p. 45). Given current literacy standards that call for high-level, rigorous instruction, teachers and coaches may spend time thinking about how to address the call for shifts in literacy instruction to help students meet expectations. Finally, at this level, coaching is focused on helping teachers become lifelong learners who are reflective about their teaching and recognize, like Atul Gawande, that as professionals they can continue to improve.

Throughout the book, these activities are discussed and specific ideas for implementation are described. Remember, however, that the Levels of Intensity are *suggestive*, not *prescriptive*; in other words, they are a guide, not a recipe. Coaches are not expected to work in a linear fashion through the activities, beginning at Level 1 and marching lockstep to Level 3. Rather, we hope that coaches will use the Levels of Intensity to help them plan *intentionally* which activities might work well at a particular time with a specific teacher or group. Furthermore, the lines between levels often blur. For example, as a coach, you might be asked to observe (Level 3) all first-grade teachers early in the year to learn more about how they are implementing the new core program and how you can support them at this early stage of implementation. Although being observed may cause some anxiety for these teachers, the post-conversations can be ones in which you, as a coach, practice good listening skills, reinforce positive practices, and begin building a relationship of trust (Level 1).

REFLECT

Look at the Levels of Intensity and think about your most recent experiences in schools. Where have you spent the majority of your time (as a literacy leader or as a participant in professional learning)? Which activities felt most comfortable? Any that felt uncomfortable? What might be best to try next?

Tenet 4: Developing a Culture Conducive to Coaching

How often have you heard someone say, "Morale is low in this school"? Or, "These parents won't get involved in any school activities"? Such statements reflect views about the culture in a given school or district. As stated by Reeves (2009), culture could be defined simply as "the way we do things around here" (p. 37). More explicitly, it is "reflected in the behavior, attitudes, and beliefs of [the] individuals and groups" (Reeves, 2009, p. 37) in an organization.

Developing a culture conducive to coaching is so critical to coaching success that we devote an entire chapter to discussing schools as places of learning and how to develop a positive culture (see chapter 4). Essentially, a coaching initiative (and the coach) has little chance of succeeding unless there is system-wide readiness for coaching (City, 2007). Key aspects of such readiness include support from administration at both district and school levels, a climate in which teachers are encouraged to work collaboratively and to make their work public, and an acknowledgment that teachers are both targets and agents of change (i.e., there is shared leadership and expertise in the school). Fullan (1993) says it well: "Change in teaching for more effective learning requires major transformation in the culture of the school" (p. 54). Coaching can provide the impetus for such transformations, but oftentimes coaching is only effective if the transformation toward a positive, collaborative, reflective school culture is already underway.

Major Assumptions About Coaching

In this section, we introduce several assumptions that we hold as central to successful coaching. We then continue to refer to these assumptions throughout the book.

> **VOICES FROM THE FIELD**
>
> Business flows because coaching comes with a "no judgment" guarantee.
>
> —Linda DiMartino, literacy supervisor

Coaching Is Nonevaluative

Most educators who write about coaching do not view it as an evaluative process, in which coaches participate in formal evaluations of teacher practices or performance. Yet, in some districts, coaches are being asked to assume such a role, especially with the current emphasis on teacher performance evaluation. For example, in one district, teachers identified as "exemplary" were assigned as consulting teachers or coaches to work with and then monitor the work of beginning teachers and veterans who were experiencing teaching difficulties (Goldstein, 2009). Such responsibilities may make it difficult for coaches to develop trusting relationships with teachers (Toll, 2006). In our view, coaches are colleagues who work with their peers to solve problems, reflect, and collaboratively make decisions about how to best improve instructional practices. Although they can support teachers who have been identified as needing to improve, from our experience, we believe coaches should not be responsible for identifying or evaluating such teachers.

At the same time, when educators, such as coaches, are asked to assume such an evaluative position, they can learn much from the coaching literature and from this book about how to work with teachers in positive ways, provide constructive feedback, and encourage teachers to become more reflective about their teaching and learning. We suggest, however, that individuals who have such evaluative positions be given titles other than "coach."

Coaching Should Develop Teacher Capacity

Many coaches with whom we have worked have indicated their surprise that teachers in their schools continued to seek the same sorts of support from them, even though these teachers had participated in various coaching activities over several years. There may be many reasons for this, including that the coaching perhaps focused almost entirely on Level 1 or Level 2 activities, without slowly nudging teachers to internalize the work and take more ownership of their own professional learning (Level 3). How often have we reverted back to practices with which we are familiar or comfortable when we didn't have the continual support to keep using new practices (e.g., learning a new way to grip a tennis racket or a golf club)?

Coaching initiatives are not meant to—nor can they—*inoculate* individuals so that eventually there is no need for coaching. There are always new students, new frameworks, and new dilemmas for coaches and teachers to discuss. Moreover, at all stages, educators, including coaches, can learn from others. At the same time, the coaching emphasis should be on helping teachers grow professionally. As stated in the report by the National Center for Literacy Education (2014), teachers should be seen "as master crafters of learning challenges that deepen literacy learning for students across a school day and academic year" (p. 4); the role of the coach is to provide the guidance and support that builds teachers' capacity to become those professionals.

Differences Between Elementary and Secondary Coaching Are a Matter of Degree

As we have written elsewhere (Ippolito & Lieberman, 2012), we believe that there are real differences between coaching at elementary and secondary levels, but we see those differences more as differences of *degree* rather than of fundamental distinctions. Literacy leaders who coach in the early grades and in the later grades must think both about the content of instruction and the coaching processes they might use. They need background knowledge and preparation about literacy curriculum and instruction, and they need to know how to work with individuals, groups, and systems. Further, scheduling is a challenge for all coaches, with both elementary and secondary coaches struggling to find time to work with teachers (as opposed to getting bogged down in administrative work).

While both elementary and secondary coaches have more in common than not, there are some differences in degree that seem to matter. For instance, secondary coaches are often expected to work with much larger groups of teachers, both within and across disciplines. Secondary coaches often need deeper background knowledge and preparation in content-area curriculum in order to best support content-area teachers in history, science, and so on. Finally, we often see the largest differences when we look at elementary versus secondary coaches' pathways into coaching: more elementary coaches come to the role with a reading specialist background, while more secondary coaches come to the role with a deeper content-area instructional background (e.g., former high school English, history, or science teachers). We believe that differences between elementary and secondary coaching are important to consider in both initiating and sustaining coaching programs; however, we also caution readers to not overemphasize the differences, and instead to look for commonalities across all roles that require literacy leaders to coach.

Context Makes a Difference

Coaching programs will look different, depending on the context in which they are implemented. School size, student demographics, experiences and backgrounds of teachers, experiences and backgrounds of coaches, and the existing culture of the school all have an impact on coaching initiatives. Other factors, such as union issues or written job descriptions, also influence the ways in which coaching initiatives function. Such factors can affect the type of coaching model implemented (e.g., directive, responsive, or balanced), responsibilities of the coach (e.g., working with all teachers or only those who request support), and even the workload of the coach (e.g., full-time or part-time hours). These variables, across contexts, account for some of the difficulty in evaluating the effectiveness of coaching.

Coaching Can Have an Impact

Over the past several decades, researchers have been studying various aspects of coaching, including the roles and responsibilities of coaches and the effects of coaching on teacher practices. As mentioned, given the complexities of coaching, obtaining unequivocal evidence about its impact, especially on student learning, has been difficult (Walpole & McKenna, 2009). However, there appears to be growing evidence that coaching, if implemented effectively, can in fact influence and change teacher practices and student learning (Bean, Draper, Hall, Vandermolen, & Zigmond, 2010; Biancarosa, Bryk, & Dexter, 2010; Elish-Piper & L'Allier, 2011; Matsumura, Garnier, Correnti, Junker, & Bickel, 2010; Matsumura, Garnier, & Spybrook, 2013).

Coaching can also influence teachers' beliefs and attitudes (Kinnucan-Welsch, Rosemary, & Grogan, 2006; Vandeburg & Stephens, 2010). However, there continues to be a need for ongoing, rigorous studies that investigate coaching's multifaceted dimensions (e.g., coach preparation and qualifications, coaching activities, and the context in which coaching appears) (Swan Dagen & Bean, 2014).

Content Matters

Those who coach must have a deep understanding of students' literacy-learning needs, a variety of literacy-oriented curricula, and effective literacy instructional methods. Literacy coaches who have this foundational knowledge are better able to facilitate teacher learning and to assist in the design and evaluation of effective school literacy programs. For example, literacy coaches unfamiliar with the research about effective phonics instruction will be less able to identify specific "trouble spots," or areas where the teacher might have provided a different type of learning experience for students. Likewise, at the secondary level, literacy leaders without an awareness of the differences between general content-area strategies and strategies for improving disciplinary literacy will be limited in what they can share with their teacher partners.

In chapter 3, we provide a more in-depth discussion about the *content* of 21st century literacy instruction and some of the challenges that face educators responsible for providing high-quality instruction that meets the needs of all students (prekindergarten through twelfth grade). In this chapter, we highlight some of the major changes in society that influence educational practices, especially those related to literacy learning:

- The fast-paced changes in digital communication that offer new opportunities for student and teacher learning
- The evolving standards movement, resulting most recently in the Common Core State Standards (CCSS) and similar standards adopted and adapted by states, calling for more rigor in expectations in the content of what we teach as a means of increasing students' knowledge and skills to meet the challenges of the workplace and the world in which they find themselves

- The access to information from multiple sources, calling again for critical thinking as a means of assessing the credibility and trustworthiness of this information

- The increasingly diverse population of students in schools today, including more students of color, English learners (ELs), students with learning differences, a wider range of cultural traditions, and so on

All of these factors call for rethinking how we teach students and support teachers. For example, although more and more schools acknowledge the value of collaboration among teachers, too often neither the structure (i.e., scheduling) nor the support (e.g., availability and capacity of teachers to collaborate) are available. According to the report titled *Remodeling Literacy Learning Together: Paths to Standards Implementation* (National Center for Literacy Education, 2014), American schools do many things right, but at the same time, there is a need for *remodeling* to continually build an even better system. This is especially true if we are to create schools in which all students have equal access to educational opportunity. It is widely agreed that opportunities to learn are limited for students of color, English learners, and those who come from high-poverty backgrounds (Darling-Hammond, 2010). There is an opportunity gap in that these students do not have equal access to quality teaching, well-resourced classrooms, and effective literacy programs. Achievement test results nationwide (Barton & Coley, 2010; Hemphill & Venneman, 2011; National Assessment of Educational Progress, 2015) indicate that many students are still not achieving at or above the proficiency level. We believe all the conditions are right, and we have a perfect storm for remodeling schools to achieve the goal of excellence for all students. Literacy leaders who are able to think and work like coaches are primed to lead the way.

Summary

After providing a definition of coaching, we described our Framework for Thinking and Working Like a Coach to develop foundational knowledge about coaching. The four tenets of the framework, and the assumptions that followed, provide readers with an understanding of our beliefs and values relative to literacy coaching in schools.

Activities

1. Download and read the position statement and research brief *The Multiple Roles of School-Based Specialized Literacy Professionals* (www .literacyworldwide.org). In what ways does this document expand your

thinking about the role(s) of literacy leaders? What questions does it raise? What are your major "take-aways"?

2. Read the report *Remodeling Literacy Learning Together: Paths to Standards Implementation* (www.literacyinlearningexchange.org/remodeling-together). Be prepared to discuss the report with colleagues, especially the finding that teachers believe they are not prepared to instruct in ways that help their students meet the new, rigorous standards. Relate this to your own work with teachers—what are the implications for coaching in your school or district?

3. Talk with two individuals with coaching responsibilities. Use the following questions to guide the discussion. Be prepared to discuss the similarities and differences in how these individuals respond to your questions and to how their responses compare to the content of this chapter.

   a. How do you—and your district—view or define coaching? Are your definitions similar? Different? In what ways?

   b. What do you see as the major focus or foci of your role(s): working with students, teachers, leaders, systems (e.g., school, district, etc.)?

   c. What are your major coaching activities (i.e., how do you spend your days)? Do you spend more time with individuals or groups of teachers?

   d. To what extent do teachers understand your coaching role (i.e., how would other teachers define your role)?

   e. What are the stated goals that you are trying to achieve as a result of your coaching work (e.g., increased student achievement, changes in literacy practices, etc.)? To what extent are these goals related to the literacy goals in your school?

   f. How is your coaching work supported? What supports would you like to see put into place?

CHAPTER 2

Cultivating Coaching Mindsets: Ways of Thinking and Working Like a Coach

GUIDING QUESTIONS

1. What are some of the habits of mind and ways of working adopted by those who coach adult learners?

2. How might these ways of thinking and working support individuals and systems across different levels of intensity?

3. Which big ideas and fields of research support our Framework for Thinking and Working Like a Coach?

Melinda had confidence that she was a good teacher and knew how to engage her fourth-grade students in active learning, but she was not as confident about working with her colleagues. What shifts in thinking and working might Melinda adopt to help her step into her new role and responsibilities? In this chapter, we expand upon the big ideas and habits of mind that guide coaching work, shape how coaches think about their work, and greatly impact both the processes and results of coaching. We outline four frames of mind that successful coaches employ as they think about and enact their roles. The subsequent chapters in this book focus on how coaches' ways of working map onto these frames. The four frames that we see as most essential are:

1. Thinking like a leader
2. Thinking like a facilitator
3. Thinking like a designer
4. Thinking like an advocate

Frame 1: Thinking Like a Leader; Authentic Leadership and Leading Adult Learning

Much is being written about teacher leadership in schools these days (Bond, 2015; Danielson, 2006; Lieberman & Miller, 2004; Mangin & Stoelinga, 2008). And while many coaching resources suggest that leadership is a core skill, we have found preparation and support in the science and art of leadership to be limited for literacy coaches pre- and in-service. When thinking like a leader, as one of our colleagues often says, you must learn how to "jump up to ten thousand feet" in any particular conversation or situation in order to take in the larger picture—what Heifetz et al. (2009) call "getting on the balcony" to then better look down and observe the "dance floor" (p. 7) below.

When coaches are thinking like leaders, they are taking into consideration a broader vision of the work and larger goals, and they are planning pathways to achieve the larger goals that they, their colleagues, and school leaders have collaboratively set. They are looking beyond a solution for today. They are thinking about the long-term. We have found two big ideas from the field of educational leadership to be particularly helpful to literacy leaders: recognizing the difference between management and leadership, and leading with an eye toward encouraging adult learning and development. We discuss each in the upcoming sections and then expand on several of these notions when talking about organizational culture and learning in chapter 4.

Managing Versus Leading

By thinking about the distinction between management and authentic leadership, literacy leaders can begin to prioritize their work. Management can be broadly thought of as the more technical, logistical aspects of literacy leadership work such as creating observation and feedback schedules, sorting books in a guided reading library, managing standardized test administration, or devising a weekly schedule for working with teachers. Leaders who operate strictly in management mode fall into what Heifetz et al. (2009) describe as "technical leadership" or what Argyris and Schön (1974, 1996) describe as "single-loop learning." These leaders identify problems, apply known solutions, and move forward without fundamentally questioning or changing business as usual in a school.

We recognize that management work is crucial to the successful day-to-day operation of a school, and without excellent management and efficient technical problem solving at multiple levels, most schools would quickly fall into disarray. Literacy coaches, for example, need to have a schedule that enables them to communicate on a regular basis with teachers, to be in the schools on a regular basis, and at the same time, to be flexible enough to address urgent issues that may arise (e.g., a teacher is ill and has been replaced by a long-term substitute who needs help with literacy instruction). However, excellent management *alone* rarely helps teachers and students do their best work. Literacy leaders who get *stuck* in management mode are ill-equipped to help teachers engage deeply and reflectively in the work of instructional improvement.

To truly influence teaching and learning, we need a different form of leadership, a form of leadership that weaves together vision, goal setting, logistical savvy, and an ability to inspire trust and followership through open, reflective dialogue. This second mode of leadership is what Robert Evans (2007) terms "authentic leadership." Evans describes authentic leadership this way:

> Leaders who are followed are authentic; that is, they are distinguished not by their techniques or styles but by their integrity and their savvy. Integrity is a fundamental consistency between personal beliefs, organizational aims, and working behavior. It is increasingly clear that leadership rests on values, that commitment among constituents can only be mobilized by leaders who themselves have strong commitments, who preach what they believe and practice what they preach. But they must also know what they are doing. Savvy is practical competence, a hard-to-quantify cluster of qualities that includes craft knowledge, life experience, native intelligence, common sense, intuition, courage, and the capacity to "handle things." Most of us seek in a leader this combination of genuineness and effectiveness. It makes him authentic, a credible resource who inspires trust and confidence, someone worth following into the uncertainties of change. (Evans, 2007, p. 136)

Unlike the logistical, technical work of learning to manage a budget, write a grant proposal, or write an evaluation report, this second form of leadership is difficult to learn in graduate school or from a series of workshops. Instead, it is a form of leadership that comes from practice in collaboratively crafting a vision of the future, articulating that vision to community members, and then supporting and nudging colleagues to bring the vision to life (all the while remaining open to the possibility that the vision may need alteration). It is a form of leadership that comes from consistently following through on promises that have been made, from listening carefully to teachers and students, and inviting them into the process of crafting a vision of the future. Sounds great, but this is not easy work. This form of leadership is what Heifetz et al. (2009) term "adaptive leadership" and what Argyris and Schön (1974, 1996) describe as "double-loop learning." This form of leadership requires the careful analysis of a school's culture, the collaborative diagnosis of the many factors involved in perpetuating a particular practice or trend, and collective design work and experimentation to create new ways of thinking and working together. Leading larger change efforts, such as making the schoolwide shift from a *reading* focus to a *literacy* focus, or from a basal reading program to a guided reading model, requires authentic, adaptive leadership in which literacy leaders' integrity is on the line. This is what Evans (2007) eloquently describes as the "consistency between personal beliefs, organizational aims, and working behavior" (p. 136).

Ultimately, one of the keys to the success of literacy leaders who coach is the balancing of managerial with visionary leadership work. A coach who solely focuses on vision and is unable to roll up her sleeves and lead a professional development workshop or set a schedule for observing and debriefing lessons is unlikely to shift teachers' practice. Alternatively, a coach who focuses entirely on scheduling, testing, and material details will find herself unable to dive into deeper conversations with teachers about their assumptions, beliefs, and practices. We know from research that coaches and literacy leaders often find themselves drowning in a deluge of managerial work (Deussen et al., 2007; Smith, 2007; Walpole & McKenna, 2009). Thus, coaches need to forge strong relationships with school and district leaders and have open conversations about roles, time management, and the need for protection from management overload (see chapter 4 for more about coach-principal relationships).

One effective tool for beginning to balance commitments is a simple whiteboard hung in a shared teacher space, or perhaps a coach's or leader's office, with outlines of broad goals for the marking period or year followed by a list of logistical details that need to be addressed. Some refer to this as the balance of the *urgent* (the day-to-day logistical details that need to be addressed) versus the *important* (the long-term, broad goals that sometimes are not addressed because of the laundry list of daily chores). Literacy leaders who make their important and urgent lists public with formal and informal leadership teams are better able to enter into a conversation with colleagues about how time is being spent and which details and logistics are most critical to helping define and reach ultimate goals. Some coaches post broad goals and essential questions on all their meeting agendas—signaling that even small, daily work can contribute to larger, longer-term goals.

Becoming an authentic and effective literacy leader means recognizing and balancing how your time is spent, taking control of that time, and not drowning in the daily list of to-dos. In the following Voices From the Field, Linda DiMartino, a literacy supervisor, discusses the ways in which she manages the week's activities and communicates with teachers. Notice that DiMartino has some routines, but she recognizes that at times she may need to juggle her schedule to meet urgent needs.

VOICES FROM THE FIELD

I keep a daily planner in which I record all of my teacher leader meetings, administrative meetings, and classroom appointments. I visit one school a day, Monday through Thursday and try to keep Friday for meetings and other duties. On a typical day, I could be modeling a lesson in three or four classrooms. The "preconference" occurs at a meeting or transpires over e-mail. I model classroom management techniques if needed, in addition to all components of a lesson. I assist students working, observe with the teacher, and discuss what we observed. I engage in conversations about student goals and plans for the next lesson. If I need to support a teacher on consecutive days, then I need to juggle more than one building. This is a challenging task. In between classroom visits, I check e-mail, which is a main way I communicate with teachers or complete another task. I never have "down time," and the trunk of my car is full of educational materials. I am available by cell phone only, because I am always on the go!

—Linda DiMartino, literacy supervisor

Leading for Adult Learning

Another critical component of thinking like a leader is adopting the mindset of *leading for adult learning* (Breidenstein, Fahey, Glickman, & Hensley, 2012). While many resources and standards for literacy coaches suggest that an understanding of adult development and learning is imperative, few resources actually offer guidance on how to make sense of and lead adult learning. Breidenstein et al. (2012) argue that "the work of school reform—or improving student learning—is inextricably connected to the learning of the adults who work in schools" (p. 12). In other words, without a clear vision for how to lead adult learning processes, and without a culture of adult learning in place, there is little hope for significant student growth over time. Breidenstein et al. go on to argue that we need to "support the learning not only of individual educators but also of the teams, groups, departments, schools, and districts in which they work . . ." (p. 8). But how might a coach productively think about organizing all of this adult learning?

Breidenstein and her colleagues build on the adult development work of Robert Kegan (1998) by proposing adult learning structures and routines that map onto the diverse ways in which adults in schools make sense of their work. Kegan's original constructive-developmental theory suggests that "(1) adults continually work to make sense of their experiences [constructive] and (2) the ways that adults make sense of their world can change and grow more complex over time [developmental]" (Breidenstein et al., 2012, p. 5). While Kegan (1998) proposes different stages of adult development focused on how adults' meaning-making systems grow more complex over time, Breidenstein and colleagues map the theory onto the experiences of groups of educators in schools. They propose that Kegan's original stages, or ways of knowing (see figure 2.1), can be translated into ways that leaders might work with groups of educators who need particular types of learning experiences (see figure 2.2).

Instrumental Knowers	Socializing Knowers	Self-Authoring Knowers
• Have concrete needs • Believe that rules are important and always search for the "right way" • Are most comfortable with concrete, specific processes • Have limited interest in reflection or collaboration when their own needs are not met	• Focus on others • Believe that group needs are important • Can put a group's needs before their own • Can be collaborative and reflective • Are uncomfortable with conflicting opinions, values, and behaviors	• Are reflective about themselves and their context • Can live with ambiguity • Evaluate their own actions according to internal standards; expect and accept conflict • Consider their personal goals and ideas very important • Are able to stand in opposition to a group

Figure 2.1: Ways of knowing.

Source: Reprinted by permission of the Publisher. From Angela Breidenstein, Kevin Fahey, Carl Glickman, and Frances Hensley, Leading for Powerful Learning: A Guide for Instructional Leaders. *New York: Teachers College Press. Copyright © 2012 by Teachers College, Columbia University. All rights reserved.*

Breidenstein and her colleagues' big contribution is not distinguishing among instrumental, socializing, and self-authoring "knowers" (or individual adults) but focusing leaders' energy on thinking about the *types of learning* that groups of adults in a school might need. The authors focus on three of the most prevalent ways of knowing and ways of learning identified among adult professional groups: instrumental, socializing, and self-authoring learning. We review each briefly:

- Instrumental learning can be thought of as technical, concrete learning that educators need when first adopting new practices (e.g., formulating effective strategies for literacy lessons involving SMART Boards or iPads and for when and how to conduct an interactive read-aloud). In instrumental-learning situations, literacy leaders can act in more directive ways, relying on their own expertise and presenting best practices. Ultimately, instrumental learning in schools is about learning specific practices.

- Socializing learning is learning that harnesses the power of a group or team. In socializing-learning situations, coaches set up and facilitate experiences where teachers can learn with and from one another. As opposed to the content knowledge and technical knowledge a coach might need to lead instrumental learning, a coach leading socializing learning needs to know how to build and support professional learning communities. Ultimately, socializing learning in schools is about learning to collaborate.

- Self-authoring learning is the kind of learning that questions business as usual, in which members of teams and groups can stand with and apart from the group simultaneously as they question deeply held assumptions about teaching and learning, as well as engage in self-directed collaborative inquiry. Coaches attempting to lead self-authoring learning must be willing to model risk taking and self-reflection. They must be able to ask tough questions of groups. A coach leading self-authoring learning supports teachers as they learn to live with tensions, such as the increased need to differentiate and create personalized learning experiences while simultaneously aligning practices with common standards and assessments. Ultimately, self-authoring learning in schools is about learning to question assumptions and become a more reflective practitioner.

A coach's stance shifts as she leads the different kinds of learning experiences (see figure 2.2), and every coach (based on her own experiences, work environment, relationships, and developmental arc) will find these stances more or less comfortable. However, we agree with Breidenstein et al. and Kegan that leaders who are able to lead from these different positions over time are better positioned to make large changes in teaching and learning.

School Learning Needs	Leadership Stance
Instrumental Learning	Leaders understand issues of teaching and learning; they have considerable knowledge about "best practice" and know how to help teachers find necessary expertise.
Socializing Learning	Leaders understand how to build collaborative groups, support reflective practice, and build school cultures that are focused on issues of teaching and learning.
Self-Authoring Learning	Leaders not only understand instructional issues and how to build reflective, collaborative cultures but also take an inquiry stance toward their own practice. Leaders become self-authoring learners themselves.

Figure 2.2: Leadership stance and school learning needs.

Source: Reprinted by permission of the Publisher. From Angela Breidenstein, Kevin Fahey, Carl Glickman, and Frances Hensley, Leading for Powerful Learning: A Guide for Instructional Leaders. *New York: Teachers College Press. Copyright © 2012 by Teachers College, Columbia University. All rights reserved.*

> **REFLECT**
>
> Think about your own leadership experiences. What do you see as your strengths? Possible needs? With which of these stances would you be most comfortable? Least comfortable?

Leading from each of these different stances suggests slightly different coaching practices. For instance, when thinking back to the Levels of Intensity we introduced in chapter 1, some coaching practices lend themselves much more to instrumental learning than to socializing or self-authoring learning. If we consider one of the goals of coaching to be supporting individuals and groups as they move from instrumental to socializing to self-authoring learning (Drago-Severson, 2009), then we might look for opportunities at the different Levels of Intensity to support learners in each of these ways. Moreover, at the group level, we might consider offering more opportunities for instrumental learning early in a coach's work, bridging slowly to socializing learning, and then slowly moving toward self-authoring learning (akin to moving across the Levels of Intensity).

Another resource that provides useful information about coaching behaviors is Moran's (2007) continuum of literacy coaching behaviors. Again, some coaching practices lend themselves much more to instrumental learning (e.g., resource management, demonstration lessons); others might appeal to those interested in socializing learning (e.g., co-planning, study groups); and others are much more indicative of self-authoring learning (e.g., peer coaching, co-teaching).

One quick, important caveat about these various ways of learning: they can be thought of as situational; that is, while individuals may predominantly need or prefer a particular form of learning, we must keep in mind that all individuals and groups also have a need for *different* forms of learning, depending on the knowledge, experiences, skills, and will they bring to any given situation or problem. Therefore, one of our goals as coaches is to always work toward expanding individuals' and groups' opportunities for learning and knowing as well as ways of learning and knowing. Ultimately, by adopting a leadership mindset, coaches position themselves to think and act more intentionally as they lead adult learning experiences within and across schools.

Frame 2: Thinking Like a Facilitator; Coaching Roles, Stances, and Positionality

One of the frames that many literacy leaders and coaches have struggled to adopt and define since the 1990s relates to thinking like a facilitator. Much debate in both the field and research literature has centered on the particular roles that literacy coaches have or should have in schools (Bean et al., 2015; Deussen et al., 2007; International Literacy Association, 2015). However, we view a great deal of this debate as a matter of the stances and positionality of coaches and teachers. Teaching has long been described as a profession governed by norms of autonomy, egalitarianism, and seniority (Donaldson et al., 2008; Lortie, 1975), norms which undermine coaching work that is built upon collaboration, shared goals, and efforts to make teaching practice public. Thus, how coaches position themselves in relationship to teachers and leaders matters a great deal. Much of the debate about the roles of coaches can be understood as a tension between coaches operating fundamentally in responsive, directive, or balanced ways (Ippolito, 2010), or what McKenna and Walpole (2008) describe as "soft" versus "hard" coaching (pp. 14–15).

Coaches who operate from a fundamentally *responsive* stance see their role as responding to teachers' needs, following teachers' interests, and encouraging teachers' self-reflection as they analyze and improve their practice in ways that teachers themselves articulate. This stance is built on a history of cognitive coaching (Costa & Garmston, 2002). On the other hand, coaches who operate from a fundamentally *directive* stance see their role as guiding teachers toward particular practices, sharing their own expertise, and holding teachers accountable. This stance is more closely aligned with the kinds of coaching associated with particular literacy models or programs, where the implementation of set practices is key. Recent evidence suggests that some *balance* of these stances is important, as coaches and literacy leaders shift back and forth between more responsive and directive ways of interacting with colleagues in order to achieve goals (Ippolito, 2010; Mangin & Dunsmore, 2015).

While the notion of balancing responsive and directive stances makes a great deal of sense, we have found that it is a complex mental model for literacy leaders to adopt and hold on to as they go about their daily work. Moreover, in some schools, the stance has been determined by a specific change initiative mandated by the district, as evident in many schools that participated in the large-scale federal Reading First initiative. A school or district administration might adopt a more directive approach overall, requiring schools to implement particular literacy programs or models, yet coaches and teacher leaders might still find ways to balance responsive and directive stances in their daily interactions with teachers. Coburn and Woulfin (2012), in a study of coaches in a Reading First school, discuss ways in which those coaches were able to support teachers in their efforts to implement the literacy framework adopted by the school, and at the same time, address the needs of individual teachers. In our most recent work with coaches and literacy leaders, we have sought an even more succinct way of talking about stance, positionality, and how best to balance the competing commitments of teachers' individual interests with larger school, district, and system-wide plans.

Having watched literacy leaders and coaches in action for over a decade, we now believe that the most successful mental frame to adopt when considering stance and positionality for coaches and teachers is the frame of "thinking like a facilitator." When a coach or literacy leader thinks and behaves as a facilitator, she naturally moves toward the balanced ways of working that seem to produce the best coaching relationships. Coaches who operate as facilitators:

▶ Provide safe learning opportunities for individuals and groups, with the goal of increasing collective capacity to reflect on student learning and instructional practice

▶ Focus on creating opportunities for genuine, deep learning (and understand that this can sometimes produce short-term confusion, frustration, and the questioning of deeply held assumptions)

▶ Create opportunities for colleagues to draw their own conclusions and craft their own responses, rather than always attempting to provide quick, *right* answers

▶ Focus on encouraging "participation, ensuring equity, and building trust" (McDonald, Mohr, Dichter, & McDonald, 2013, p. 11)

▶ "[Ask] difficult questions of the group, [take] responsibility for the arc of the group's learning, and persistently [push] towards deeper learning" (Fahey & Ippolito, 2015, p. 4)

▶ Use clear agendas and discussion-based protocols (an "agreed upon set of discussion or observation rules that guide coach/teacher/student work, discussion, and interactions") (Ippolito & Lieberman, 2012, p. 79) (see chapter 5)

▶ Respect and value the contributions of teachers, encouraging them to participate as colleagues in conversations and decision making

As can be seen from this short, partial list of the role of a facilitator, coaches and literacy leaders who operate as facilitators are always seeking to build shared ownership and understanding of instructional practices and student learning among teachers. Facilitators are neither entirely directive (introducing and prescribing specific instructional moves) nor entirely responsive (catering to individual and group requests). In fact, operating as a facilitator can free coaches from feeling as if they must always have all of the *right* answers at their fingertips. Instead, they can focus on *how* to help teachers find *better* answers, through individual and group processes that promote ownership and build confidence. One of our coaching colleagues calls this "finding the right tool for the job," signaling that, ultimately, facilitation is about matching purpose with participants and learning processes. Facilitative work is the day-to-day work of a literacy leader who coaches. Those who do not focus specifically on improving their facilitative skills are limiting their ability to positively influence colleagues.

Frame 3: Thinking Like a Designer; Considering Form and Function

Another powerful frame a literacy leader who coaches can adopt is that of a designer. Design thinking focuses on collaborative problem solving, addressing both technical and adaptive challenges (Heifetz et al., 2009) by collaboratively surfacing hidden assumptions, sources of confusion, structural and logistical obstacles, and procedural inefficiencies and then engaging individuals and teams in a process of *designing* effective responses. Literacy leaders who approach student learning and instructional challenges with a design mindset are able to engage colleagues in a process that builds reflective and problem-solving capacity—helping coaches position themselves as facilitators instead of sole experts.

There are roughly three areas that we have seen effective coaches address when they adopt the mindset of a designer: teaching and learning routines, collaborative learning structures, and assessment. We discuss each briefly here, and then we elaborate on each in later chapters:

- When coaches are helping teachers adopt, adapt, and invent teaching and learning routines, they are best served by thinking as designers. When thinking about how to best support teachers in their own design work of crafting instructional units and lessons, coaches often consult state and professional standards, consider the students' needs in their particular school and district, and the skills, knowledge, and practices of their teaching colleagues. When coaches recommend a particular practice or co-develop a new routine with a teacher, all of the aforementioned factors are in the back of their minds, and they are in fact acting most like designers who are thinking strategically about end results and efficient routes to those results. We explore this kind of thinking further in chapter 6.

- When coaches are choosing and creating collaborative learning structures for teachers, they are best served by thinking as a designer and then as a facilitator. Choosing whether to offer a content-based workshop, a study group, or a series of co-teaching opportunities requires coaches to adopt a design mindset and consider which dilemmas are most pressing and which collaborative learning structures might most efficiently address the dilemmas at hand. Sometimes a particular protocol or collaborative learning routine may not work without a bit of adaptation. Adapting a traditional routine to fit the needs of a particular group can benefit from design thinking. We explore this kind of thinking further in chapter 7, where we zoom in on group coaching.

- When coaches are considering assessment issues, they are best served by thinking as designers. Most literacy leaders know that excellent teaching and learning begins with sound assessment practices. When thinking like a designer, coaches might strategically use Google Forms or other tools to design targeted needs-assessment surveys to help faculty determine which areas of teaching and learning are most in need of improvement. Assessment work is also focused on the analysis of student data, including both formative and summative assessment results. All these data become part of the initial stages of design work, wherein a coach can lead teams of teachers through analysis, design, and implementation phases. We dive into the coach's role in assessment work in-depth later in chapter 8.

All of these ways of thinking and working map onto what has recently been called *design thinking*, and we highlight one of our favorite resources that helps educators and coaches adopt this frame. We have used and pointed many coaches to the free set of resources offered by Design Thinking for Educators (www.designthinking foreducators.com) and its accompanying downloadable resource guide, the *Design Thinking for Educators Toolkit* (www.designthinkingforeducators.com/toolkit). These materials encourage teachers and instructional coaches to engage in a five-step process (discovery, interpretation, ideation, experimentation, and evolution) that helps individuals and groups move from identifying and understanding a challenge to designing possible solutions. Along with a description of the five-step process for participating in and engaging others in design work, the *Design Thinking for Educators Toolkit* (2012) suggests particular ways of thinking about design work that are most productive, including:

- Thinking of yourself as a designer by being intentional in your creative problem-solving work

- "Embrac[ing] your beginner's mind" (p. 16) by adopting a learning stance, allowing for mistakes along the way, and not expecting the "right" answer to emerge immediately

- "Stepping out of your comfort zone" (p. 16) by leaving your classroom, routine, and established patterns of thinking and collaborating in order to try something entirely new

- Understanding that "problems are just opportunities for design in disguise," focusing us optimistically on a better future and helping us to ask, "What if?" instead of, "What's wrong?" (p. 16)

Notably, by adopting a design mindset, literacy leaders and coaches can shift the way they work with both individuals and larger groups to focus on productive problem solving instead of getting stuck in less productive cycles of blame and avoidance. At the systems level, adopting a design mindset might mean the collaborative design of group cycles of collaborative inquiry, action research, and coaching across grades and content areas. It means moving from the strategic large-group parsing of standards and deliberation about a set of core instructional practices that might meet those standards to design work that pushes beyond standards to meet particular students' needs, such as the needs of ELs or students with learning differences.

Adopting a design mindset as an organization suggests that the answers to both technical and adaptive challenges lie within the expertise and skills of the teachers and leaders in schools (perhaps with some assistance from outside resources as well); however, it positions literacy leaders and teachers as agents of change and designers, as protagonists in their own stories instead of extras on a movie set.

Above all else, thinking like a designer allows literacy leaders and teachers to try new approaches with an eye toward tinkering and refining, without expecting excellence or success immediately upon implementation. The related notion of "prototyping" is powerful (Scharmer, 2009). Coaches and teachers can try new ways of working, with some impunity to say, "Well, that didn't quite work the way we expected; let's figure out what didn't work and try something slightly different tomorrow!" It is this kind of design thinking that fosters a positive, collaborative, inventive culture where teachers begin to turn to each other to discuss and collaboratively solve instructional dilemmas. Ideally, over time, if a literacy leader promotes this way of working, teachers can engage in design thinking more autonomously, without needing constant feedback from the coach.

Frame 4: Thinking Like an Advocate; Standing for Something

You likely have heard the adage that "if you don't stand for something, you'll fall for anything." This has never been truer than for literacy leaders and coaches who are, by nature, stuck between students, teachers, principals, directors, and superintendents. More often than not, coaches have little formal authority, yet they are perhaps in the best position to influence teachers and leaders alike. This is why it is critically important to "stand for something" as a coach; in other words, to know what is most important to you and then to advocate for it.

VOICES FROM THE FIELD

I see my role as providing the support teachers need as they work to guarantee the academic success of their students. Teachers have so much responsibility, and they need the support [*and advocacy*] of others to make that a reality.

—Marsha Turner, literacy coach

Some scholars have suggested that advocacy work is a vital part of literacy leadership work (Smith, 2009), because when coaches are able to adopt the frame of thinking like an advocate, they are in a powerful position to leverage research, personal experience, and relationships not only to *improve* but also to *transform* teaching and learning. When thinking like an advocate, coaches engage in the following: advocating for students, advocating for teachers, advocating for community partnerships, and advocating for particular practices, models, and programs. We briefly discuss each stance next.

PUT INTO PRACTICE

In what ways do you as a literacy leader serve as an advocate? Talk with colleagues about the sorts of specific advocacy efforts that would improve literacy instruction in your school or district.

Advocating for Students

At the heart of all professional learning and improvement work is a laser-like focus on student access, opportunity, and success. Literacy leaders are well positioned to be advocates for individuals or groups of students. Hamilton (1993) found that reading specialists viewed themselves as advocates for students experiencing difficulties with reading. They made certain that these students weren't penalized for incomplete work by keeping them from recess or gym class, were recognized for their special talents in the classroom, and had opportunities to view reading as enjoyable and as a means of learning.

Regardless of their formal titles, literacy leaders can serve a vital role in schools by advocating for rights for students, including early identification of students' needs, multiple tiers of instruction and intervention (typically as part of a response to intervention [RTI] or tiered instruction system), and authentic reading, writing, and communication tasks and associated resources. For more about the advocacy for students' rights, we suggest looking at the position statement "Making a Difference Means Making It Different" (International Reading Association, 2000).

One of the most frequent queries we receive from pre-service and practicing literacy leaders is: "Should I raise concerns when I believe that current materials, instruction, schedules, or systems aren't truly meeting students' needs?" While the devil is in the details, our answer is almost always yes! Students' needs are the highest priority, and often, reading specialists, literacy coaches, and teacher leaders have extensive, specialized knowledge and experience to identify dilemmas and support colleagues as they begin to address gaps. Of course, every school has limitations regarding its budget, space, staffing, and materials; however, if current conditions are not meeting students' needs (as evidenced by both quantitative and qualitative data), then literacy leaders can confidently and respectfully advocate for change with teachers and leaders. In fact, advocating for change based on clear documentation of students' needs (and gaps between needs and current practices) is perhaps the strongest advocacy position to adopt.

Advocating for Teachers

While many literacy coaches and informal literacy leaders report feeling like "neither fish nor fowl" (Ippolito, 2010, p. 169), operating neither as formal classroom teachers nor as formal school leaders, this middle-road position can be a powerful place from which to advocate for the betterment of conditions, so that teachers can deliver the best literacy-focused instruction possible. This kind of advocacy work is delicate and must always be grounded in evidence related to students' needs; however, there are times when literacy leaders are completely justified in arguing for lengthier instructional blocks of time, common planning time for teams of teachers to meet and review literacy data and practices, or particular professional learning experiences to support new instructional practices.

When advocating for teachers' needs, we have found it best to:

▸ Draw clear connections between students' needs and teachers' needs. If teachers' needs are presented unrelated to students' needs, then little change can be expected.

▸ Build a coalition before approaching administrators. Do the informal relationship-building work of talking with both allies and possible naysayers before going public or making a case with administration. Not all teachers necessarily need to completely agree with a recommended change, but without broad support, literacy leaders will find themselves fighting a battle on multiple fronts at once.

▶ Do the homework of looking for implementation examples in the literature and in schools and districts nearby to paint a clear picture of the future after a proposed change has been adopted. If arguing for longer literacy instructional blocks, guided reading groups, classroom libraries, and so on, be prepared to demonstrate how these elements have proven successful elsewhere.

▶ Develop a rough plan before approaching administration, including possible benefits and rationales for drawbacks related to proposed changes. Going to an administrator with a problem without also brainstorming some possible solutions will likely lead to frustration and wasted time.

Advocating for Community Partnerships

Beyond advocating for students and teachers, literacy leaders are also often in a position to advocate for stronger school-community partnerships. While we expand on the coach's work with the community in chapter 10, we note here that literacy leaders are well positioned to advocate for better school-community connections.

Some have argued that strong school-community relationships are the key to school reform, particularly in our neediest urban schools (Warren, 2005). We completely agree. The more invested parents, politicians, and business leaders are in a community's local schools, the stronger a school's position to seek and receive support in the form of funding, volunteers, and wraparound services that provide students with the targeted assistance they need beyond school hours. The more that literacy leaders know about community-based services, and the more that community members are invited into schools, the better equipped both the school and community will be to meet students' needs. However, literacy leaders advocating for stronger school-community partnerships must do so with the knowledge, consent, and support of school- and district-based leadership, as well as a broad coalition of teachers. We have seen literacy leaders design and advocate creative, ongoing literacy-focused programs: volunteer reading-tutoring programs that invite retired community members to partner with elementary school students; bilingual-family education support services that invite parents to join their students at different times of day to learn a language together; and community members offering elective mini-courses for students, freeing teachers for short periods to engage in professional learning experiences. More frameworks and examples for school-community advocacy work can be found in chapter 10.

Advocating for Particular Practices, Models, and Programs

Finally, we have witnessed literacy leaders judiciously advocating for particular practices, models, and programs. While we find ourselves agnostic when it comes to particular practices, models, and programs, we believe that both homegrown and prepackaged curricula must be created, chosen, and adapted based on a synthesis of research-based best practices and a deep understanding of each school's context and its students' needs. Given this, there are times when literacy leaders are well positioned to advocate or oppose particular programs.

Many schools and districts seek to purchase and implement prepackaged literacy programs. We certainly see the value in terms of providing teachers with guidance, aligning practices, and offering students (particularly in schools and districts with high degrees of student mobility) similar experiences across grades and schools. However, not all literacy-focused programs and models are created equal. Literacy leaders are well positioned to help teachers and school leaders evaluate existing (and homegrown) literacy programs and models in order to ensure that authentic materials, rigorous cognitive tasks, and research-based practices in literacy learning are forefront.

While not all schools or literacy leaders will have complete freedom in choosing literacy-focused programs or models, it is perfectly reasonable for literacy leaders (as part of routine self-assessment practices) to collaboratively assess whether a particular program or model is in fact meeting students' needs. If not, then advocating for change makes sense.

We end this section with a short list of tenets for literacy leaders engaged in advocacy work:

> ▶ Marshal research, policy, and site-based data and evidence to support your position—don't simply assume that colleagues will adopt your stance without well-supported documentation.

> ▶ Adopt an evidence-based stance—encourage experimentation and the testing of hypotheses, with a willingness to move in a different direction when classroom-level evidence is suggesting that something is or isn't working.

> ▶ Passion is important, but reason will win the day. Try to avoid battles of will, petty disputes, or personality conflicts.

> ▶ Always remain open to the possibility that you're wrong—nothing works 100 percent of the time across all contexts, and something you *know* is right might work differently in different contexts.

> ▶ When a final decision is made, by a formal leader or group of colleagues, accept the decision and show your support through words and actions. It is always better to advocate for the next change than to spend time mourning the loss of a current debate.

Now that we have reviewed our four coaching mindsets, we want to introduce a quick tool to use as you reflect on your own coaching work and continue reading this book. Appendix A provides a simple template that allows you to take notes as you read, keeping track of which habits of mind are dominant in each area of coaching work and which habits of mind you have already adopted (or might consider adopting). We will refer back to appendix A throughout the book, but you may want to make a copy of it or create your own version now before reading on.

Summary

In this chapter, we described why savvy literacy leaders adopt the mindsets of leader, facilitator, designer, and advocate in order to best support students and teachers as they engage in literacy-based work. These mindsets not only help literacy leaders to adopt a coaching stance but also suggest productive ways of working to support the improvement of teaching and learning in individual classrooms as well as across entire schools and districts. In the following chapters, we elaborate on and illustrate these mindsets in action.

Activities

1. Look at, print, or create your own version of the chart in appendix A. Before reading further in the book, conduct a quick self-assessment. As you look across the columns of the template, which mindset comes most naturally to you? From which mindset do you typically engage in literacy leadership and coaching work? Which frame of mind is your biggest blind spot at the moment? What actions are you already taking to build that set of skills?

2. Next, as you look down the rows of the chart in appendix A, consider the topics of the upcoming chapters. Which domains (e.g., knowledge of literacy instruction, working with individuals, working with groups) are areas of strength? Any blind spots?

3. Then, look for overlaps by viewing the intersections between ways of thinking (column headings) and ways of working (row headings) addressed in the book. Look for strengths. Similarly, note possible blind spots, where your ways of thinking and ways of working may both need bolstering (e.g., thinking like a leader when leading school-change initiatives). How might doing this quick self-assessment shape your reading of the book and your subsequent work as a literacy leader who coaches?

4. Finally, look at appendix B, where we have provided additional resources related to many of the chapters in this book. Select one of the resources to read and discuss with colleagues.

Coaching for Student Success: What 21st Century Literacy Leaders Need to Know

> ### GUIDING QUESTIONS
>
> 1. What might effective literacy instruction look like in the 21st century? What are we coaching for?
>
> 2. How might current standards be used as drivers for developing curriculum that meets high expectations?
>
> 3. In what ways can literacy leaders assist teachers in thinking about the marriage between content and process, the what and how of literacy instruction?
>
> 4. How might technology be used as a tool to support teacher and student learning?

Melinda felt very comfortable with her fourth-grade curriculum and with providing literacy instructional advice to other fourth-grade teachers; however, when her principal asked her to expand her role to coach kindergarten, first-, second-, and third-grade teachers, Melinda grew nervous. What did she *really* know about those grades' needs in terms of reading, writing, and communication skills? What were the *most* important aspects of literacy instruction Melinda should focus on *now*, in light of demanding standards and pressures to improve student performance? What exactly was Melinda expected to *know* about literacy teaching and learning more generally?

In chapter 3, we turn our attention to exploring the *content* of literacy instruction, or what 21st century literacy leaders need to know about the core skills and knowledge at the heart of literacy instruction and achievement improvement efforts occurring nationwide. We begin with the end in mind—highly effective literacy instruction for student learning. Our goal in this chapter is to highlight major recent shifts in literacy instruction and point readers (such as Melinda) to the wealth of research and resources available to guide decisions about effective literacy instruction across grades. Given the many changes in the field of literacy during the latter part of the 20th century, 21st century literacy leaders must be able to navigate their way through heaps of suggestions and instructional advice. Where better to start than a brief discussion of the role of standards in literacy-focused professional learning and improvement efforts?

Standards as the Driver for Developing Curriculum That Meets High Expectations

Goals and standards adopted by a school or district can serve as the driver for developing or selecting curriculum (prekindergarten through twelfth grade), planning instruction that enables students to achieve these goals, and designing related professional learning routines. One of the responsibilities of literacy leaders, therefore, is to help teachers wrestle with and understand current literacy-focused standards; only then will they be able to develop or select curricula and instruction that enable them to support students in meeting those standards. We often point literacy leaders to a white paper written by curriculum design experts McTighe and Wiggins (2012), who discuss what they call "five big ideas" for translating high-level standards into curriculum, instruction, and assessment practices (for a more extended discussion of the following ideas, please see https://ldc.org/sites/default/files/mctighe_wiggins_final _common_core_standards_0.pdf). Our adapted versions of their "five big ideas" include:

▶ Make time to study the standards. The standards require careful reading, not only at one grade level, but at various levels, to determine how the requirements change over time and across domains. McTighe and Wiggins (2012) suggest that teachers, in groups, compare and contrast new standards with previous ones to determine how they differ and what these differences might mean for instruction (pp. 1–2). They may spend time unpacking what a specific standard means, examining the concept, the skill (verb), and the context. Teachers would then need to design experiences that enabled students to meet that standard. See this example:

  ▷ Standard item: "Ask and answer questions to demonstrate understanding of a text, referring explicitly to the text as the basis for the answers" (Reading Standards for Informational Text K–5, CCSS, p. 14) (NGA & CCCSSO, 2010)

▷ Concept: Understanding of a text, specifically using text as the basis for answers

▷ Verb/Skill: Ask and answer questions

▷ Context: Informational text

▶ Recognize the need to understand that standards identify outcomes or long-term goals. The standards do not describe or specify a particular literacy curriculum; rather, they identify long-term goals or expectations for students. Schools must make decisions about how they will achieve those goals. For example, how does the specific aforementioned standard relate to other standards? What teaching and learning activities would be appropriate?

▶ Involve teachers in unpacking the standards to develop curricula for a unit or grade level. McTighe and Wiggins (2012) suggest four types of "unpacking" tasks: long-term transfer tasks, overarching understandings, overarching essential questions, and cornerstone tasks (p. 4).

▶ Design or map the curriculum backward. Perhaps McTighe and Wiggins's most popular and widely cited contribution to the field is the notion of *backward design*. Here, we are encouraged to think about eventual student *outputs*—what can students produce or do?—and end goals as related to particular standards. We are then encouraged to think like designers and carefully plan the instructional *inputs*—what activities will the teacher plan for the lesson?—that will guide students toward successful enactment of the standards. This suggestion encourages coaches and teachers to begin curriculum selection and design conversations with the question, "Having learned key content, what will students be able to do with it?" in order to guide the answers to what is often teachers' more pressing question: "What will we teach and when should we teach it?" (p. 7).

▶ Use assessments wisely to determine students' growth toward goals. Here, McTighe and Wiggins (2012) remind us that it is only through careful and local *assessments* that teams of coaches and teachers can reveal where we are meeting our instructional goals, as evidenced by student performances of understanding across a variety of tasks (pp. 9–11). While new high-stakes tests will almost certainly accompany new standards, some of the most powerful assessments are those that help teams of teachers to refine their instructional practices in order to more efficiently guide students toward effective demonstrations of standards-based work.

In this era of the CCSS, effective literacy leadership teams are using the standards as levers to engage teachers in deep, meaningful conversations about long-term literacy goals for students across grade levels and content areas. Literacy coaches working with a leadership and design mindset are asking teachers to join them in cycles of inquiry around the standards, analyzing which instructional practices most efficiently meet those standards and the needs of their particular students (see a partial example from the Long Beach School District in Bean, 2015, pp. 298–300). Another resource for literacy teams involved with professional learning experiences related to standards is the guide produced by the Aspen Institute, *Implementation of the Common Core State Standards: A Transition Guide for School-Level Leaders* (published September 2013), which can be retrieved from www.aspeninstitute.org/publications /implementation-common-core-state-standards-transition-guide-school-level-leaders.

The CCSS, and other standards like them, appear to be a step in the right direction toward producing sophisticated readers, writers, and communicators within and across disciplines. The inclusion of Reading Foundational Skills (K–5) in the CCSS speaks to the importance of the initial literacy skills of "concepts of print, alphabetic principle, and other basic conventions of the English writing system" as a means to an end, that of developing proficient readers who can "comprehend text across a range of types and disciplines." As stated in the International Reading Association's document *Literacy Implementation Guidance for the ELA Common Core State Standards*, "Early, systematic, and explicit teaching of the foundational skills is required" (International Reading Association, 2012, p. 2).

Nevertheless, we have seen enough standards come and go (as well as ongoing debates in the research literature) that we always encourage schools to develop teachers' capacity at the local level to become critical consumers of both standards and research. It is only as a group of collaborative, critical consumers that teams of teachers are able to align their teaching with standards and research while also adopting and adapting sensible practices given the particular population of students at hand.

Major Shifts: How *Now* Is Different From *Then*

In the spirit of adaptation, invention, and creating ownership at the local level, we introduce two ways of thinking about highly effective literacy instruction. First, we introduce a few working hypotheses about effective literacy instruction. Every district, school, and teacher has their own set of beliefs about what works and what doesn't; therefore, we wanted to take a moment to show our own cards and reveal our own working hypotheses about modern instructional efforts. Second, following our working hypotheses, we review what we believe to be the most important major shifts in literacy teaching and learning that have occurred at the outset of the 21st century. These are shifts that every literacy leader should be aware of in order to effectively prioritize professional learning and support work.

REFLECT

As you read the hypotheses and shifts that follow, note which you agree and disagree with. What would you add to the lists? What would you subtract? Which of these hypotheses and shifts might be most pressing for your school or district? (You might share this list with teachers in your school as a means of stimulating a discussion that enables teachers to discuss their beliefs and perspectives.)

A Few Working Hypotheses About Effective Literacy Instruction

- There is no single set or definitive list of literacy instructional practices that will be equally effective for every school, grade-level team, or student. Standards and research are useful guides but will never *completely* reflect what is most effective for each group of students in each and every school. Local adjustments, adaptations, and interpretations will always be necessary in order to respond to students' needs.

- Acknowledging that there is no perfect *silver bullet* set of instructional practices, highly effective schools and teams of educators must continually seek to align their literacy instructional practices with both emerging research and evolving state literacy standards.

- The most effective schools and teams will continually and collaboratively review, refine, and redesign teaching and collaborative practices in order to come to a common, shared understanding of what *effective practice* means in their school for their students.

- Effective schools and teams will focus on the kinds of materials, experiences, and tools (including digital tools) that help students bridge from their own linguistic, cultural, and economic places of origin to an expanded sense of self and place in the global community.

- Finally, the most effective schools and teams will continually evaluate and improve upon their instructional practices through a process of self-study focused on students' actual learning outcomes (e.g., collaboratively collecting and analyzing student work and data and altering teaching practices as a result).

It is with an acknowledgment of the power of standards, and with these working hypotheses in mind, that we now review what we see as major shifts in literacy instruction in the 21st century. Some of these shifts have been prompted by current standards for literacy, whether those are the CCSS or those adopted or adapted by states and districts. We then provide examples that illustrate what we might expect of students when they are working in classrooms that exemplify these instructional shifts.

Major Shifts in Literacy Instruction in the 21st Century

Literacy teaching and learning has undergone several major shifts during the first decades of the 21st century. A number of societal factors have challenged the way we think about teaching reading, writing, and communication in the United States. Related instructional shifts follow:

- An integrated view of literacy that calls for attention to reading, writing, and communications has arisen. No longer is the emphasis only on reading, but there is recognition of the interrelationships between and among all of the language arts. For example, early oral language skills lead to and facilitate the development of later reading and writing skills. Talking about what one has read or written and listening to others discuss what they have read or written develops deeper understanding and learning (Chapin, O'Connor, & Anderson, 2013; Michener & Ford-Connors, 2013; Zwiers & Crawford, 2011).

- Literacy is the foundation for all learning. All teachers have a responsibility for understanding how literacy impacts learning in their classrooms. The term "disciplinary literacy" (Shanahan & Shanahan, 2008; Moje, 2015) has come to represent the ways in which teachers, at both elementary and secondary grade levels, apprentice students in the ways of thinking and working in a discipline, increasing content learning by focusing on disciplinary literacy skills. For example, a history teacher asking students to discuss a chapter about factors leading to the Civil War can use specific disciplinary literacy strategies to help students think like historians. Students might consider particular features of a secondary source, the author and his perspectives and biases, and how to discuss the content of the chapter as a historian might, taking a stand about the content and the form in such a way that students can disagree without being disagreeable.

- A comprehensive, systematic literacy program is needed. An effective literacy program calls for a well-articulated approach with increasing expectations and rigor as students move through the grades. Some refer to this as the "staircase of complexity" as specifically related to increasing textual challenge.

- There is an increased emphasis on the literacy learning needs of children across all ages and grade levels, from birth through twelfth grade (and even after). States and districts now recognize the importance of working closely with providers of preschool education to support efforts to develop the language and literacy skills of young students. Also, much more attention is being given to integrating literacy instruction in secondary schools as essential for preparing students for college and career success. All of these efforts are focused on the importance of language and literacy as the bases for all learning.

- There is a need for students to read text, both print and digital media, critically and to understand how to evaluate the credibility and trustworthiness of such text. The widespread availability of technology requires schools to guide and support students, so that they are able to use a wide variety of digital devices and software wisely as tools for literacy learning and communication.

- Students need to learn both general academic and discipline-specific vocabulary to support their wide reading, discussion, and writing work. Teachers can assist students in learning words by establishing classrooms that are language-rich, through explicit teaching of words, and by teaching students *how* to learn words (Dobbs, 2013). Helping students learn both general academic vocabulary (e.g., "abstract," "categorize," and "summarize") and discipline-specific words (e.g., "precipitation" and "photosynthesis") will facilitate their ability to learn new, unfamiliar concepts.

- Students need to consume a balanced diet of literary fiction and informational texts from prekindergarten through twelfth grade. While literary fiction has an important (and more accepted) role in literacy instruction, experiences with informational texts are important from the early grades on. Such experiences may provide a necessary entry to literacy, helping students develop the background knowledge necessary for disciplinary learning.

Next, we describe some of the types of activities that students would be undertaking in classrooms that exemplify these shifts:

- "Writing-to-learn" tasks include activities like structured note taking, interactive reading guides, and written responses to short prompts. Students could also produce a moderate amount of "writing-to-demonstrate-knowledge" projects in the form of longer, process-focused essays, reports, feature articles, data presentations, and so on—these would be polished final products, the results of lengthier workshop processes, ideally meant for dissemination or display to a larger, real audience. Students of all ages could be guided through a process of brainstorming, drafting, revision, editing, and publication, all with a target audience in mind, such as parents, the classroom next door, or online forums.

- Students could use digital tools, strategically and substantively, to demonstrate their understanding of content as well as their mastery of digital media. This might include creating PowerPoint presentations, websites, blogs, tweets, Facebook posts, mashups, and so on.

- Real-world products valued by various disciplinary experts, in forms that approximate what professional artists, authors, historians, musicians, mathematicians, and scientists might create themselves, could be the end-goals. Again, this is all with an eye toward age appropriateness; however, there is great power in asking second graders to create their own science notebooks in which they record (in words and diagrams) the differences and similarities between butterflies and moths. Likewise, tenth graders might collect and analyze (in a more sophisticated notebook) and then present in a mock research paper their own data about the success or failure of different designs meant to prevent an egg from breaking when dropped from different heights.

REFLECT

In what ways have the shifts in literacy instruction, described previously, affected instruction in the schools in which you work? What challenges have these shifts created for teachers, administrators, and students? What additional shifts have you experienced, and what have been the effects?

Marrying the Content and Processes of Effective Literacy Instruction

Given that literacy leaders, in their work with teachers, must think both about content and process—for example, inferential comprehension skills (the content) and use of high-level questioning (the process)—we discuss key notions about these two aspects of literacy instruction. One of the first questions that any literacy leadership team and instructional coach might ask themselves is: What knowledge and skills do we expect students to master as the result of literacy-focused instruction?

While intelligent people continue to differ in how they think and talk about the content and skills that students need to acquire in school (Hirsch, 2006; Perkins, 2014), we take the long view of literacy-focused instructional work. Often, students' acquisition and application of a set of reading, writing, and communication skills are meant to stretch far beyond a particular text and beyond a single instructional activity to larger ways of working and thinking within and across disciplines. Instruction is meant to support students in making connections well beyond the classroom. This idea is comforting in many ways—as former teachers, we have had moments where we could comfort ourselves at the end of a tough day by saying, "Well, that *one* activity or *one* day is just a drop in the bucket for these kiddos, so don't panic!" While this notion can be comforting in the moment, it can pose a dilemma for coaches and teachers in the long-run as they might disagree about particular sets of texts and artifacts to engage students (the content) as well as how best to engage students deeply with that content (the process). As coaches and literacy leadership teams wrestle with this tension—about how the *content* and *processes* of literacy-focused instruction might best be married—we find ourselves pointing coaches to two sources. The first is a brief rubric designed by Newmann, Secada, and Wehlage (1995), which helps

guide our thinking about the quality of instruction. (The simple four-item rubric can be found at http://schoolreforminitiative.org/doc /classroom_instr_rubric.pdf.) The other resource is the emerging literature on the teaching of disciplinary literacy (Moje, 2015; Shanahan & Shanahan, 2008).

We have found the Newmann et al. (1995) rubric helpful when talking with coaches and coaching teachers directly. It focuses on the following dimensions of instruction: higher order thinking, deep knowledge, substantive conversation, and connections to the world beyond the classroom. The rubric supports literacy leaders, teachers, and teams in choosing excellent textual materials and designing highly engaging related learning activities. The result is rigorous, impactful work that boosts students' literacy and content learning. Consider an instructional task that requires students to engage in higher order thinking such as discovering, analyzing, critiquing, or synthesizing; focuses students on pushing for deeper knowledge through problem solving, explaining their thinking using evidence, and so on; engages all students in substantive conversation with each other and the teacher; and connects the task at hand to their own lives and world beyond the classroom. This is the kind of instruction that marries content and process, connects to Common Core standards, and ultimately harnesses students' literacy skills in service of deep content learning.

Additionally, while disciplinary literacy was first conceptualized primarily as a way of teaching in the upper grades, recent work points to the power of elementary school teachers introducing informational texts and multiple texts in ways that prepare students to more carefully consider disciplinary habits of mind and ways of working (Brock, Goatley, Raphael, Trost-Shahata, & Weber, 2014; Shanahan & Shanahan, 2014). Let's consider further how a focus on disciplinary literacy across all grade levels might help teacher teams make sense of marrying content and process goals.

Disciplinary Literacy as a Way of Selecting Authentic Content

Disciplinary literacy asks teachers to model for students of all ages and grade levels ways of thinking and working like historians, literary critics, mathematicians, scientists, and so on with the purpose of preparing students to eventually attain the highest levels of literacy (Shanahan & Shanahan, 2008, 2014). One of the goals of teaching with a disciplinary literacy mindset is selecting authentic, real-world texts and artifacts that provide students with opportunities to engage in the kinds of reading, writing, thinking, and discussion that mirror (in age-appropriate ways) how professional artists, authors, critics, historians, mathematicians, and scientists work (Brock et al., 2014; Phillips Galloway, Lawrence, & Moje, 2013). We find this way of thinking about the content and processes of literacy-focused instruction helpful, particularly by asking and answering the following questions when choosing instructional materials:

> ▶ Is this text, artifact, data set, or problem something that professionals in their respective fields would consider to be authentic, pedagogical, and connected to real-world phenomena in age-appropriate ways? (Again, we emphasize *age-appropriate* here, not meaning to suggest that second graders analyze *War and Peace* or advanced data sets related to infectious diseases.)

> ▶ Are the habits of mind and ways of working like an author, critic, historian, mathematician, or scientist evident in the material at hand?

> ▶ How can students examine this text, artifact, data set, or problem and see the hallmarks of a larger genre?

> ▶ How can students read, write about, and discuss this text, artifact, data set, or problem in ways that approximate (in age-appropriate ways) how professionals in their respective fields might interact with the material?

> ▶ Are students' own lives, languages, and cultures reflected in at least a portion of the texts, artifacts, data, or problems being introduced across content areas?

By asking and answering these questions in grade-level or subject-specific groups, we believe that literacy leaders and teams of teachers are able to substantively evaluate informational and literary materials used to teach content. From this way of thinking, the true rigor of any literacy-focused instructional work can be measured by the degree to which high-quality content and strategic processes interact to help students work in deep, meaningful, disciplinary-specific ways. When authentic, real-world content is introduced in such a way that students are able to read, write, talk, and think deeply about it (disciplinary literacy juxtaposed with Newmann et al.'s rubric), then we would be hard-pressed not to call the work rigorous.

So where might coaches and literacy leadership teams turn, specifically, as they continue to think about the content of their disciplinary literacy-focused instructional work? For a more fine-grained sense of high-quality disciplinary literacy content that students might need to master at elementary and secondary grade levels, literacy leadership teams might do well to consult the standards produced by the major disciplinary professional education organizations:

- National Council of Teachers of English (www.ncte.org/standards)
- National Council of Teachers of Mathematics (www.nctm.org /Standards-and-Positions/Principles-and-Standards)
- National Council for the Social Studies (www.socialstudies.org /standards)
- National Science Teachers Association (http://ngss.nsta.org)
- National Core Arts Standards (www.nationalartsstandards.org)

These organizations provide excellent starting places for coaches and teams to catalog and choose which disciplinary literacy habits of mind, ways of working, and canonical texts, artifacts, data, or problems students should encounter across grades and subject areas. However, while these standards suggest major concepts that students might need to master by particular grade levels and stages of schooling, they rarely suggest particular texts or media through which students must learn these concepts. They merely provide starting places for teams to consider the foundational ways of thinking and working that each disciplinary community values, which could and probably should guide teaching teams' selection and use of materials and instructional tasks.

Looking to Research for Promising Practices for Teaching Literacy From Prekindergarten Through Twelfth Grade

While content and process are clearly linked, there does exist a great deal more research about promising practices (processes) of literacy instruction that serves students well over their college and career lives. As coaches and teams consider which skills students need and which instructional practices support the acquisition of those skills, the first place teams might turn is the set of standards identified for their specific state. Standards are a rich source for literacy leadership teams to consult as they consider the procedural skills that will likely undergird much of students' literacy-based work in the coming decades. However, the standards do not dictate *which* model texts or instructional strategies teachers must use to introduce and refine important skills. The particular disciplinary content used to meet the standards is left to the discretion of teachers and literacy leadership teams—which we think is just right! This provides teachers the opportunity to select appropriate texts and pedagogical moves in response to students' backgrounds, stages of reading development, and interests.

Another way of thinking of the literacy procedural skills students need (and related instructional practices that introduce and refine them) is to turn to major literacy research syntheses and reports. We identify several here:

- The 2000 report of the National Reading Panel (NRP) (National Institute of Child Health and Human Development, 2000) is perhaps one of the most influential literacy-focused reports in recent US educational history. The report has been widely cited, and as a result (somewhat predictably), also critiqued (Coles, 2003). The NRP research group conducted a meta-analysis of literacy research to make recommendations for which instructional practices result in successful literacy outcomes for young students. Their findings included a focus on phonemic awareness, phonics, fluency, vocabulary, and reading-comprehension strategy instruction. Of course, much like the CCSS, these represent more procedural skills (e.g., fluency and flexible use of comprehension strategies) as opposed to an argument for the teaching of particular texts or content-area concepts.

- *Reading Next* (Biancarosa & Snow, 2006), *Writing Next* (Graham & Perin, 2007), and *Time to Act* (Carnegie Council on Advancing Adolescent Literacy, 2010) each focus on adolescent learners. In *Reading Next*, *Writing Next*, and *Time to Act*, we see clear extensions of the early recommendations for procedural skills, with perhaps a bit more attention paid to disciplinary literacy, explicit comprehension instruction, motivating adolescent learners, engagement with a wider diversity of texts, and engagement with technology in reading and writing tasks. Elsewhere, we have written that these domains of procedural skills (and related instructional practices) shift slightly across age ranges, with older students needing a clearer focus on disciplinary literacy, general academic and discipline-specific vocabulary, academic language and discussion skills, synthesis of multiple texts, digital literacy skills, and writing-to-learn as well as writing-to-demonstrate-knowledge skills (Ippolito, Lawrence, & Zaller, 2013). Again, however, all of these domains map onto literacy *procedural knowledge* as opposed to particular disciplinary-specific concepts.

Connecting Content and Process in a Quick Example

Coaches and teams of teachers we have worked with often ask which literacy program or framework is best when considering content and process goals. Unfortunately, this is not an easy question to answer, because the marriage of content and process is most effective when it is carefully crafted by teams of teachers in particular schools responding to specific groups of students. However, there are some frameworks that do indeed skillfully marry content and process goals. The Literacy Collaborative framework (based largely on the work of Irene Fountas and Gay Su Pinnell) is one such set of processes that has demonstrated success across schools over time, with a dedicated coaching component supporting the continual improvement of teaching and learning (Biancarosa, Bryk, & Dexter, 2010). In the following Voices From the Field, you will hear a bit about how one district utilized the Literacy Collaborative framework to jumpstart its creation of literacy leadership teams across levels.

VOICES FROM THE FIELD

Our district used the grant funding to participate in the Literacy Collaborative through Ohio State University (OSU). This philosophy of literacy instruction is based on the theories within Marie Clay's Reading Recovery program, which had long been established in our district. Through the Literacy Collaborative at OSU, we created a building-level Primary (and later Intermediate) Literacy Team. This team was supportive to the coaching positions as it included teachers and administrators. This team analyzed data, looked at curricula, and made instructional decisions and plans for the school. Much of the coaching need or focus also came through this team and was supported by the team.

—Annette Vietmeier, Director of Curriculum, Instruction, and Technology

—Tracy Toothman, Reading Recovery teacher/literacy coach

—Fran Hardisty, Reading Recovery teacher

In figure 3.1 (page 50), we provide a quick vignette illustrating how a third-grade guided reading session neatly marries content and process. Also notice how it is connected to Newmann's rubric and disciplinary literacy considerations.

A third-grade teacher is facilitating a guided reading group with six students around Scieszka and Smith's (1998) *Time Warp Trio: Knights of the Kitchen Table*, and she is working to address both English language arts and social studies standards. Before beginning to read, the teacher asks the students to quickly brainstorm, looking at the front cover, what events they might expect to read about in the book. She asks what comes to the students' minds as they think about King Arthur and the knights of the round table. She asks whether students believe King Arthur was real or fictional, and what a historian might consider and ask himself as he would begin to read the fictional account. Then, with this group, who has been practicing guided reading for several months, the teacher sets them reading individually, with a few reminders of the skills she would like them to practice as they read (e.g., writing questions, summarizing, and noting any places of confusion).

As students begin to read the first chapter of the book, the teacher poses three questions to guide them to think "within," "beyond," and "about" the text (Fountas & Pinnell, 2006, pp. 32–44). She asks students to find, record, and talk about particular vocabulary words within the first chapter that foreshadow the impending time travel back to King Arthur's realm. She asks individual students to share with her one at a time, whispering quietly while the others read, about their predictions based on their understanding of words and phrases they identify in the text. After students have finished reading, the teacher focuses students' attention on and "beyond" the text by asking comprehension questions related to the chapter and connecting to students' lives, about their own views of time travel, and which aspects of the adventure would produce the most excitement or anxiety. Later, in their reading journals, the teacher asks the students to write a few sentences about the text, talking about the story's structure, the author's use of language, or initial impressions of characters. Connecting to social studies standards, the teacher asks the students to critique the text as historians, offering Scieszka advice about how to better bring history to life.

Figure 3.1: Vignette illustrating the marriage of content and process.

REFLECT

- Fountas and Pinnell (2006) suggest guided reading practices that focus both teachers' and students' attention on particular disciplinary content and asks them to wrestle with it in meaningful ways. Where do we see that equal attention in the previous vignette?

- Thinking about the Newmann et al. (1995) rubric, where in the previous vignette do we see instruction that promotes higher order thinking, deep knowledge, substantive conversation, and real-world connections?

- Finally, what disciplinary literacy connections are to be found?

In the previous vignette, one can easily see the interaction of the procedural skills emphasized by the National Reading Panel (NRP) report and literacy research, such as attending to vocabulary and focusing on comprehension, with the kinds of instructional practices that Fountas, Pinnell, and Newmann et al. consider to be most effective. Of course, all of this wonderful marrying of content and process is also now increasingly supported by students' use of digital resources, a 21st century eventuality. Modern literacy leaders cannot ignore their roles in supporting teachers' and students' effective use of digital tools and systems.

Technology as a Tool to Support Teacher and Student Learning

Technology, perhaps more than any other domain, has made a dramatic difference in how we communicate and learn in and out of schools. Many young students today come to school with much experience using tablets, smartphones, computers, and a wide array of touch screen devices; moreover, most older students will have spent a great deal of their free time engaged in gaming, social networking, and texting. They have experience playing games on their iPads, using Skype or FaceTime to communicate with friends and family, and often have their own cell phones. Most students will have experience with using the Internet, but many often do not know how to use it effectively and critically. Thus, more emphasis is being placed in schools on both computer programming as well as helping students to use the Internet and a wide number of personal devices as learning tools, especially as teachers provide students with opportunities to engage in rigorous and authentic assignments required to meet the expectations of state standards. For example, in the CCSS, students are expected to be able to conduct online searches, use multiple sources (both print and digital), assess the reliability and validity of these sources, and communicate what they have learned from their work. The *Framework for 21st Century Curriculum and Assessment* (National Council of Teachers of English, 2013) identifies a list of questions addressing what students should be able to do to develop proficiency and fluency with the tools of technology (for the full position statement, see www.ncte.org/positions/statements/21stcentframework). The six overarching questions include:

1. Do students use technology as a tool for communication, research, and creation of new works?

2. Do students evaluate and use digital tools and resources that match the work they are doing?

3. Do students find relevant and reliable sources that meet their needs?

4. Do students take risks and try new things with tools available to them?

5. Do students, independently and collaboratively, solve problems as they arise in their work?

6. Do students use a variety of tools correctly and efficiently?

To support students' development of digital literacy skills, Castek and Gwinn (2012, p. 301) identify four strategies essential for online reading comprehension:

1. **Reading to locate online information:** Students need to know how to ask questions, to identify key words, and to revise search terms. They must know how to navigate websites effectively.

2. **Reading to evaluate online information:** Students must be able to identify the accuracy of online information and know how to verify its trustworthiness.

3. **Reading to synthesize online information:** Students must be able to synthesize information from different online sources, to locate what is important, to eliminate the nonessential.

4. **Reading to communicate online information:** Students must be able to share what they have learned in a meaningful way (e.g., in oral presentations and in writing). Sometimes students use technology such as PowerPoint or SMART Boards to share information—again, this is an important aspect of what teachers need to emphasize in their instruction.

Literacy leaders who coach will surely want to keep a professional learning focus on students' use of technology to achieve higher level reading, writing, and communication skills. One important first step is for colleagues to collaboratively read and discuss potential differences between students' online and offline reading, writing, and communication options and experiences. Coiro (2009) offers five good starting places for such conversations, identifying research-based tenets for technology-focused literacy instruction with students:

1. Understand and make explicit for students the relationships between offline and online reading comprehension strategy use.

2. Honor the literacies that students bring to school from their daily lives.

3. Explore and clarify expectations for new classroom roles and relationships embedded in problem-based online collaborations.

4. Provide time for students to develop positive dispositions toward learning and communicating via the Internet.

5. Use self, peer, and teacher assessments as inquiry to inform online-reading strategy use and classroom instruction.

Coiro (2015) goes on to provide several recent examples of how elementary teachers can provide their students with opportunities to develop understanding through online inquiry. One suggestion is the use of Internet inquiry baskets, in which students write questions on index cards that are placed into a special basket. At a specific time, the teacher selects one card, and then develops a plan for working with students to help them search and navigate the Internet, looking for answers to that question.

Helping Teachers Learn to Use Technology in Their Instruction

Literacy leaders who coach can do a great deal to support a community of educators learning together about best teaching practices that include technology, especially in an effort to address high-level, rigorous standards. Indeed, the CCSS emphasizes the importance of "new literacies" and, specifically, the importance of being able to read information from multiple print and digital sources, assess their accuracy and credibility, and integrate information across these forms.

For literacy leaders wishing to support teachers in this domain, it is no longer enough to simply make technology available; rather, teachers need to be supported in their efforts to incorporate technology in their instructional practices when appropriate. In other words, technology should not drive instruction—it should be a tool that helps teachers reach their identified goals. Coiro (2015) suggests three guiding principles for those involved in supporting teachers' use of technology:

1. Recognize that teachers are at different stages as users of technology. Some use technology to teach in traditional ways while others are willing to embed technology in their current practices, making adaptations in how they teach. Other teachers use technology in new, creative ways. In other words, in all schools, there will be a range of expertise from novices through sophisticated users; thus, coaching support will almost necessarily differ.

2. Teachers will have different perspectives about technology, its value, and their willingness to use it. These perspectives can range from "I don't see a need for it" to "Technology has made a difference in how I teach and how students learn." Also, perspectives will affect the specific recommendations made by literacy and school leaders and the success of those recommendations.

3. Job-embedded learning that includes opportunities for collaboration is essential in advancing teacher learning and enthusiasm for technology in the classroom. (See chapter 7 for more ideas about working with small groups.)

While there is much more that could be said about the role of technology in a modern, effective literacy instructional program, this is an emerging field best held by literacy leaders as an ongoing focus of collaborative inquiry. Thus, we offer two key resources for further exploration: the University of Connecticut's Neag School of Education New Literacies Research Lab (http://newliteracies.uconn.edu) offers a variety of research-based readings and resources related to digital literacies; and the International Society for Technology in Education (2007) describes standards for students (http://www.iste.org/standards/ISTE-standards/standards-for-students).

Thinking Ahead to School-Wide Literacy Programming

Before we move on to chapter 4 and the rest of the book, where our focus is more squarely on the work that coaches and literacy leaders can undertake to help produce the kinds of teaching and learning outlined previously, we want to acknowledge that, ultimately, *rigor* and *highly effective instruction* are achieved through the integration and interaction of a number of leadership and instructional actions. Highly effective literacy instruction for students is not often produced through adoption of a single program or framework, nor is it merely an additive process of continually piling one more initiative or intervention onto the heap, what Bryk (2015) terms "solutionitis" (p. 468). Instead, effective school-wide literacy teaching and learning is achieved through the systematic self-study and responses of literacy leaders and their colleagues. Researchers Bryk, Sebring, Allensworth, Luppescu, and Easton (2010) talk about this phenomenon as baking a cake, needing not only the sum of the ingredients, but the interaction of the elements to produce something new. Bryk et al. (2010) talk about five key ingredients: leadership as the driver for change, parent-community ties, professional capacity, a student-centered learning climate, and instructional guidance. The researchers go on to explain that the "overall coherence of improvement efforts . . . is akin to a recipe. It provides guidance about how one should mix and blend the ingredients . . . to make reform truly add up to systemic change" (p. 203). We couldn't agree more. Coaches who think and act like leaders are continually focusing on system-wide coherence and integration of services for students.

Moreover, in our own work helping schools implement and evaluate highly effective literacy programs, we have found that rigorous, effective instruction is often part of a larger school-wide program that includes attributes similar to those identified by Taylor (2011):

- Using collaborative instructional delivery models that provide for coherence (e.g., aligning core classroom instruction with specialized instruction provided by Title I special education teachers [horizontal], or providing for a seamless transition from elementary to middle school literacy instruction [vertical])

- Maximizing the amount of time for reading instruction (e.g., developing a common literacy block across classrooms)

- Using school-wide data to inform instruction

- Providing interventions for students who struggle

- Collaborating with peers in professional learning and change efforts

- Having strong links to parents

Notice the emphasis on collaboration in Taylor's list, both in how instruction is delivered and also in the ways in which teachers work with each other to increase their professional expertise. We would add to these attributes the importance of effective leadership (specifically, shared leadership that includes all educators in decision making related to a school's literacy program). We expand on many of these ideas in chapters 4, 9, and 10, where we dive more deeply into the work of the coach as related to school culture, school-wide literacy programming, and school-community partnerships.

Summary

In this chapter, we discussed the end products of effective literacy leadership and coaching work—highly effective, rigorous teaching and learning that marries content and literacy processes. We reviewed the importance of providing time and support to deeply analyze standards, in order to then use standards as a driver for instructional change and refinement. Next, we talked about some of our working hypotheses of literacy instruction and described some of the major shifts in literacy instruction. We ended with a brief discussion of the importance of students' use of technology to support literacy learning, which must be mixed and blended a little differently for each school and district.

Activities

1. Using the chart found in appendix A, note ways that literacy leaders can support teachers' investigation of current standards and the development of a shared understanding about what highly effective and rigorous literacy instruction looks like in your context. How can you as a literacy leader serve as facilitator, leader, designer, and advocate when involved in standards analysis and implementation?

2. Discuss with colleagues the questions raised in the National Council of Teachers of English's (2013) *Framework for 21st Century Curriculum and Assessment* found in the section of this chapter titled Technology as a Tool to Support Teacher and Student Learning. Where does your school or district currently stand with respect to these questions? Are students capable of working with technology effectively? What areas might need additional work? Which coaching activities might best support continued conversations on this topic?

3. Finally, look at appendix B, where we have provided additional resources related to many of the chapters in this book. Select one of the resources to read and discuss with colleagues.

CHAPTER 4

Analyzing and Shaping School Culture: All Systems Go!

GUIDING QUESTIONS

1. How is culture defined in this book? In what ways are culture and leadership related?

2. In what ways does the culture of the organization affect literacy leaders' ability to improve literacy teaching and learning?

3. In what ways can literacy leaders work with teachers to develop an understanding of and appreciation for the diversity that exists in their schools? To design instruction and curriculum that provides for the needs of all students?

4. In what ways can literacy leaders and principals work together to improve literacy learning in the school?

Melinda, identified by her principal as a teacher leader, was excited about her new coaching role. She valued the perspective of her principal, who consistently reminded the teachers, "I need and value your input. We are in this together. Tell me what you need to be able to improve student literacy learning." In Melinda's school, teachers were encouraged to work collaboratively to identify and solve problems; the culture was conducive to coaching, or in Melinda's words, "the school is viewed as a place of learning for students and adults." But what roles should Melinda play in continuing to encourage and expand her school's culture of learning and continual improvement? What aspects of culture should Melinda attend to most closely? Who might be her allies in continuing to shape the larger culture of literacy learning?

As mentioned in chapter 1, such a collaborative learning culture is one of the key tenets of our Framework for Thinking and Working Like a Coach. In this chapter, we elaborate by first defining "culture" and its influence on life in a given school or district. We then provide some background on its importance and describe features of schools found to be important when initiating any literacy reform or "remodeling." We identify ideas for improving the culture of schools. We then address diversity as an important dimension of culture and provide ideas about how to develop an awareness and understanding of diversity. Included in this chapter is a specific section on the principal's role in facilitating coaching, highlighting ways literacy leaders and principals can work together. We conclude with a specific example of a whole-school organizational change initiative to improve student literacy learning.

Professionals in schools, like those in other organizations, have specific views or beliefs about the culture in which they work. They may believe that "teachers in this school really enjoy working with students," or unfortunately "teachers don't believe their students can learn" and behave in ways that reflect their attitudes toward students and colleagues. They may interact with peers by seeking advice or resources about how to improve instruction, or perhaps they close their classroom doors and ignore school-wide efforts to change curricula or instruction. In some schools, the cultural norms are such that teachers readily participate in community events, or they are willing to stay after school to attend a special professional learning activity—even if it occurs beyond required hours. Schein (2010) views culture as almost a living thing:

> Culture is both a dynamic phenomenon that surrounds us at all times, being constantly enacted and created by our interactions with others and shaped by leadership behavior, and a set of structures, routines, rules, and norms that guide and constrain behavior. (Schein, 2010, p. 1)

Schein elaborates on three distinct levels of culture. The first level, that of *artifacts*, is observable; for example, the banners or signs on display when one enters the school (e.g., "We are better together," or "Focus on literacy"), the ways in which the classrooms are organized (e.g., small-group settings for discussions, tables and chairs set in rows), or even the ways in which teachers interact with their students or their colleagues.

The second level, that of *espoused values*, includes those goals or ideals identified by the group (e.g., the written mission or vision statements that indicate literacy is the key to learning in all subjects).

The third level, the most difficult to discern, is that of the *underlying assumptions* of a group (e.g., what do we believe about the students we teach and their parents, and how supportive are we of the direction of the school, the efforts of administration, and so on?). Much of what makes up "culture" is invisible, similar to that of an iceberg, where only a small portion is visible. For example, although teachers in a school where the student population has changed over the years might not verbalize any negative views about the students they teach, there may be an implicit, unstated set of beliefs that current students don't have the background, motivation, or ability to learn. And teachers may behave in ways that reflect these beliefs. They may only call on certain students to answer questions, plan assignments that require little challenging or high-level thinking, or teach in ways that ignore the backgrounds and knowledge that students bring to the classrooms.

Those who write about culture often discuss the importance of leadership and its influence on the culture and climate of an organization. We agree with Schein (2010) that leadership is critical to creating and managing the culture in an organization and is not a single role assigned to a specific individual. All personnel in an organization have leadership responsibilities that include developing trusting relationships among colleagues. The principal plays a major leadership role, especially in facilitating and supporting others as leaders. There is general acceptance of the principal as "the leader," given the authority of the position. However, those who have coaching responsibilities also have leadership responsibilities, although their leadership roles are informal and they often lack the formal authority to require compliance; rather, they must encourage, inspire, nudge, and convince others to support organizational goals and visions. Those who coach must develop an understanding of the ever-shifting culture in a school and the meaningful role of leadership as critical to creating organizational or systemic change. Effective leaders know how to manage and change the culture rather than having the culture manage them.

School Culture: How Important Is It?

Although there are many efforts in today's schools to improve the quality of teaching in individual classrooms—for example, "measuring" teacher performance and then rewarding or penalizing teachers for their efforts—there is research evidence that such efforts alone are not sufficient; more emphasis needs to be placed on improving the organization in which teachers work (Bryk et al., 2010; Leana & Pil, 2006; Marzano, 2003; Taylor, Raphael, & Au, 2011). Leana and Pil (2006), based on their large-scale research, identified and discussed two important constructs that influence organizational culture: human capital and social capital. Human capital, relates to the human resources in the school—the staff (e.g., teachers, administrators, and specialized personnel) and their experiences, backgrounds, education, and dispositions. The second construct, social capital, can be subdivided into *internal* and *external* social capital. Internal social capital refers to the patterns of interactions and relationships between and among all individuals in the school. (For example, how committed are teachers to the goal of improving student literacy learning? Do they have high expectations and a shared vision for student outcomes? To what degree have all been involved with establishing common goals and visions?) The second, external social capital, refers to the relationships of the school with its families and to other community agencies or organizations (e.g., libraries and businesses) that have an impact on the school's success.

Several key notions related to social capital are essential to the work of literacy leaders. First, building social capital relies on building trusting and low-risk relationships in which teachers feel comfortable discussing problems or needs. For example, Leana and Pil (2006) found that teachers, faced with a problem, tended to seek out their peers for advice more than they did a coach or principal. Second, building social capital relies on providing opportunities for interaction so that such collaboration can occur.

To answer the question in the heading of this section, culture is *extremely* important! Meaningful, long-term, and sustained change will not happen when efforts are focused at the individual level only. As described by Leana (2011), one can use the analogy of Tinker toys when thinking about school culture. The circles or nodes represent human capital, but one must also use the rods to make connections between and among the circles. It is here that real and sustained change occurs.

In figure 4.1, we illustrate the importance of both human and social capital, highlighting the need for both. If a school has high human capital but low social capital, it falls in the box in the upper left-hand quadrant (e.g., there are effective teachers in schools but little collaboration or a sense of collective effort to achieve a common goal). These are schools where quality teaching is occurring in isolated classrooms. Often, parents will request a specific teacher or teachers for their children. Teachers who are experiencing difficulties with instruction may feel as though they have little guidance or direction and aren't sure exactly where they can seek help.

If the school has high social capital but low human capital, it falls in the lower right-hand quadrant. Teachers in these schools collaborate, but only a few have much experience or knowledge about the content or pedagogy for which they are responsible. Teachers may be involved in professional learning communities, but the leaders lack facilitation and leadership skills to guide thinking and learning; thus the meeting times are unproductive. Conversations aren't focused on matters related to instruction, or there may be a lack of support and follow-through with implementation ideas.

If both high social and human capital are evident in the school, it falls in the upper right-hand quadrant—the place to be! Teachers in these schools participate in meaningful dialogue in which they raise questions about their own work and that of others, with a focus on providing effective instruction for all students. Experienced, knowledgeable teachers and novices learn from each other in a risk-free environment, and literacy leaders provide necessary resources, guidance, and support. The principal provides leadership that encourages and supports this work by establishing the structure and facilitating the collaborative work of teachers and coaches.

The least desirable situation is one in which there is both low social and human capital (the lower left-hand quadrant). Much has to be done to improve or remodel these schools. Moreover, coaches who work in such environments will have a difficult task; they will need to work with administrators, perhaps at the district level, or even bring in external consultants to assist in developing a strategy to create better working conditions.

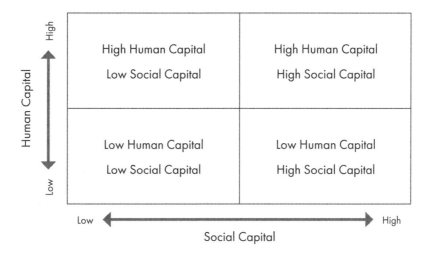

Figure 4.1: Human and social capital relationships.

PUT INTO PRACTICE

Introduce figure 4.1 to your colleagues. Ask them to think individually about where they would place your school in terms of human and social capital. Then ask group members to discuss their individual responses and the rationale for them. How similar or different were the responses? Discuss whether there is a need to make changes in the school and how.

Creating Change at the Organizational Level: Improving Literacy Instruction

Taylor, Raphael, and Au (2011), in a synthesis of school reform efforts, identified and described four important components of any overall effort to improve student literacy learning. Each of these is described and elaborated upon in the paragraphs that follow.

Need for a Vision and a Commitment to Achieving Specific Student Goals

Both short- and long-term goals must be identified, and there must be recognition that change occurs over time. In Reading First schools in Pennsylvania, Zigmond, Bean, Kloo, and Brydon (2011) found that some schools were able to change in ways that increased student literacy learning in two or three years, while others took longer to achieve their goals. Taylor et al. (2011) suggest that five years may be needed to make large-scale changes in a school reform effort. Achieving a vision requires more than "buy-in" from teachers. When teachers are involved in decision making and work collaboratively to craft the vision, there is much more potential for a successful and sustainable change effort. Further, there will be greater awareness of the need for additional learning, changes in teaching, and ways of thinking.

Several ideas for helping teachers in a school work toward a common vision follow:

▸ Establish a literacy leadership team that has the responsibility for facilitating discussions about where a school is and where it wants to be, relative to student literacy learning. We write about this more in-depth in chapter 9.

▸ Provide opportunities for teachers to reflect collectively about what they do well and what they think needs to change if they are to improve literacy learning in the school. Reflective dialogue is one of the keys to sparking transformation (Mezirow, 2000). Start by working in small groups, such as grade-level or departmental teams, and then share information in large groups, so that there are opportunities to look both vertically and horizontally at the curriculum and instruction in the school.

▸ Focus! There is strong evidence (Collins, 2001; Schmoker, 2011) of the importance of having a laser-like focus that addresses what needs to be done, based on current strengths, to achieve literacy goals. For example, a school that recognizes the importance of improving writing instruction at the middle school in all curricular areas, has a coach with deep knowledge and understanding of writing instruction, and has a committed group of teachers interested in doing a better job should be given the opportunity to *focus* on the goal of improving student writing. One of our oft-repeated adages to coaches and school leaders is that if a new initiative or project is being put *on* teachers' plates, then what is going to come *off* their plates? Effective change does not occur simply by adding more and more initiatives, a common mistake.

▶ Provide top-down as well as bottom-up support. When a school is implementing a specific initiative, it needs support from the district; that is, top-down support. If a district is moving in a different direction from that identified by the school, there will be little chance of success. School personnel such as coaches, principals, and teachers need to know that their vision and goals are recognized as important and that they will receive the necessary support to work toward their goals. And as stated previously, any change initiative at the school level will be more successful when there is teacher involvement and decision making.

Leadership

Throughout this book, we emphasize the importance of leadership or "the capacity to translate vision into reality" (Bennis, 2009, p. 185). As mentioned in chapter 2, literacy leaders support teachers by listening to them, helping them solve problems, and keeping them focused on identified goals and action steps necessary to achieve those goals. And an important assumption in this book is that there are many leaders in schools, from the principal (who has a key leadership role in developing a collaborative environment in which teachers feel empowered to make decisions) to teachers (whose role as leaders is too often understated). As mentioned in chapter 2, leaders must be able to see the big picture (that is, they must be thought leaders), and at the same time, they must manage the day-to-day occurrences that can facilitate or hinder progress toward a specific goal.

Collaboration

There is strong evidence of the importance of collaboration as a means of developing collective efficacy in schools. Teachers need opportunities to work together to address real, meaningful problems. Such collaboration requires administrative leaders to develop schedules that enable groups of teachers—grade-level and departmental groups—to meet together on a regular basis. But allocating time for meeting is not enough. To be effective, administrative leaders must establish both time and cultural norms that allow for literacy leaders to facilitate meetings in which there are clear norms for group work, protocols for guiding discussions, and agreed-upon approaches for managing conflicts and arriving at decisions. As mentioned in chapter 2, such group work requires coaches and colleagues to engage in problem-solving issues about students, curriculum, instruction, and so on. In chapter 7, we elaborate on ways that literacy leaders can facilitate small-group work.

Before undertaking systemic change efforts, literacy leaders, administrators, and teachers might consider crafting a shared understanding of their own school culture or climate, creating a starting point for a school-wide dialogue about and common vision for literacy learning and curriculum that is evidenced-based and meets the needs of students in context-specific ways. The NCLE Framework for Capacity Building in their report, *Remodeling Literacy Learning Together: Paths to Standards Implementation* (NCLE, 2014, p. 33), might be a great place to start. The NCLE Framework identifies six conditions and practices that support effective collaboration and have an impact on student learning: deprivatizing practice, enacting shared agreements, creating a collaborative culture, maintaining an inquiry stance, using evidence effectively, and supporting collaboration systematically. It provides an Asset Inventory (http://bit.ly/ncleassetinv) that groups can use to assess their perceptions about each of these conditions and the degree to which they are present in a school.

Literacy leaders might consider using the inventory to facilitate discussion about collaborative work and how it can be improved. Another similar resource is the Professional Learning Communities Survey provided by the School Reform Initiative (http://school reforminitiative.org/doc/plc_survey.pdf).

Use of Data for Decision Making

Taylor et al. (2011) use the term "principled" use of data, which identifies data as tools, not as goals. They indicate the need to use a broad array of data sources, from student work samples to standardized test scores. Further, they highlight the importance of student, teacher, and school data as important sources of information to guide decisions. (See more about data use in chapter 8.)

In thinking about school culture and all that it encompasses, a discussion of diversity in schools, communities, and in our society overall is essential. Our society is becoming increasingly diverse along all dimensions, and regardless of the locale of the school, students must be engaged in activities and curriculum that help them understand diversity as a source of strength and potential. Literacy leaders have the responsibility of supporting teachers in implementing instructional practices that promote equity and social justice and advocating for change if inequities exist.

Diversity: Human Capital

As defined by Coleman, Negron, and Lipper (2011), diversity is a "multidimensional, broadly inclusive concept that acknowledges and embraces the richness of human differences . . . the term 'diversity' is not code for race, ethnicity, or gender by themselves" (p. 20). Rather, it is more encompassing of many different attributes, including academic achievement, reading abilities, gender, age, religion, sexual orientation, marital status, as well as race and ethnicity. Diversity of students, teachers, and staff in schools and in the surrounding community contribute in positive ways to the culture of the school, providing opportunities for learning.

To establish a culture that builds on diversity, literacy leaders can support teachers in working effectively with all learners and their families to change from "business as usual to unusual business." We view diversity as a topic central to any discussion about developing the school culture as an effective place for learning, so we encourage literacy leaders to go beyond the brief ideas presented in the upcoming list and consult the additional resources in appendix B for a more in-depth study of diversity, its influence, and its impact on schools. Here are three key ideas to consider in your work with educators:

1. Develop an awareness of and appreciation for cultural differences and bring the topic of diversity to the surface. A large majority of the teachers in US schools tend to be white, middle-class English speakers, and often they have not had the experiences that prepare them to work with the increasingly diverse student body in their schools. Too often, they aren't given the opportunity to talk about culture (their own and their students') in a meaningful way. Some specific ideas for developing awareness and appreciation of diversity follow—

    a. Ask educators to share their own stories, their cultural traditions, biases, and perceptions as a means of raising issues and discussing the diversity that exists in the school. Talking about our own cultural experiences can often open the door to even more meaningful conversations about how to develop learning activities that build on students' experiences.

    b. Bring in external consultants to lead discussions about the topics of diversity and culture.

    c. Give teachers opportunities to read articles about culture and diversity and then hold discussions about them. The School Reform Initiative (www.schoolreforminitiative.org) provides a number of discussion-based protocols designed to support adult educators committed to meaningful work around diversity issues (e.g., Diversity Rounds, Equity Stances) that literacy leaders can use to initiate discussions about diversity in schools.

    In sum, by developing an awareness and appreciation for cultural differences (in our view a first step), literacy leaders can then work with teachers to develop curriculum and instruction that builds on what students bring to their classrooms and helps them make connections between that knowledge and what they are learning.

2. Develop and transform curriculum and instruction to build on students' assets. Literacy leaders and teachers together can discuss where curricular gaps exist and what activities or instructional strategies might address those gaps. For example, is there a need to improve instruction for English learners? Is there a need to help students understand and value diversity (in its broadest sense)? Is there a need for more culturally responsive curriculum that addresses issues related to ethnic diversity, especially as it involves literacy learning?

3. Engage families and the community. The positive relationships found in the research about parental involvement and student learning call for even closer attention to developing effective partnerships among families, communities, and schools. However, too often school-parent relationships have been built on a deficit model that reinforces the "school knows best" mindset and positions the school as the expert, ignoring the strengths that families bring to the conversation. Boutte and Johnson (2014) call for strength-based involvement programs that place schools in the position of learners who acknowledge, value, and learn about the funds of knowledge (Moll, 2000) that families bring to schools. As stated by Boutte and Johnson (2014), "instead of viewing families as 'struggling,' perhaps it is useful for educators to think of the struggles that they are facing . . . and how to circumvent and transcend these" (p. 179). For a more in-depth discussion of family and community involvement, see chapter 10.

Much has been written about diversity beyond the scope of this book, and again we encourage literacy leaders to refer to the resources identified in appendix B. Now, we turn our attention to the critical role of the principal in supporting literacy leadership and coaching work. Without strong building-based leadership, issues of diversity and culture writ large cannot be adequately addressed.

VOICES FROM THE FIELD

As new principals were hired, they would attend state-sponsored coaching trainings, which typically focused on a purely directive approach. The principal began seeing the coaching role as that of compliance monitor, data manager, or assessment coordinator. Once a principal developed this mindset, it was incredibly difficult to change that perception. During my second year, I focused more attention on building the principals' understandings of effective coaching practices. Slowly, this helped to build a shared model of coaching, and I learned the importance of including principals in building our system of coaching.

—Christina Steinbacher-Reed, supervisor of coaches

The Principal and Coaching

Substantial evidence exists that principals play a key role as leaders and have a powerful effect on both teaching and learning in schools (Bean & Lillenstein, 2012; Berebitsky, Goddard, & Carlisle, 2014; Breidenstein et al., 2012; Bryk et al., 2010; Leithwood & Jantzi, 2008; Supovitz, Sirinides, & May, 2010). Effective principals are also learners who gain a better understanding of classroom literacy instruction by interacting with teachers.

Steinbacher-Reed and Rotella (www.teachershipus.com) have created a new term, *teachership*, that describes the quality that emerges when exceptional teaching is interwoven with exceptional leading. In their view, leaders such as principals must continue to learn about instruction, especially some of the newer shifts and approaches, while teachers must be willing to step up and become more involved in leadership roles—hence, the term *teachership*. For example, principals, teachers, and coaches might shadow one another to learn more about instruction or about leadership. The principal might watch a coach lead a guided reading group; later, the principal might teach such a group on his or her own (while the teacher meets with a coach). Or a coach or teacher might shadow a principal who is leading a learning walk as a means of developing proficiency in facilitating this type of professional learning experience. This notion of *teachership* promotes a culture of leadership and learning school-wide.

One of the important leadership tasks of principals is that of developing and distributing leadership in schools; that is, identifying and supporting teacher leaders, creating schedules that allow for collaboration, supporting teachers in their change efforts, and providing support for those changes. Effective principals understand, facilitate, and support both formal and informal coaching efforts. In a recent study (Bean & Lillenstein, 2012) of the implementation of RTI systems in five schools, the principal was the "central person for promoting a risk-free environment, leading the effort in establishing norms for collaborations, and facilitating shared responsibility and accountability" (p. 497). Matsumura, Sartoris, Bickel, and Garnier (2009) found positive and significant relationships between specific behaviors of principals and high implementation of coaching in schools. When principals became actively involved in the change initiative, identified and supported coaches as sources of expertise, and trusted coaches to manage their own schedules, teachers were more frequently involved in coaching activities.

In this section, we discuss first how principals can support the work of coaches and then ways that coaches can most effectively work with principals. For additional resources related to coach-principal relationships, see appendix B.

The Principal's Role in Supporting Coaching

In all coaching efforts with which we have been involved, coaches have identified first and foremost the key role of principals in ensuring that the coaching initiative will be successful (Bean, Dole, Nelson, Belcastro, & Zigmond, 2015; Bean & Lillenstein, 2012; Carroll, 2007; Ippolito, 2009). In the following bullets we identify and describe ways that principals can facilitate the work of coaches. Principals can:

▸ Understand the role of coaches and the importance of coaching. This includes understanding not only what coaching is and can do but also what it is not and what it cannot do. For example, principals must understand that effective coaching relationships cannot be forged if the coach is asked to serve in an evaluation role. Likewise, principals should not ask coaches to identify the weaknesses of specific teachers. At the same time, effective principals recognize they can learn much from the coach relative to literacy instruction if they listen to the coach describe literacy needs in the school broadly (e.g., "Student work samples indicate need for more in-depth comprehension work at the fourth-grade level"; "The eighth-grade team wants to learn more about how to actively engage their students in discussions"). The focus of any coach-principal interaction, in other words, is on the needs of the group as a whole rather than on "reporting" specific problems of individual teachers.

▸ Support the work of coaches and identify them as a source of expertise. Principals can speak positively in school meetings or with individual teachers about coaching and its value for improving student literacy learning; they can suggest ways that teachers may choose to work with the coach or identify topics for discussion. (A caution: recommending coaching only for specific teachers who have been identified by the principal as having weaknesses can be problematic for both coaches and teachers. Such recommendations may cause teachers to view coaching as an activity designated for "ineffective" teachers only. An excellent teacher at one school mentioned that the literacy coach in their building never approached her, indicating that she, the teacher, had no need of coaching. Yet, this teacher believed that an opportunity for interaction with the coach would have given her a chance to raise some questions about specific students and discuss new instructional ideas.)

▸ Facilitate the work of coaches by co-developing schedules (with the literacy leadership team) that provide time for the coach to work with teams of teachers, or volunteer to substitute in a classroom when the coach wants to hold a debriefing conference with a teacher.

▸ Communicate routinely with the coach. The type (oral or written) and timing of conversations may differ, depending on the principal's and coach's preferences, but regular communication is essential. Some principals may prefer a written, weekly summary of activities and a set of recommendations and questions. Other principals may suggest that the coach set a regular time to meet each week or every two weeks. In addition to conversations that include only the principal and the coach, regularly scheduled meetings for the principal and the literacy leadership team can be especially useful for sharing perceptions, clarifying and elaborating upon any recent decisions, and deciding which members of the team are responsible for specific tasks. Principals can be especially supportive if they make it clear that, if circumstances warrant it (i.e., there is a specific problem or concern), the literacy leader is welcome to stop by for a meeting.

▶ Provide feedback to the literacy leader. Coaching can be a lonely job, and although we recommend that coaches form networks where they can interact informally with others in a similar role, getting feedback (warm and cool) from the principal can be helpful. The principal can share with the coach the fact that several teachers were very excited about their work with the coach, make suggestions about how the coach might reach out to teachers, or advise the coach on how to use time more productively. Taking the time to ask the coach how he or she can be helpful—for example, rearranging schedules or putting the coach on a meeting agenda for a brief mini-lesson—can be part of this interaction.

▶ Involve the coach in leadership activities. As mentioned earlier, principals can support the leadership learning of coaches. They might work with the coach in planning and conducting professional learning workshops. Or they can ask the coach to serve on specific leadership teams. The key is that principals and coaches work collaboratively in designing schedules, assigning students or teachers to specific instructional groups, discussing assessment results, or discussing the implementation of a specific literacy program.

How Coaches Can Support Principals

Leadership in a school can be distributed in different ways, depending on the experience and knowledge base of the principal. As mentioned previously, and as we hear from many principals, coaches knowledgeable about literacy can be a source of learning for the principal who may not have that knowledge base. In such instances, the principal may ask the coach to take on more responsibilities for leading literacy efforts in the school in collaboration with the principal. Both can discuss data results and their implications for instruction. Together, they can take informal walkthroughs through the school, gaining a deeper sense of the students in the classrooms and teaching and learning practices. In schools where the principal has a strong literacy background, the coach and principal can work together with teachers to make short- and long-term decisions about literacy instruction at the classroom and school levels. Specific ideas for those who coach and how they can support the principal follow. Coaches can:

▶ Develop with the principal a systematic plan for providing feedback about how literacy instruction can be improved in the school. Such feedback should include specific ideas for improving instruction at specific grade levels, departments, or the school as a whole. As mentioned previously, feedback should not be specific to an individual teacher, unless there are unusual circumstances where a teacher's behavior is detrimental to the welfare of children.

▶ Have a tight, clear agenda for your meetings with the principal, so that time is used wisely. The agenda should highlight positive occurrences in the school (e.g., "The interactive read-alouds in first grade are really helping students develop their listening and reading comprehension skills"); raise questions about possible concerns (e.g., "The middle school social studies team is struggling with how to hold effective small-group discussions"); and identify ways in which the principal can help you do your job better (e.g., "It would be helpful if you could attend the fifth-grade team meeting where we are going to review work samples; we are going to need to make some instructional changes, and this may affect scheduling").

▶ Be honest with the principal about your needs as a coach, identifying any concerns you have or any support you need to do your job more effectively. For example, perhaps you are being taken away from your coaching responsibilities in ways that reduce your effectiveness (e.g., entering data results for all students). Ask the principal if there are ways to address this problem and be prepared to suggest possible solutions, such as having a paraprofessional enter the data. The principal might not be aware of the problem and how it is affecting your work; it is important to raise the issue rather than stew about it.

▶ Break "confidentiality" only as a last resort. Coaches often ask what to do when they have tried, over and over, to work with a specific teacher or group and have had little or no success. The teacher's or group's negativity has affected student learning and progress toward meeting school goals. There is no perfect solution for situations like this, and although they aren't necessarily frequent, they can be detrimental to any school-change efforts. Given the impact of this negativity, the coach might decide, as a last resort, to have a private conversation with the principal to discuss the situation and generate possible next steps. Often, the principal is aware of the situation and can be helpful; it also requires the principal and coach to design a plan for addressing the problem in ways that won't sabotage the work of the coach. This type of situation highlights the importance of the coach and principal having a relationship of trust, understanding that addressing an issue like this is a delicate one that can only be solved by working together.

PUT INTO PRACTICE

Meet with a small group of coaches to discuss how they might address a situation in which a teacher's negativity and lack of effort are affecting student learning in his or her classroom. The coach has tried to work with this teacher in many different ways, but there has been no change in the teacher's behavior or attitude. Should the coach talk with the principal? If he or she does, how might the principal and coach address this issue together? Think about this as requiring a number of steps: What could be done first? If little success, what next? Discuss ways by which such negativity can be prevented. What can be done to improve the overall climate in the school?

Working With Other Specialized Professionals

Given the ways in which schools function in today's world, there are many more opportunities (and a need) for literacy leaders to work collaboratively with various teams of educators beyond classroom teachers. Often literacy leaders serve on teams with allied professionals such as special educators, the school psychologist, or the speech and language teacher (the principal may also be a member of the team). These teams may be responsible for analyzing data and making decisions about instruction. They may be discussing the needs of specific students identified as having difficulties with reading or writing. They may also be responsible for discussing the implementation of intervention systems such as RTI or similar systems designed to differentiate instruction to meet students' needs. In fact, in the Bean and Lillenstein (2012) study of five schools successfully implementing an RTI initiative, principals took the "lead role in establishing conditions for effective implementation . . . being on the sidelines was not an option" (p. 497).

Those who were interviewed, including specialists and coaches, highlighted the importance of learning to work as a team and indicated how much they learned from colleagues with different expertise. The psychologist in one school talked about how much he had learned about literacy by working with the reading specialist and coach. Reading specialists and special educators were excited about opportunities to exchange ideas about instruction. Reading specialists and coaches appreciated the opportunities to use a team approach to coaching, with each of them, based on their experiences, working with specific teachers or focusing on a particular area of literacy. These educators identified the importance of providing constructive, as well as positive, feedback to teachers and identified three guidelines as important for their work:

1. Treat teachers with respect and value their input.

2. Use data to support the message.

3. Focus on student learning.

Two major conclusions were drawn from this study. First, to implement an initiative such as RTI, educators in schools must work collaboratively, to learn with and from each other. Second, all educators in the school need to develop the leadership skills that enable them to collaborative effectively.

Example of a School Change Initiative: The Importance of System-Wide Change

In the upcoming paragraphs, we briefly describe an example of a change initiative led by a principal and his colleagues at two underperforming high schools. Note the similarities between the research presented previously and the specifics of this initiative (Reed, 2015). Rather than searching for specific programs or external solutions, these educators decided to build their own capacity and develop the learning environment from the *inside out* (Elmore, 2004) in ways that improved both teacher and student learning. In both schools, student test scores improved in just a few years. Reed discusses the importance of focus, describing three areas of emphasis.

Collaboration

Informal collaborative meetings held quarterly, called "Coffee and Conversations," provided opportunities for teachers to share their views with the principal and each other. Groups of teachers stopped by during their planning periods to raise issues and suggest solutions. Similar informal conversational meetings were scheduled with parents and students. Other collaborative efforts included teacher leader meetings with the principal to discuss areas of need. Follow-up meetings to discuss next steps were facilitated by teacher leaders with their teams. Electronic surveys were also conducted to receive feedback from stakeholders when specific issues arose (e.g., a change of graduation venue).

Use of Data

Data were shared with teachers in an easy-to-understand format, and the focus was on discussing what the data results meant in terms of improving the system or organization. As a result of data analysis, changes were made in the types of classes being offered, teaching assignments, and length of the instructional day. The school also implemented a literacy plan that emphasized reading and writing in all courses.

Building Faculty Capacity

Instructional coaching became an important approach for facilitating instructional change, with coaches helping teachers reflect on their practices. Teachers participated in informal, voluntary learning walks, facilitated by a fellow teacher or a coach. Following these learning walks, e-mails with positive feedback about effective strategies seen in the classrooms were sent to all faculty. Based on learning walks, faculty observed the need for alignment among teachers teaching the same course. Administration then redesigned the schedule to provide teachers from the same discipline a common planning period to realign the curriculum.

This is only one brief example of a concerted, long-term effort to remodel a school; that is, to change the organizational culture in ways that facilitated learning of both faculty and students. Schools may use different approaches to achieve organizational change, but the broad notions of establishing shared vision, collaboration, meaningful use of data, and effective leadership from multiple sources are important foundational elements.

REFLECT

Think about the description of this school and how a group of committed educators, in a shared leadership model, created an environment that produced learning changes for both students and teachers. Would this work in your school or district? What questions or challenges does it raise? What other ideas or approaches might be used to get to the ultimate goal: improving student learning at the school or district level?

Summary

In this chapter, we defined "culture" and then discussed the importance of establishing an organizational culture that promotes shared leadership and collegiality as a means of moving toward a common vision and goals for literacy learning. We provided specific suggestions about shaping the school's culture for improving literacy instruction. We followed that with a discussion about diversity and ways that literacy leaders might help design and facilitate school practices that build on the strengths coming from diversity in schools and society. We then discussed notions for how principals and other specialized professionals can collaboratively support the work of the coach. We concluded with a specific example of a school remodeling effort at the high school level that emphasized cultural changes as a means of improving student literacy learning.

Activities

1. Using the chart found in appendix A, note ways that literacy leaders can support the development of a culture that is receptive to collaborative

learning for both adults and students. How do you as a literacy leader already serve as facilitator, leader, designer, and advocate when involved in establishing such a culture in your school? Which activities might you consider adopting that would further these ways of thinking and working?

2. With your colleagues, conduct an inventory of the culture in your school, using one of the tools suggested in this chapter (e.g., Asset Inventory, Professional Learning Community Survey). Which aspects of the inventory might be most important to share with other colleagues and school leaders? What short-term and long-term actions might your group suggest?

CHAPTER 5

Overview: Ways of Working With Teachers

> ## GUIDING QUESTIONS
>
> 1. What do coaches need to know about the power of language and its importance in working with individuals and groups of teachers?
> 2. What are discussion-based protocols, and how can they be useful in facilitating discussions between coaches, individuals, and small groups of teachers?
> 3. In what ways can coaches develop relationships of trust with individuals and groups of teachers?

Although Melinda knew the novice teachers that she was asked to coach—she had attended meetings with them and talked with them about school routines and rules—she wasn't quite sure about how to begin this more intense relationship. Should she just tell them she was going to coach them? Should she begin by asking them where they need some help? What structures and routines might she establish initially to start the relationships off on the right foot? In this chapter, we provide an overview that highlights the importance of communicating with teachers in ways that encourage reflectivity and a sense of inquiry, regardless of whether coaches are working with individuals or groups. Although we mentioned discussion-based protocols in earlier chapters, we provide more detail about their use and potential in coaching contexts. Finally, we conclude with a discussion of coaching activities useful for developing a trusting relationship between coaches and teachers—probably a good place for Melinda to begin!

The Power of Language: Talking With Individuals and Groups of Teachers

Given that language is key to the success of any coach-teacher interaction, we describe a few critical notions about language as a tool for facilitating conversations with teachers. (See appendix B for additional resources related to facilitation and the language of coaching.)

Be an Active Listener

As an active listener, attend to more than the words being spoken and listen for the deeper meaning behind what is being said. Listen for what Heifetz et al. (2009) call the "song beneath the words" (p. 76). A teacher who says, "My students can't work well in small groups" may be expressing frustration, confusion, anger, or may even be reaching out for help. Likewise, in group settings, listen for the intent of the comment. In conversations we have with coaches, being an active listener is always first on their list of important characteristics of effective coaching. As active listeners, coaches should probably be doing less speaking and more listening. *Pausing* is an important aspect of being an active listener. Give teachers time to reflect and respond rather than answering your own question.

Be Aware of the Impact of Your Nonverbal Communication

Smile, use some humor, or nod affirmatively when others make key points. Too often, literacy leaders are so focused on their goals that they forget to carefully manage their own nonverbal communication (e.g., crossing their arms, frowning, tapping their foot, or otherwise signaling impatience). Try to maintain a positive or neutral physical presence as much as possible. Think about how positively you respond when an airline representative seems eager to help you solve your traveling needs and presents you with several options that will save you money or time.

Use Effective Questioning Techniques

Although questions are an important tool, be careful to not use them in ways that make conversations seem like interrogation sessions. Rather, they should be used to facilitate or co-construct understanding and build shared meaning (i.e., so that participants are on the same page). According to a quote attributed to Einstein, if he had an hour to solve a problem, he would spend fifty-five minutes of that time deciding on the right questions to ask, ones that would enable him to solve the problem in the remaining five minutes. Think about how and when to use the following types of questions in conversations with either individuals or groups:

- *Focus questions* can highlight the key points or issues in a discussion. They may be generated by the coach or the teacher and are often helpful at the outset of a coaching conversation. Focus questions or statements can also be helpful when a group has moved away from the topic being discussed and there is a need to get back to the intent of the conversation. An example of a focus question is: "Let's think about the ways in which students were engaged in the lesson. How did you provide for active learning?"

- *Clarifying questions* are helpful for providing a clearer understanding of a teacher's instructional context or of the topic being discussed, helping all participants in a conversation to "get on the same page." Examples of clarifying questions include: "What texts are you using to introduce the unit on neighborhood helpers?" and "How long is your average guided reading session?" Participants should be able to answer clarifying questions easily, without too much thinking. If anyone has to think too long and hard about a clarifying question, then the question is likely a "probing" one (see next bullet point). Paraphrasing can also serve as a clarification tool used to clarify your own remarks or those of another. Some examples of possible lead-ins to paraphrasing are: "In other words, you indicated that . . ."; "I want to be sure I understand; this is what I heard you saying."

- *Probing* or *elaboration questions* are those in which the coach is asking the teacher to say more about a topic, to expand on what was said, or to gently push the teacher to think more expansively about a topic. Probing questions are generally open-ended and seek multiple responses. Excellent probing questions may not have ready or right answers, in which case it is important to help teachers understand that the point of the probing question is not to answer it as quickly as possible, but instead to hold on to it and consider it over time. Ultimately, one coaching goal might be to help support teachers in asking their own probing questions, as a means of self-reflection. Examples of probing questions are:
  - "Can you say more?"
  - "You indicated students weren't as engaged as you had hoped— what is your hunch about why that might be happening?"
  - "What evidence would convince you that your students understand what you are trying to teach them?"

Such questions, while not always easily or quickly answered, lead to deeper teacher reflection and, ultimately, shifts in thinking and instruction. Over time, teachers are able to ask themselves these same types of questions, leading to more reflective and  meaningful teaching and learning. To read more about the crafting and use of clarifying and probing questions, consult the School Reform Initiative's *Pocket Guide to Probing Questions*, developed by Gene Thompson-Grove (http://schoolreforminitiative.org/doc/probing _questions_guide.pdf).

In figure 5.1, we provide a summary of some dos and don'ts of effective communication. You might use this list to briefly reflect on your own communication skills and habits.

Do:

- Be an active listener

- Listen for content and for feelings

- Use wait time to give speakers opportunities to finish their statements

- Be aware of your nonverbal communication patterns

- Listen more than you speak

- Use questions that are appropriate for the context

- Use exploratory or focus questions to open the conversation

- Use clarifying questions that lead to a clearer understanding of the topic or issue

- Ask questions that invite elaboration

- Ask probing (often open-ended) questions that extend and deepen the conversation

- Use statements that help "pull the conversation together"

- Use summary statements

- Paraphrase others' words

- Ask group participants for feedback about your message or to summarize what they heard

- Be quick to praise and show appreciation

- Find at least one aspect of the teacher's or group's work to praise in each session

- Thank the teacher or group for their time, flexibility, efforts, and so on

- Let teachers know what you learned from working with them

Don't:

- Interrupt the speaker

- Practice internally what you are planning to say in response (this can prevent active listening)

- Make snap judgments about the messages of others

- Turn the discussion or conversation into a "blame game"

- Monopolize the conversation

- Focus on what you would have done in a specific situation

Figure 5.1: Dos and don'ts of effective communication.

*Visit **www.learningsciences.com/bookresources** to download a reproducible version of this figure.*

Carefully considering and crafting different question types, as described previously, is useful when facilitating both one-on-one and group discussions. While some coaches have no difficulty providing warm feedback to teachers, many experience difficulties when providing cool feedback designed to help a teacher or teachers understand where there is a mismatch between their goals and their instructional actions or where there is simply room for improvement and change. Effective questioning can facilitate collaborative inquiry and move a group to deeper, more honest discourse, or as MacDonald (2011) indicates, "beyond the culture of nice" (p. 45). She suggests that team meetings should not always end with participants "feeling confirmed in what they have been doing" (p. 46); rather, there should be opportunities for participants to question their own and others' beliefs, assumptions, and practices.

Literacy leaders who coach, particularly those interested in practicing different types of questioning, will find the many forms and components of discussion-based protocols (each of which illustrate productive ways of facilitating challenging conversations) useful for their work. Next, we discuss the power of discussion-based protocols as part and parcel of coaching work.

The Power of Discussion-Based Protocols

Throughout this book, we reference discussion-based protocols; therefore, as part of this overview chapter on working with teachers and attending to coaching language, we wanted to take a moment to elaborate on the nature and utility of these tools. "Protocols" can mean different things to different educators, but we think of them as an "agreed upon set of discussion or observation rules that guide coach/teacher/

student work, discussion, and interactions" (Ippolito & Lieberman, 2012, p. 79). Some educators bristle at the term "protocols," perhaps because they associate protocols with medical terminology or believe discussion-based protocols to be overly prescriptive. This can occur if educators are introduced to discussion-based protocols in inappropriate or slapdash ways. In such instances, we are careful to use different terminology—"structures," "tools," "routines," or "agendas." Ultimately, the terminology we use is not as important as the underlying principle that coaches who plan a structure for their coaching conversations *before* having the conversations often fare much better than those who simply try to navigate the conversation in the moment.

Protocols are sometimes deceptively simple, with just a handful of steps that ask a facilitator (i.e., coach) and teacher presenter or participant to work together to define, consider, and begin to solve an educational dilemma. Consider the steps in the classic Consultancy protocol (developed by Faith Dunne, Paula Evans, and Gene Thompson-Grove), used as a tool for helping a group of teachers discuss a dilemma identified by one of their peers. The steps in this protocol are as follows:

1. A teacher describes a particular instructional dilemma or piece of work, ending with a focus question.

2. The coach and group ask clarifying questions (i.e., those that are factual and have clear answers to help a coach and group better understand the context).

3. The coach and group ask probing questions (i.e., those deeper questions that broaden thinking and do not have ready answers).

4. The presenter sits quietly while the coach and group discuss the matter at hand, mirroring back what they have heard and sometimes offering concrete suggestions for next steps.

5. Finally, the teacher or presenter is invited back into the conversation to have a "final word" before the entire group debriefs the conversation in order to improve the group's process (see http://schoolreforminitiative.org /doc/consultancy.pdf for more details).

These simple steps are not so simple. Skilled facilitation is needed to help individuals and groups understand the power of each of these steps, negotiate the differences between clarifying and probing questions, and wring the most value out of brief conversations. What does this look like with groups versus one-on-one conversations between a coach and teacher? How and when do you move a group to the next question, step, or phase of a conversation? When might you shift gears entirely? What might you do when challenged by a group member publicly in the middle of a coaching session? One of our favorite tools to help coaches consider what they might do in different real-life coaching situations, related to the use of protocols, is David Allen

and Tina Blythe's "Facilitation Scenarios," found on the School Reform Initiative website (http://schoolreforminitiative.org/doc /facilitation_scenarios.pdf). These vignettes are focused specifically on the facilitation of professional learning community discussions; however, we have also used these with literacy leaders who coach (as well as asked them to write their own vignettes) as a way to help facilitators reflect on their own larger set of facilitation skills.

Another consideration is the selection and creation of protocols and collaborative structures. Allen and Blythe's (2004) *Facilitator's Book of Questions* has a number of excellent resources for coaches thinking hard about the purpose of protocols and how to refine and design them, but two of our other favorite freely available tools

related to protocol selection are: the *Guide for Using 7 of the Student Work/Problem Solving Protocols* (http://schoolreforminitiative.org /doc/guide_7_protocols.pdf) and the *Continuum of Discussion-Based Protocols* (http://schoolreforminitiative.org/doc/continuum_discussion _protocols.pdf).

The *Guide*, revised by Gene Thompson-Grove, Amy Schuff, and Diane Leahy, is designed to help coaches consider which of the classic discussion-based protocols (e.g., consultancy, tuning, looking at student work, and so on) might be most appropriate for a given coaching conversation. As always, the *purpose* of the conversation needs to drive the decision for which protocol or structure to use. The *Continuum*, designed by Jacy Ippolito, suggests that there are some protocols that are best introduced early to teachers because they help groups get to know one another as well as how protocols work. Two examples of these "early" protocols are the Microlab, with its focus on reflective writing and conversation in trios, and Compass Points, in which group members reflect on and share their own collaboration styles and preferences when entering a new group. Over time, as comfort levels and trust increase within a group, new protocols can be introduced that push everyone to share more of their own work, their students' work, and, eventually, their own deepest beliefs and values related to teaching and learning. This continuum is important for three reasons:

1. It helps those new to protocols to consider the purposes and timing of when different protocols might be used. Hundreds of protocols can be downloaded and adapted from the School Reform Initiative (www .schoolreforminitiative.org), the Literacy Coaching Clearinghouse (www.literacycoachingonline.org/tools.html), and Harvard's Project Zero Visible Thinking Routines repository (www.visiblethinkingpz .org); however, to the uninitiated, the long lists of protocols might

seem overwhelming. Where do we start? The *Continuum* provides a reasonable guide.

2. The *Continuum* is important because we often see coaches and districts download and use the riskiest, most sophisticated protocols with brand new groups of teachers, without consideration given to group development. When groups are asked to take risks that they aren't yet ready for, they (by and large) walk away frustrated, vulnerable, and disinclined to work with protocols again. The *Continuum* helps coaches make better decisions about which protocols might be best introduced early versus later in coaching work, given teacher comfort levels and experience.

3. The *Continuum* also maps onto our own Levels of Intensity (introduced in chapter 1), and can be a concrete way for coaches to consider how they might grow their own facilitation skills over time, as group comfort and Levels of Intensity increase.

A final caveat: the more closely a protocol relates to the needs and interests of teachers in a specific school, the more receptivity there will be to participating in structured discussions. When protocols are seen as contrived or irrelevant, group members may see them as inauthentic and not useful. As a result, teachers will be less willing to participate.

VOICES FROM THE FIELD

As an extension of our interactive read-aloud study group, teachers co-planned lessons and scheduled classroom observations. While I did the majority of observations and demonstrations, a few brave teachers opened up their classrooms to their colleagues to watch lessons. At the conclusion of the study group, a teacher who had been previously resistant to coaching approached me to ask about what she and I could focus on for a one-on-one coaching opportunity next year! Slowly but surely, people are becoming more comfortable talking about their teaching and watching each other teach.

—Shauna Magee, literacy coach

Coaching Activities for Developing Relationships With Individuals and Groups of Teachers

Literacy leaders who coach often wonder how they can promote teacher involvement in the coaching process, and often, they are encouraged to work with volunteers. Yet, according to Timperley (2008), volunteering does not necessarily lead to change. Timperley identifies two important questions that identify whether teachers will engage in a meaningful and deep way: Are they learning key content by participating in meaningful activities? And is there a rationale for the activities based on identified student needs (p. 16)? Meaningful engagement, in our view, begins with establishing a relationship of trust between coaches and teachers. As Shauna mentions in the preceding Voices From the Field, and as we have mentioned previously (figure 1.2, page 10), developing such relationships with teachers is key for all literacy leaders.

Moreover, many literacy leaders who coach worry about working with so-called resistant teachers. This is certainly a legitimate concern, and all of us who have taken on coaching responsibilities have at some point found ourselves in positions where a teacher is less than excited about working with us. However, we find that it does not often help to frame the situation as "working with a resistant teacher." The frequent question asked by coaches is, "What can I do to reach *resistant* teachers?" We might reframe that question a bit, encouraging teachers and coaches instead to ask, "How can I get teachers to welcome me into their rooms? To respond in a positive way to my suggestions? To consult me when they are experiencing difficulties?" We view issues of "resistance" more as issues of trust and credibility, of being able to demonstrate to one or more teachers that you as a coach have real value and that you also understand their workload and daily concerns. Although we certainly recognize that not all teachers will greet the coach with open arms, and that there will be varying degrees of receptivity to coaching, our rules of thumb are that coaches need to convince (i.e., show) teachers that they can provide some valuable support and that differentiating the ways they approach teachers is key. Linda DiMartino talks about how she works with teachers who may be somewhat hesitant to participate in coaching activities in the following Voices From the Field.

VOICES FROM THE FIELD

I sometimes encounter the challenge of veteran teachers who say, "I'm all set," as they figuratively shut the door. I am aware that change is difficult, and I respect the knowledge and experience they have acquired. Their years of experience speak volumes. The words, "This is against my philosophy," ring loud in my ears. My approach in a situation like this is to offer a reflective statement, let him or her know that I hear and recognize how he or she feels. I provide more information, such as "Research shows that . . . " I tell the teacher that I would like to try something out, and I'd like to use his or her class as a trial run for a lesson. I place the focus on me and what I'm doing as a teacher. I ask for more opportunities to model lessons or co-plan as I work my way in. I verbalize the benefits of what I'm doing and focus on student work. I ask for questions or concerns to keep communication open and positive. I offer to get a unit or practice up and running and model the steps to success, while always maintaining a no-judgment stance. This approach works well, because the focus is not directly on the teacher.

—Linda DiMartino, literacy supervisor

What is evident in the way that Linda works with a resistant teacher is: her respect for the teacher and his or her views and experience, her willingness to try various coaching activities that may increase the teacher's receptivity, her focus on student learning, and her willingness to keep trying. We think this is good advice for all coaches faced with nearly any issue that could be labeled as "resistance." Often, when "resistant" teachers see the success that others are having, they become more willing to work with coaches. Be patient, be tenacious, and be flexible when building relationships with all teachers and especially those who are somewhat reluctant to participate in coaching activities.

Ultimately, our best advice about working with reluctant teachers is to become more diligent and deliberate in the ways you enter into and establish your coaching relationships. Bean (2015) identifies several general ideas useful for all literacy leaders, but especially for those new to a school or coaching position:

▶ Explain your role. As we have mentioned, coaching responsibilities can differ from school to school and year to year. Take the time to talk with teachers about what your role is and is not (e.g., "I'm not here to evaluate your performance"; "I don't do bulletin boards"). The best scenario is for the principal and coach together to discuss the coaching role with the faculty. To accomplish this, literacy leaders, such as coaches or teacher leaders, should have a written job description that can serve to guide their work.

▶ Be available and accessible. All coaches, especially those new to the school or to specific teachers, must make their presence known. Sitting with the teachers in the lunch room or in the teacher's lounge, posting schedules, and setting up a communication system establishes the coaches' availability. Some coaches hang a weekly scheduling chart outside their office where teachers can sign up to meet with the coach, while other coaches indicate their availability at specific times for walk-in conversations. When receiving e-mail or cell phone messages, effective coaches respond as quickly as possible, generally during the day they receive the message.

▶ Be credible. When making a commitment to a teacher, honor that commitment. For example, if you have a change to your schedule, perhaps because of an unexpected but important meeting at the central office, teachers who are affected should be notified, informed of the reason, and every attempt should be made to reschedule as soon as possible. Also, keep to a minimum the number of times that you cancel appointments with teachers.

▶ Begin immediately, but slowly. Coaches new to the role often ask what they are supposed to do in the beginning months of a coaching initiative, especially in September when teachers are busy organizing their classrooms and getting to know their students. As a coach, this is a great time to be helpful to teachers: volunteer to find or develop resources for them; set up or refresh a professional resource room with books organized by level or genre; write one or two brief flyers describing several techniques or strategies that teachers might use in their classrooms at the beginning of the year (e.g., setting norms for small-group discussions, using key classroom management techniques, introducing academic vocabulary). Importantly, get to know the school and the teachers. Arrange to meet and have brief conversations with teachers about their students and their literacy goals. Figure 5.2 (page 86) describes some ideas for these initial conversations.

Even in the early stages of coaching, when developing a relationship of trust, coaches can begin helping teachers think more deeply about their work and help them tackle instructional issues. Most importantly, the nature and timing of coaching activities is perhaps the literacy leader's best offense (and defense) when trying to overcome reluctance toward coaching. The type and timing of coaching activities should be carefully designed to build trust, credibility, and rapport. Moreover, each individual teacher might need a slightly different sequence of coaching events and amounts of support.

Schedule a time to meet with each teacher individually in a comfortable situation and when it is convenient for the teacher to talk. Below is a suggested framework for the conversation.

Breaking the ice. Share with the teacher some information about yourself—your goals as a coach, your background (if new to the school). Talk with the teacher about his or her background, interests. Sometimes, there are pictures of grandchildren, vacation trips, or pets that can spark a short conversation.

Setting a goal. Establish the reason why you are holding these conversations: Get to know the teacher's goals for the students; learn more about the students in the classroom and their strengths and needs.

Suggested questions:

- What are your goals for your students this year? (Think about broad goals of the reading program.)

- What are the skills and abilities of students in terms of achieving the goals? How can I help you learn more about your students? What strategies/approaches seem to work for you and help you achieve your goals?

- What resources would be helpful to you?

- In what ways can I be helpful?

Figure 5.2: Questions for an initial conversation with teachers.

Source: R. M. Bean. (2015). The Reading Specialist: Leadership and Coaching For Classroom, School, and Community. New York. Reprinted with permission of Guilford Press.

*Visit **www.learningsciences.com/bookresources** to download a reproducible version of this figure.*

High-Leverage Coaching Activities

Next, we share several ideas related to low-risk, low-intensity coaching activities, with the caveat that savvy readers will combine various activities in order to maximize success with individual teachers (see also figure 1.2).

Initial Problem Solving

During the day-to-day interactions that coaches have with teachers, specific questions may arise (e.g., "Tamika really has difficulty with comprehension even though she seems to read every word accurately. What do you think is causing this?"). Teachers may stop by the coach's office to talk about an upcoming conference with a parent or ask the coach to look at some writing samples. All of these instances are great problem-solving opportunities for coaches and teachers (opportunities to think like a designer). Problem solving can serve as an initial step for developing a trusting relationship between coach and teacher. More than that, when coaches and teachers work together collegially to solve a problem, they are engaged as professionals who recognize the complexity of problems and the need for adaptive and reflective thinking (thinking like a leader). Many issues and concerns arise in schools that can serve as the basis for problem-solving discussions. These concerns might include:

- Student-based dilemmas (e.g., "I'm not sure how to address the needs of Joaquin, a new second-grade student who appears to be struggling with decoding and reads very slowly.")

- Curriculum- or instruction-based dilemmas (e.g., "As a world history teacher, I'm supposed to be introducing vocabulary in rich, robust ways; I'm just not sure how to do that.")

- Classroom-environment or management dilemmas (e.g., "This class just doesn't seem to be able to work independently in learning centers—any ideas?")

- Professional learning dilemmas (e.g., "I'd like to learn more about how to integrate technology into my teaching of writing—do you have any resources or ideas?")

- Assessment dilemmas (e.g., "Here are the test results for the unit I taught on ecology. Students did well on the multiple-choice questions but really had difficulties answering open-ended questions. I'm wondering whether it relates to their knowledge of the subject or their difficulties with expressing themselves in writing. What are your thoughts about how to address this?")

PUT INTO PRACTICE

Think about each of the dilemmas identified previously. Select one and role-play a problem-solving conversation you might have with a teacher. You might ask a colleague to observe and provide feedback about your conversation.

Co-Planning

Some teachers are comfortable sitting with a coach, looking at the lesson to be taught, and discussing how modifications can be made for the students in their classrooms. Such co-planning enables coaches to raise questions related to students: Which of the suggested steps or procedures in this lesson might be problematic for your students or for some of your students? Which might not be necessary, given what your students bring to the lesson? What adaptations might be made in the lesson? Questions relative to teacher comfort and understanding of how to teach the lesson can also be generated: Is there anything in the lesson that seems confusing to you? Do you have the materials and resources you need to teach the lesson? How can I be helpful?

Co-planning can lead to co-teaching, to teacher-coach conversations about the success of the lesson, and to more in-depth coaching down the line. Essentially, it can be an initial step for developing a relationship of trust between coach and teacher.

Assessment and Working With Data

Often, coaches can help teachers by assisting with assessment tasks (e.g., screening or progress monitoring) required by the school. They can be part of a team of educators who enter the classroom to assess all students. Also, they can talk with teachers about assessment results for instructional decision making (more will be discussed about this in chapter 8).

On-the-Fly Coaching

Although coaching, in general, should be intentional and focused, coaches can also take advantage of opportunities that arise spontaneously. Sometimes, teachers will mention an issue in an informal situation, and the coach can use the opportunity to talk briefly with this teacher then schedule additional time to address the issue more fully at a later time.

Making the Rounds

Visiting classrooms informally for short periods of time, with or without students present, can be beneficial for several reasons. Brief visits can lead to discussions about necessary resources or specific student needs. Teachers can become more comfortable with having the coach in their classrooms, and the visits might provide an impetus for more in-depth coaching with specific teachers. Such visits can be made before classes begin in the morning, after classes end in the afternoon, or sometimes during teachers' prep periods. One elementary coach made it a rule to see each teacher in the building at least once a week, stopping by before classes began and chatting informally about the students or the literacy program, being sure to ask whether she could be helpful in any way.

At the secondary level, coaches might rotate classroom visits, alternately focusing on teachers in a specific discipline or at a common grade level to learn more about how students respond to the disciplinary literacy instruction being used to enhance content learning. In elementary schools, coaches might visit during the literacy block, talking with students at their seats to get a better sense of what they are doing and whether they seem to understand the goals of instruction. Coaches can also work quietly with students who might be experiencing difficulties with a task. When visiting the classroom, it is helpful for coaches to establish a routine for the visits. The following questions might be helpful:

- What is the literacy environment in the room (e.g., evidence of student work, books, and other materials)?

- What are students doing, and can they talk about their work (do they understand the task and reason for it)?

- What is the teacher doing to implement effective literacy instruction?

When leaving the classroom, consider leaving a short note on the teacher's desk with a few positive comments about his teaching and students. As a coach, it might also be helpful to jot down a few notes or questions for later reflection about the instruction in one or more classrooms, so you can look for patterns. Often these notes can indicate whether there are some common issues or even some common positives occurring across settings.

Facilitate or Participate in Faculty Group Meetings

These meetings, generally scheduled on a routine basis, provide great opportunities for literacy leaders to get to know individual teachers and how they function as a group. They also allow literacy leaders to become working members of the team focused on accomplishing a specific task, establish positive working relationships, and even generate possible coaching activities with individual teachers. Also, coaches can quickly tell which groups are working well as teams and which are experiencing difficulties. As one coach stated, "I love working with every grade-level team, except for the second-grade group. They spend their time complaining about their students, the materials they are using, and even the fact that the meeting is a waste of time!"

This team might benefit from creating norms for group work and then evaluating the use of those norms at each meeting (for more on creating norms, see chapter 7).

Participating in facilitated group meetings over time provides literacy leaders with multiple ways to develop relationships that promote openness and honesty. They also foster conversations in which coaches and teachers engage in meaningful discourse so they can identify preconceived views, understand the disconnects between those views and new learning, and apply what they have learned to inform instructional practice.

Once again, while the coaching activities reviewed thus far have all been shown to support both teacher and student learning, the sequencing and amount of activities will necessarily vary depending on contextual factors. Moreover, the focus between individual and group coaching will often shift depending on coach and teacher needs.

Summary

In this chapter, we discussed the power of language and identified some key notions about how literacy leaders can use language effectively in working with both individuals and groups of teachers. We also described the value of discussion-based protocols and gave some examples of those that might be useful in coaching work. Finally, we identified many different ideas for working with teachers to establish a relationship of trust. We elaborate on many of these ideas, providing further examples, in the next chapters on working with individuals (chapter 6) and with groups (chapter 7).

Activities

1. Using the chart found in appendix A, note ways that literacy leaders can function as facilitators, leaders, designers, and advocates when attempting to develop a relationship of trust between themselves and the teachers with whom they work. Which activities might you consider adopting that would further these ways of thinking and working?

2. Look up one of the protocols described in this chapter. Talk with a colleague about its potential for facilitating conversations with teachers. When would you use it? What benefits do you see in its use? Any concerns?

3. Partner with a coaching colleague, with each of you using one of the following prompts. The other person should serve as "facilitator," asking questions that move the conversation along. Tape this short three- to five-minute conversation. Then go back and analyze the type of questioning that was used in the conversation to facilitate the conversation. You may generate your own prompts, but here are a few to get you started:

    a. Talk about a recent trip you have taken, what you enjoyed and any unusual experiences you had.

    b. Talk about a book you read recently, your views about it, and why you would or would not suggest reading it.

    c. Talk about one of your favorite hobbies, how you became interested in it, what your goals are, and so on.

Working With Individual Teachers to Analyze and Transform Instructional Practices

GUIDING QUESTIONS

1. What is the rationale for coaching individual teachers?

2. What are key guidelines for using the coaching activities of modeling, co-teaching, and observing?

3. In what ways do coaches think like designers and facilitators when working with individual teachers?

4. In what ways can coaches facilitate post-observation conversations so that they encourage teacher inquiry and problem solving?

When Melinda stopped by the classroom of one of the novice teachers she was assigned to coach, she saw Janice peering at the teacher's guide and shaking her head. She looked at Melinda and said, "There's too much in here. I just don't know where to begin. Help!" Melinda saw this as a "coaching moment," but she wondered about the most productive way to start. Should she volunteer to sit with Janice and co-plan the next few instructional lessons? Should she take more time to observe in Janice's classroom to get a better sense of the students and their needs?

Working with individual teachers is the heart of coaching; it facilitates teachers' professional learning in ways that help them become reflective problem solvers who address instructional dilemmas as design problems. In this chapter, we describe activities specific to analyzing and transforming the instructional practices of individuals (Levels 2 and 3 in our Levels of Intensity). To illustrate more fully what we mean by an "observation cycle of coaching," we include a vignette of a coach and teacher working together during each step of the cycle. We conclude by discussing post-observation conversations as a means of developing teacher inquiry and problem solving.

In some ways, coaching in schools is similar to coaching sports—attempting to teach specific technical skills and, in team sports, encouraging and motivating individuals to work together. Coaching in schools also requires a focus on developing technical skills and on encouraging teachers to work as a team. However, coaching in schools is somewhat different from coaching on the field in that a key role of the literacy coach is to facilitate teachers' reflective thinking, help them analyze their own instructional practices, generate ideas for how to address instructional issues, and grow as professionals to *then* support their own students (a layer of learning and focus less common in sports coaching). Literacy coaches provide another set of eyes and ears, helping teachers become more reflective about their own practice, to better coach their own students. Given that quality teaching makes a difference in student learning, investing in learning experiences that help individual teachers think about, analyze, and transform their practices is a key part of a school's comprehensive literacy plan.

In the following paragraphs, we describe activities in which coaches work with individual teachers to analyze and transform instructional practices. Across these activities, coaches must think like a designer (about content) and like a facilitator (about the coaching process). By reflecting with teachers about design problems, we focus on how a lesson could better meet student needs (rather than highlighting "what went wrong"). Framing issues as design problems resonates with teachers who, as professionals, can reflect on what they already know, need to learn, and need to do to improve instruction for their students. In terms of facilitation, coaches need to consider how much direction or guidance is necessary to enhance teacher problem solving and reflectivity. Is it better to co-plan with the teacher, watch the teacher in action, or model?

A coach might begin by modeling ("I teach"), move to co-planning or co-teaching ("we co-plan and co-teach"), and then progress to observing ("you teach") to watch the teacher apply what has been learned from the previous activities. Although such a continuum can be useful, this process may not always be possible or necessary. For example, a coach might first observe and then decide upon next steps, perhaps modeling or co-teaching. With another teacher, the coach might model and then observe, skipping the co-teaching altogether. Coaching strategies can and should differ based on several factors, including students' needs. In the following Voices From the Field, literacy coach Marsha Turner describes the ways in which she worked with an experienced teacher who was somewhat resistant to school-wide efforts to change literacy instruction. We then describe three specific coaching activities, suggesting guidelines for their use. For additional resources about working with individual teachers, see appendix B.

VOICES FROM THE FIELD

Throughout the course of the school year, we had many conversations regarding the new national standards. I shared what I had observed in other classrooms, and I often wondered aloud what those same experiences would look like in her classroom. She participated in a classroom "learning lab" with me and expressed her surprise at the depth of the students' conversations, some of whom were in her classroom the prior year! Soon after, I modeled a literacy lesson in her classroom, in which students began practicing skills similar to what we had observed in the learning lab. The classroom teacher was amazed at what the majority of her students were able to do. After a little encouragement and support, she agreed to co-teach a literacy lesson with me. During this lesson, the classroom teacher would catch herself, look over at me, and laugh, knowing that she was saying or doing what we were trying to change. She explained to her students that she was learning something new and that it was hard!

—Marsha Turner, literacy coach

As you read about the suggested coaching activities that follow, think back to Marsha's experience and consider how she layered different coaching moves to make progress with the classroom teacher. Think also about Melinda, and which of the following activities might best support Janice in her classroom.

Modeling

Many of us need to see something before we understand it. That's why instructors show us how to do something, or we watch videos to see how something is done. The coach who models provides a visual example that often helps teachers reach an aha moment. Modeling is helpful when a practice is new to teachers, when they are not certain of how to implement a specific strategy; when teachers are unsure of whether it will work for their students; or when teachers are having specific difficulties with implementation. Guidelines for modeling follow (Bean, 2015).

Establish Goals

Talk with the teacher about the goals for the modeled lesson. What are the expected outcomes for students? What are the goals for the teacher (the teacher's expectations for learning)? Be sure the modeling is focused—for example, the coach could agree to model for a second-grade teacher how to use Syllasearch (Beck & Beck, 2013), a strategy for helping students focus their attention on the syllables in multisyllabic words.

Involve Teachers as You Model

In the modeled Syllasearch lesson, the teacher can assist in management, handing specific syllable cards to the coach. Teachers can also monitor the work of specific students, especially those who may have some difficulties with the lesson content. If students spend some time working in small groups, the teacher can work with one group while the coach works with another. Teacher and coach can also agree upon some "look-fors," and teachers can record their observations and questions on a tool similar to the one in appendix C.

Talk and Reflect With the Teacher Soon After the Lesson

Were goals achieved? If not, why? The fact that some goals may not have been achieved is often a great talking point. Both teacher and coach can learn a great deal by discussing difficulties, and teachers often breathe a sigh of relief when they see that coaches too can experience teaching dilemmas.

Follow Up

What are the next steps? Do you move to co-teaching? Should the teacher now try to use what has been learned and then talk with you as the coach? Together, the coach and teacher can make decisions about activities that make the most sense.

While modeling is a powerful coaching activity, there are a few cautions to consider when modeling or demonstrating. First, teachers can become reliant on modeling—they may be very willing for *you* to model, but don't necessarily want you to watch *them* teach.

Second, when you go back to observe in the classroom, you may see little application of what was modeled in classroom practice. Teachers may not have valued what was modeled, or perhaps they worry that they cannot do what the coach has done. Talk with the teacher about other possibilities for improving classroom practice, asking him or her to indicate what might be most beneficial. For example, instead of modeling, the two of you might co-plan the lesson or co-teach it.

A third caution: the experienced teacher may be less receptive to modeling than the novice who appreciates seeing a specific strategy or approach in action. The experienced teacher, on the other hand, may be somewhat resentful about being told or shown how to teach. In fact, the savvy coach is always attending to power dynamics within coaching work, particularly when age, seniority, or power imbalances are in play (Rainville & Jones, 2008). At the same time, in our coaching work with Reading First teachers, modeling was the activity most valued by teachers. Modeling, then, can be useful; but as with all coaching activities, decisions about when, how, and with whom to use this coaching activity are important.

PUT INTO PRACTICE

Ask a teacher if you can model a specific instructional strategy or approach in her classroom to learn more about the students in the classroom and their response to the strategy (in a pre-observation conversation, identify the purpose and teacher activities for the modeled lesson). Hold a debriefing conversation with the teacher to discuss the lesson, reflecting on what made the modeling experience a valuable one. What might you, as a coach, do differently next time?

Co-Teaching

Co-teaching is often considered to be a bridge between modeling and observing—a bridge that can lead in either direction, with either the modeling or observing coming first. Co-teaching is not always necessary, but it is useful in many ways. First, it promotes teacher and coach working together as colleagues to address an educational issue. The coach can learn more about teachers' beliefs, values, and understandings. Second, it helps to build the trusting relationship so important to coaching and often is seen as less threatening than the coach observing. Third, the coach can learn much about the students in a classroom and gain a sense of what they need to be successful literacy learners.

Some literacy leaders who coach may be assigned instructional responsibilities as part of their position; therefore, co-teaching may be an important aspect of their role. A part-time coach, for example, might have teaching responsibilities for part of a day. Also, some reading specialists or special education teachers working in elementary schools within an RTI program may be responsible for Tier 2 interventions in the classroom, providing rich opportunities for coach and teacher to learn from each other. In the points that follow, we share some possible approaches to co-teaching, many of which are similar to those used by reading specialists who have teaching responsibilities.

One Person Teaches and the Other Assists or Monitors

One teacher acts as the lead teacher, presenting a lesson (e.g., teaching a phonics lesson or teaching a specific strategy for learning vocabulary). The second teacher serves as a monitor, observing and supporting students as they work. For example, in the early grades, when students are being asked to practice blending and segmenting words using letter tiles, the monitor can quickly and efficiently provide needed support. In the later grades, especially with project-based learning, having two teachers in the classroom can be quite helpful. A coach in a middle school social studies classroom can assist students in close reading primary sources and taking notes, as part of a larger interdisciplinary research-writing project.

Parallel Teaching

Each adult is responsible for teaching the same lesson to a small group of students in the classroom. Each teacher differentiates instruction by providing more or less scaffolding or modifying instructional techniques (e.g., in one group, students read segments of the selection silently, stopping to discuss at specific points; in the other group, students read aloud to a partner). Given the smaller number of students in the group, there is more opportunity to focus on students' individual needs and to modify the lesson.

Station Teaching

Students are learning at centers or stations, and each of the two instructors—coach and teacher—develop goals and activities for specific stations. In an intermediate classroom, for example, there may be four stations and students rotate from one to another during an extended block of time. Students might be working independently at the writing and reading stations. At the third station, the teacher might be working with a group on vocabulary activities specific to an informational text to be read the following day. The coach might be working at the fourth station with a small group, discussing a fiction piece related to the informational text.

Turn Taking or Team Teaching

The teacher and coach plan a lesson that requires each of them to assume teaching responsibility in the lesson. In some cases, there may be turn taking. For example, the coach might introduce and explain a vocabulary word, using the notion of student-friendly definitions (Beck, McKeown, & Kucan, 2002); the teacher might do the same with another word. There may also be more sophisticated uses of team teaching, where both teachers introduce concepts and then lead students through the various steps of a lesson. Some colleagues have indicated this sort of teaching works best when instructors know each other and their styles well, and in the words of one coach, "I can finish the sentence of my teaching partner."

Co-teaching might also be used as an optional coaching activity, perhaps focused on helping a teacher understand how to implement a new strategy or approach. In one situation, three days a week for a month, a coach and teacher taught together during the literacy period; the teacher had been transferred from the middle school to the primary grades and was having difficulty making that transition. According to the coach, the time was well spent because the teacher, by the end of the month, was able to effectively handle literacy instruction on his own.

At the secondary level, co-teaching might be an effective way of helping content-area teachers as they learn to use various disciplinary literacy strategies appropriate for developing students' content knowledge. The coach and teacher can co-plan and then co-teach a lesson in which students are asked to work collaboratively in small groups. This provides ample opportunities for coaches to learn more about discipline-specific content and habits of mind (e.g., in a chemistry class, how to think about similarities and differences between covalent and ionic bonds), while the classroom teacher learns more about literacy-focused instruction (e.g., modeling word-learning strategies in dense, technical texts). Again, the key to successful co-teaching is to reflect with the teacher after the lesson to discuss its effectiveness, talk about what each educator learned about literacy instruction for students, and discuss how it might be improved.

PUT INTO PRACTICE

Ask a teacher with whom you are working if you can co-teach with him. Think about which of the models described earlier would work best, and plan the lesson with the teacher. After teaching the lesson, take time to talk about what went well and the lessons learned. Possible questions to discuss include:

- Were the students able to achieve the goals of the lesson?

- In what ways did co-teaching contribute to those goals?

- What worked effectively? What changes might be made?

Observing

Observing teachers as they work with students provides information about whether teachers can "walk the talk." That is, to what extent can teachers use specific strategies or approaches, manage classrooms, or provide a literate environment conducive to literacy learning? Periodic observations can help coaches pinpoint what feedback would be helpful to individual teachers in making changes in their instruction. At times, observations may be used to determine the extent to which a specific strategy or instructional approach is being implemented in classrooms. For example, a coach might observe in all fifth-grade classrooms to get a better sense of how teachers are implementing a newly adopted writing workshop initiative. Results of the observations can help coaches plan for teachers' professional learning. Also, observations may be used as a follow-up after each modeling or co-teaching session to support teachers in their efforts to transform instruction. Coaches may also observe in classrooms where student performance, perhaps on progress-monitoring tests, has been low and there is a need to get a better sense of the instruction. Following are some key notions about observing.

Observations Should Assist in Improving Instruction

Coaching observations are not conducted for evaluation purposes, and results are not to be shared with principals or supervisors. What coaches see, and the feedback they offer, should be confidential and shared only with the teacher being observed. In fact, we suggest that coaches closely monitor the ways in which they observe in order to de-emphasize any potential evaluative messages. To what extent does the coach focus on describing rather than evaluating or making judgments about what she sees? We encourage coaches to observe in a "descriptive mode," taking note of what is happening and sharing it with teachers, without adding the layer of normative values. Note this example:

> A tenth-grade history teacher, during a lesson, asks individual students to read aloud paragraphs of a specific chapter in the textbook. This goes on for the entire period. The coach, in a debriefing conversation, is careful to stay in "descriptive mode," describing the activity and lack of student attention in purely factual terms. For example, the coach says, "During a fifteen-minute reading time, eight students were called upon to read. Each student read for less than two minutes. Seven other students were observed reading something other than the textbook or looking at papers on their desks. Twelve additional students were observed interacting with each other, nonverbally or quietly, but not with the text." The coach is cautious not to immediately criticize round-robin reading as an instructional practice. Instead, when the teacher indicates that the students can't read the book on their own as a rationale for

asking students to read aloud, the coach discusses research-based alternatives to round-robin reading, such as partner reading, that might be more effective.

A One-Time Observation Is Just a Snapshot

An observation reflects just one moment in time of both the teacher's and students' actions. Many things can affect what is seen: the particular topic or skill that is taught, the behavior of a specific student on one day, activities going on in school (holiday time), and so on. Also, as the coach, you don't have as much information as the teacher about the purpose of the lesson, particular classroom dynamics, and the attributes of specific students that may affect instruction. Pre-observation conversations can help coaches get a better understanding of the lesson's context.

The Observation Cycle

Implicit in much of what we have written so far is the foundational observation cycle that many literacy leaders who coach use across all of their activities and work. As shown in figure 6.1, we suggest four steps in a complete observation cycle.

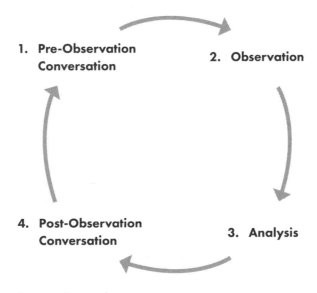

Figure 6.1: The observation cycle.

*Visit **www.learningsciences.com/bookresources** to download a reproducible version of this figure.*

We recognize that time and workload may limit the degree to which coaches can actually implement this cycle; further, it may not be necessary to go through the full cycle for all observations. When working with a single teacher over time, the pre-observation conversation (often used for planning) can occur during the post-observation conversation (i.e., teachers and coaches can plan what to do next). In the sections that follow, we discuss the four steps in more depth, illustrating the work of a coach and teacher through a series of boxes ("Paul and Shannon") and revealing their interactions during each phase of the process. We begin with an example, which sets the context for the observation. Think about yourself as the coach and how you might move through this observation cycle.

PAUL AND SHANNON:
THE CONTEXT FOR THE OBSERVATION

The school had recently decided to introduce kindergarten students to more informational texts to increase students' world knowledge and academic vocabulary. Specific books and accompanying activities were developed by a team of kindergarten teachers. Shannon, a new teacher, was experiencing difficulty in using these materials and asked Paul, the literacy coach, if he would observe a lesson and provide her with some feedback. As they finished their conversation, Paul reminded Shannon that he would be taking notes to help him remember important points. Paul and Shannon agreed to meet during a planning period soon after the observation. In addition, Paul asked Shannon to jot down some of her thoughts and questions about the lesson before that conversation.

Pre-Observation Conversation

The goal of meeting with a teacher before the observation is to develop a focus or goal for that observation and possible subsequent coaching conversations. Because Shannon requested the observation and identified the focus, most likely the post-observation conversation and follow-up will be positive. In other instances, the coach may be the one to suggest the focus, such as observing a specific strategy required by the school or conducting a routine observation to observe teachers' implementation of the new core reading program. At times, the coach and teacher together may decide on the focus. What is important is that there *is* a focus: trying to observe all that is going on in a classroom during a single lesson is difficult (if not impossible). This pre-observation conversation can also serve to reinforce the notion that the coach and teacher are co-learners and have the same goal or focus in mind. The teacher and coach can also talk about the protocol to be used for taking notes, if any are to be taken. This conversation does not have to be lengthy, especially if the teacher and coach have participated in an observation cycle previously.

Observation

Before observing, the coach, perhaps with the teacher, should develop or select a tool or strategy for collecting data as a source of evidence for discussion after the observation. Coaches may design or propose a particular protocol (e.g., a checklist, a rubric, or even an open-ended procedure). Several comments about each follow:

- Checklists that include a "scale" can be useful (e.g., a three-point scale ranging from "evident to some degree" to "not all all"). Such checklists provide you with direction and enable you to be consistent in how you think about what you see. You may choose to focus on only one or two sections of the checklist if you have selected a specific focus. You and your colleagues may have developed or selected one that is aligned with a particular literacy program or initiative. It is possible to develop a template that addresses only one aspect of an initiative: What would you expect to see when a teacher is leading a discussion aimed at encouraging active engagement and high-level thinking? Appendix D illustrates a checklist that can be used for observing in a content-area classroom (Bean, 2015, p. 293).

- Descriptive or scripted approaches are also helpful. Coaches using this approach write down as much as they can of both the teacher's and students' words and actions. An important advantage of this system for coding an observation is that results can be shared with teachers to provide evidence of what the teacher and students actually said or did. Thus, in many ways, this type of coding can be less subjective than checklists. Data from the notes can be readily used to describe what went on in the lesson and identify discussion topics. Some guidelines that may help when using a scripted or descriptive approach follow (see the example in figure 6.2, page 102):

  - Develop abbreviations or create symbols to represent words (e.g., "OB" for "observed"; "NE" for "not engaged"; "OC" for "observer comments").

  - Use a T-chart to indicate the teacher's and students' words and actions.

  - Draw a line to indicate a change in activities or a specific time period (e.g., draw a new line after every five minutes).

Teacher	Students
9:00 So, where does a chicken live?	Ss – shout out: Nest, yard, coop, outside.
What does the book say about where chickens live?	Ss – silence OC – Kids confused?
Look at this word. – (T. points to "coop.")	
It says "coop." Chickens live in a coop.	Ss – shout out "Coop"
9:05 Tell me about the picture on this page. (Points to pigs in sty)	S – I know, I see pigs!
	Three kids get up, stand in front of the big book
Please sit down!	

Figure 6.2: Partial example of descriptive coding.

Often, teachers who see the results of this sort of observation are amazed, surprised, or stunned. For example, sometimes they don't realize how much talking they do during class, while others are pleased to see improvements in areas they've been working on in their instruction. This type of data collection lends itself well to a more descriptive rather than judgmental approach to coaching, which can sometimes produce resentment or resistance on the part of the teacher. In place of this type of scripting, the coach and teacher may decide to videotape part of the lesson and obtain similar information. One of the advantages of the video is that it can be shared with the teacher and, if the teacher grants permission, used for a discussion with peers. Additionally, given the recent national focus on making teaching public, videos of classroom instruction can be especially helpful to guide coach-teacher debriefing conversations. Note, however, that the use of video as a coaching tool can be intimidating and is considered Level 2 or 3 on our Levels of Intensity scale (see figure 1.2, page 10).

Sample observation protocols can be downloaded from the Literacy Coaching Clearinghouse (www.literacycoachingonline.org/tools.html) and the School Reform Initiative (http://schoolreforminitiative.org). In addition, two broad guidelines for observing follow:

1. Make arrangements with the teacher before entering the classroom about where you will sit and the degree to which you will be an unobtrusive

observer. The two of you may decide that you will not interact at all in the lesson, or, if there is an appropriate time (and request from the teacher), you might be able to participate in the lesson. Regardless, the decision should be one that helps both of you address the goals of the observation, and it should be agreed upon before the observation.

2. When leaving the classroom, thank the teacher for letting you visit. If possible and appropriate, thank the class and indicate how much you enjoyed being there; be as specific as you can (e.g., "I really enjoyed hearing everyone read aloud; you are really wonderful readers").

In the next installment of Shannon and Paul's journey, Paul observes Shannon's lesson and takes explicit notes, using a descriptive approach.

PAUL AND SHANNON: LESSON OBSERVATION

Shannon was reading an informational book about types of houses to her group of eighteen kindergarten students that included a student new to the class. (Miguel, a student whose first language was not English, had arrived just that day.) Shannon had written the various content words to be taught ("sty," "coop," "nest") on large cards. When the words appeared in the text she was reading, she would show the card to the students, say the word, explain the meaning of the word, have the students read it, and resume reading.

Paul took notes as he watched. He noted that students, clustered around the big book, were antsy, wiggling, touching each other, and not looking at the big book or the word cards. Shannon cautioned them at least five times to be good listeners and pay attention. She stopped the lesson on several occasions to discipline Miguel for standing or walking around. Also, Shannon read in a flat, unexpressive manner and did not stop reading except to introduce and explain the vocabulary words when they came up in the text. She continued the lesson for twenty-some minutes, except when she called the paraprofessional over to remove Miguel, who had wet his pants. Shannon rolled her eyes at Paul and shrugged her shoulders. Paul, when he left at the end of the lesson, whispered quietly to Shannon, "Hang in there; we've all had days like these."

Analysis of the Observation

This step is key in that it enables the coach *and* the teacher to think about the lesson—and each should reflect on the lesson before they meet. Always, the goal is to refer back to the planning meeting: What was the focus of the observation, and in what ways did the lesson address that focus? In appendix E, we provide a Lesson Analysis Guide to help coaches reflect as they prepare for a post-observation conversation. The guide can be used both when preparing for and facilitating the conversation with the teacher. The coach can also ask the teacher to analyze the lesson, using a similar protocol. Two key points to think about when analyzing the lesson are: How can the data (checklist, scripts) be used as evidence to identify essential elements of the lesson? Are there any critical or pivotal incidents that warrant discussion, such as good use of an open-ended question or a student raising a question about another student's comment?

Remember the teacher can often, but not always, identify a problem and assist with the solution. Consider the following questions in making decisions about the follow-up conversation:

▸ How can I work with the teacher to co-construct and develop a shared understanding of the observations?

▸ What changes do the teacher and coach view as most important for student learning? Which changes do the teacher and coach see as most urgent? Most doable?

▸ What resources or supports does the teacher need to make changes?

▸ What were the effective elements of the lesson? In what ways did the teacher achieve the goals?

▸ What are possible alternatives or options to address any difficulties (generated by coach and teacher)?

▸ What are the key points for discussion with the teacher? Identify only two or three, so that there is more probability of follow-up and implementation. Also, include points that reinforce positive aspects of the lesson.

Consider carefully your opening statement in the conversation. It can often set the tone for the discussion. It may be problematic to begin by asking the teacher, "What do you think about the lesson?" Teachers may think the lesson was great, which puts you in the uncomfortable situation of disagreeing with that view. Some better possibilities include:

• Responsive coaching: "I appreciated having an opportunity to visit your classroom. Let's use this opportunity to think about those aspects of the lesson that helped you achieve the lesson goals and raise questions about those aspects that you may want to change. Perhaps you can share your thinking first?"

• Directive coaching: "I really enjoyed being in the classroom today. I jotted some notes about aspects of the lesson that seemed to really work well for you—and also raised some questions for you to think about. Let me share a few of those with you."

PAUL AND SHANNON: ANALYSIS OF THE LESSON

After leaving the room, Paul sat down in his office to reflect on the lesson design, thinking about what appeared to work well and what could be changed to meet students' needs. He also thought about how to approach his conversation with Shannon, scheduled for the next day. In other words, Paul was thinking like a designer ("How can this lesson be improved for these students?") and as a facilitator ("How can I work with Shannon to elicit her ideas, learn more about her students, and collaborate in ways that support Shannon's learning and enhance student literacy learning?").

Paul realized that there were several design elements to consider. In reviewing his notes, he identified three possible focus topics: material being used (was it appropriate?); instructional approaches (reading of text, introduction of vocabulary); and classroom management (grouping, length of lesson). As he reflected, Paul identified some questions:

What made the text difficult for students? Would a "first and complete read" of the text be a useful strategy to help students get a sense of the book before working with complex vocabulary? Were there other ways to involve students in the discussion of the vocabulary words? If Shannon made adjustments in her oral reading, would students have been more involved? Could she work with a smaller group (having her paraprofessional work with the other children) so that all students could see the big book easily? Could the lesson have been shorter—perhaps divided into two parts over two sessions?

Paul's goals were to work collaboratively with Shannon to think about the lesson and possible options for improving its effectiveness and to capitalize on Shannon's willingness to learn and reinforce what she was doing well. Paul made notes about the possible content of the post-observation conversation, using a protocol similar to the one in appendix E.

Post-Observation Conversation

This conversation requires perhaps the deftest facilitation skills of the entire cycle. The points raised about urgency and feasibility are key; coaches need to help teachers focus on important issues. Simultaneously, coaches need to consider which changes in teacher beliefs and knowledge are necessary and possible at this point in the teacher's professional learning process. Next, we provide some general guidelines for the post-observation conversation:

- Make the setting a comfortable one. If possible, sit next to the teacher rather than across a desk to develop an atmosphere that establishes the two of you as co-learners. It's also easier to review data when sitting side-by-side.

- Establish the goals and purpose for the conversation. Understand the limits of time, making certain that important items are addressed first.

- Provide balanced feedback. Help teachers understand what was effective and where changes might have a positive influence on lesson outcomes. The example in the sub-bullet illustrates what we mean by balanced feedback:

  - "Giving students opportunities to talk with others about their views about fracking and its effect on the environment is an effective approach for encouraging active involvement and high-level thinking. I wonder whether the conversations might be more productive if initially some of the pros and cons had been identified by the group and perhaps written on the SMART Board. What do you think?"

- Make plans for follow-through. What will the teacher plan to do? What does the coach need to do to support the teacher's efforts? Select priority goals, perhaps only one or two so that the teacher will be successful in these change efforts.

Providing feedback can be difficult for coaches, and receiving feedback can be equally difficult for teachers. At times, coaches find themselves focusing on the positive, minimizing teachers' need to address specific areas of concern, or dominating the conversation. Too often, the common pattern for feedback is to first provide positive feedback and then to *tell* teachers what is wrong or ineffective. Timperley (n.d.) suggests that these feedback sessions be seen as learning conversations in which coach and teacher collaboratively design solutions for identified problems. Peterson, Taylor, Burnham, and Schock (2009) and Duncan (2006) both provide examples of such conversations, notably guided by simple discussion protocols. These conversations are demanding (not demeaning), and there is respect for each other's views and a focus on developing reflectivity and inquiry as habits of mind. Further, in planning these conversations, coaches must consider each teacher's ways of knowing and leadership stances (Breidenstein, et al., 2012) as identified in chapter 2 (i.e., instrumental learning, socializing learning, self-authoring learning). The savvy coach will listen carefully to the kinds of questions the teacher is asking, and which stance she might be adopting.

- Is the teacher asking for quick, concrete solutions, and looking to the coach for explicit, expert advice (suggestive of an instrumental-learning approach)?

- Is the teacher asking for support from colleagues, thinking about ways to bring a dilemma to the weekly professional learning community meeting, or perhaps asking to observe others in action (suggestive of a more socializing-learning approach)?

- Is the teacher asking the coach to respond to ideas that the teacher has generated as a way of solving a problem, wanting the coach to act more as a sounding board or extra set of eyes (suggestive of a more self-authoring stance)?

Which of these ways of knowing and ways of learning might be in play during the post-observation conversation? What might help the teacher feel most comfortable? What might the coach do to help create an environment in which the teacher can safely stretch a bit? (For example, not simply *giving* the instrumental teacher an answer but instead suggesting that she observe a colleague or talk with her instructional team; or asking the teacher who is quick to lean on her team to instead suggest a few alternatives that she imagines her team might provide). It is always important to take into consideration the skills and knowledge of the teacher and the goals for student learning.

In the paragraphs that follow, we describe three particular stances toward providing feedback that can be useful in conversations between coaches and teachers (adapted from Robbins, 1991; Ippolito, 2010), when to use them, and examples of language that illustrates each. Again, selecting a stance (or multiple stances) is dependent on the teacher's knowledge, experience, and disposition, as well as the strength of the relationship between the coach and teacher. Also, a conversation is often a mix of the various stances, with a coach moving from one stance to another as needed.

Expert (or Directive) Stance

Coaches bring their expertise to the conversation, providing ideas, resources, or materials teachers might find helpful. When using this stance, the coach supports teachers by suggesting ideas or resources. This stance can be helpful when engaging with teachers who are interested in a more instrumental-learning experience. The expert or directive approach is useful when teachers lack the knowledge or experience of a specific strategy or approach, or when they are seeking immediate information (e.g., "I need to try something different *tomorrow* to help four of my students, who can't read the texts I'm using in my classroom").

Coaches may also use this stance when the teacher asks, "What do you think?" or, "How would you handle Sammy, who is disrupting my lessons by getting out of his seat and refusing to participate?" The following reply is an example of a coach adopting a more directive stance: "You asked about how to help a child become more fluent in his reading. There is research evidence suggesting that lots of practice reading and re-reading connected text really helps. Here are some specific ideas that seemed to have worked well for other teachers. Would any of these seem to be workable for you?"

The coach, even from this expert or directive stance, is providing options for the teacher and soliciting teacher input about the feasibility of those options. Again, with any design problem, there are always a number of ways to solve it. Serving as an expert, or responding in a directive manner, may be useful when addressing technical issues, but less advantageous when dealing with changes that require adaptive thinking.

Coach-as-Peer (or Balanced) Stance

When using this stance, the coach uses language that enhances the ability of the two participants to work collaboratively to identify and solve problems. This stance is useful for promoting teacher reflectivity and for addressing changes that require adaptive thinking about specific and often complex classroom problems (as well as potential solutions). This stance might be more commonly found in use with teachers engaged in socializing or self-authoring learning. When there is a high level of trust and a low-risk environment, the teacher will most likely be willing to talk openly. An example of the language in such a conversation follows:

> **Teacher:** "What do you think if I include more nonfiction materials using the approach discussed in the article by Nell Duke? I know my third-grade students need more opportunities to read nonfiction."
>
> **Coach:** "Great idea! Let's think about what that approach means in terms of putting it into practice. What specific ideas is Duke recommending? What are your thoughts about how you might start? What questions do you have, and how can I help? Do you need some nonfiction selections? I might suggest you start with a few familiar nonfiction picture books to open the conversation about genre features."

Coach-as-Mirror (or Responsive) Stance

The metaphor of a mirror is one that illustrates the key role of the coach as a listener or as someone to serve as a facilitator, helping the teacher move to more complex ways of thinking about her reflections. Often, this stance is used with a teacher comfortable with a more self-authoring learning stance (or a teacher the coach is trying to encourage to become more self-authoring). This stance is perfect for those who are able to self-reflect and who want the opportunity to talk through a lesson with a knowledgeable peer; the coach can help by asking probing questions that raise the level of thinking. Such questions provide guided-inquiry experiences that help develop reflective thinking. In a conversation using this stance, a coach might say, "You've identified the goal of increasing student engagement by asking questions that require higher level thinking. As you look at the transcript of the lesson, where do you see that goal being met? Where do you see room for tweaking? How might I help you get to the next level regarding your goal?" Notably, this stance may be less effective with a novice teacher (or more instrumental learner) who is eagerly seeking a concrete answer from the coach; instead, the teacher might potentially find this line of guided questioning evasive and frustrating. Again, it is very important for the coach to gauge what the teacher needs both substantively and procedurally during these conversations.

Remember that all three of these stances may be used in one conversation. Think about a conversation as an intricate dance—one with many steps, with participants moving forward, backward, and sideways. Each conversation is an opportunity to encourage different ways of learning and knowing, with both the coach and teacher pushing each other to adopt more complex stances toward reflecting on their practice. The key is the ability of the coach to listen to the response of the teacher, feed off that response, and provide comments or questions that facilitate thinking for both parties. Of course, using note-taking guides or protocols (similar to the one in appendix E) can help guide your thinking. One quick example of such a protocol, designed for use when a coach and individual

teacher are planning reading and writing workshop instruction, is the "Into/Through/Beyond" protocol designed by Judy Blanco and found on the Literacy Coaching Clearinghouse website (http://www .literacycoachingonline.org/briefs/tools/Into_through_beyond_tool _1.11.09.pdf).

In the next "Paul and Shannon" installment, we summarize Paul's post-observation conversation with Shannon. As you read the text, think about how Paul and Shannon work together to solve the design problems in the lesson. Also, note how Paul's questioning and comments help facilitate the conversation.

PAUL AND SHANNON: POST-OBSERVATION CONVERSATION

In their post-observation conversation, Paul began with a comment about how a student new to the group (like Miguel) can create a new set of issues and how difficult that is for any teacher. He asked Shannon to talk about the students in the class and their familiarity with this type of lesson. He also asked her to talk about Miguel and how he was adjusting to the class.

continued →

Using a set of focus questions, Paul then asked Shannon to talk a little about the text being used, how she selected the words, and what other texts and resources were available to her (thus focusing the conversation on Shannon's teaching materials). Paul reiterated the value of introducing these young literacy learners to informational text to develop their academic vocabulary and content knowledge; at the same time, given students' lack of familiarity with this type of text structure, they would need ongoing experiences and probably more scaffolding (an example of balanced feedback). They both agreed that students would need additional support with these types of lessons, now part of the kindergarten curriculum. Shannon then asked Paul for some suggestions.

Paul and Shannon discussed possible options for improving the lesson design: reducing the size of the group so all could see the big book clearly, shortening the length of the lesson, and increasing student engagement. Although Paul offered some possibilities, Shannon added ideas about how she might reduce the size of the group, suggesting that the paraprofessional could work with half the class while Shannon worked with the other half. Shannon also described how she might divide the lesson into two shorter lessons taught over two days.

The final focus topic, classroom management, was raised by Shannon, who talked about her difficulties in that area. In response, Paul used clarifying and probing questions: When does she experience difficulty? During what types of lessons? What are her current management strategies? What is her hunch about the relationship between group size and engagement? Length of activity and engagement?

Paul and Shannon then discussed the connection between instruction and classroom engagement. Were there elements that could be changed to increase student engagement? Shannon and Paul together identified some possible instructional changes: reading the selection all the way through the first time, pointing to the pictures that illustrated some of the vocabulary words, and reading in a more expressive manner.

Together, Shannon and Paul summarized what was discussed and formulated next steps. They agreed that the two of them would co-plan a lesson using an informational text. Shannon wanted to teach this lesson on her own, and Paul agreed, with the proviso that the two of them would talk after the lesson.

Note that both directive and responsive coaching (i.e., balanced coaching) was used in the post-observation conversation just described. Paul shared his expertise and also asked clarifying and probing questions that required Shannon to think critically about literacy instruction. In many ways, the conversation leaned a bit toward an instrumental-learning focus to support Shannon as she learned new strategies for adopting (what were for her) new practices. At the same time, Paul asked questions that required Shannon to take an inquiry stance, encouraging a bit more of a socializing or self-authoring learning stance. We can imagine Paul suggesting that Shannon bring these same issues to her weekly grade-level team meeting for further discussion and reflection, or engage in a bit of self-study by keeping a journal of instructional results and writing her own reflections at the end of each day. These coaching moves are designed to help edge Shannon, bit-by-bit, into more socializing and self-authoring ways of working.

In the observation cycle described in the preceding sections, Paul and Shannon collaborated to address an instructional issue of importance to Shannon and to develop a shared understanding of both identified problems and potential solutions. Further, Paul used his facilitation skills of active listening and questioning to learn more about the students, the lesson, and the teacher, recognizing that teachers themselves bring their own funds of knowledge (Moll, 2000) to the conversations. These coaching moves are critical, as classroom teachers often have a deeper understanding of the specific classroom context and students than does the coach. As one teacher talking about the differences between herself and a reading specialist said, "*She's* a reading specialist; *I'm* a kid specialist!"

Summary

In this chapter, we discussed the rationale for coaching teachers one-on-one and then described the coaching activities of modeling, co-teaching, and observing. We delved deeply into an illustrated example of the coaching observation cycle (including pre-observation conversation, observation, analysis, and post-observation conversation steps). We also provided specific guidelines about how coaching can promote teacher learning and an inquiring habit of mind. We concluded by discussing the importance of providing feedback in ways that show respect for teachers' views and knowledge, while challenging them to think reflectively about how they can improve the literacy learning of their students.

Activities

1. Using the chart found in appendix A, note the ways that literacy leaders function as facilitators, leaders, designers, and advocates when working with individual teachers. List some possibilities that you might consider in your current position.

2. Watch a video of a classroom lesson, either by yourself or with some coaching peers. (Many sample videos, across grade levels and literacy-focused activities, can be found on The Teaching Channel [www.teachingchannel.org]). Assume the teacher is a coach modeling

instruction. Identify some prior look-fors and then take on the role of the teacher who is watching this modeled lesson. When you finish, think about your experience watching this lesson. What did you learn by watching this modeled lesson that can help you develop your ability to model and talk with teachers after the lesson? If you are watching with your coaching peers, discuss what you learned and compare your experiences.

3. Read one or both of the following briefs found on the Literacy Coaching Clearinghouse (www.literacycoachingonline.org/briefs.html); think about or discuss ideas and take-aways with colleagues that may support your work as a literacy leader:

    a. "What Teachers Say They Changed Because of Their Coach" by Vanderburg and Stephens

    b. "Do's and Dont's for Literacy Coaches" by Bean and DeFord

4. Think about the coaching sessions in this chapter and the ways that Paul and Shannon worked together. In what ways did Paul facilitate the conversations? In what ways did Shannon and Paul work together to solve design problems? What questions come to mind? What are some take-aways? Talk with a colleague about your reflections.

CHAPTER 7

Working With Groups to Establish Schools as Places of Learning

GUIDING QUESTIONS

1. Why and when is group coaching effective?

2. What do coaches need to know about facilitating small-group meetings? Making presentations to large groups?

3. In what ways can literacy leaders help establish schools as places of learning for both students and teachers?

Melinda, in her new role as literacy teacher-leader, was asked to serve as the leader for her grade-level team of five teachers. This group of experienced and novice teachers had varying views about literacy instruction and classroom management. A few were wedded to the core program, moving through it with little variation. Two teachers, who had just attended workshops about reading and writing workshops, were eager to make some changes in how they used the core program; in fact, they wanted to work as a team, regrouping students across their two classrooms. Melinda knew she needed to develop some facilitation skills that would help her work effectively with this team of teachers. What routines and structures might prove most successful with her group? How might she make sure that she started on the right foot?

In this chapter, we focus on how literacy leaders who coach can work productively with groups of teachers. First, we discuss the rationale for working with small groups, present related guidelines, and elaborate on how literacy leaders can effectively facilitate the work of small groups. Next, we present ideas for working effectively with large groups, including making school-wide presentations. Finally, we end with a section on developing professional learning communities (PLCs), in which we suggest specific approaches for developing schools as places of learning for both students and teachers.

VOICES FROM THE FIELD

I do know that my thinking on coaching has changed. Gone are the days when I spent most of my time providing one-on-one support to teachers. I still support some teachers independently; however, my coaching support has evolved into that of a facilitator in a group setting. I still ask the same reflective questions and push everyone's thinking [just like] I did in an independent format—I'm just doing it with groups of teachers rather than one-on-one. I have found that when working with a group, the conversations are richer, the thinking is deeper, and teachers value the time spent with their colleagues. I'm introducing structures, such as peer coaching or classroom learning labs/instructional rounds, as a way for teachers to support one another in daily job-embedded professional learning, resulting in learning that still continues without my presence. I then follow up with individual teachers as needed. As I reflect on my support, I always ask the same question, "Do my words and actions promote dependence or independence?"

—Marsha Turner, literacy coach

Why Coaches Work With Groups

Although literacy leaders who coach spend much of their time working with individual teachers, many also work directly with groups of teachers. They collaboratively discuss the vision and goals for the literacy program for a grade-level, specific subject area, school, or district; analyze data to inform instruction; develop curriculum; and make large-group presentations to develop background information about a literacy topic. The reasons for working with groups of teachers, from just a few to an entire faculty, are many and multifaceted—you can probably think of several ways in which you have been involved in group work during the school year. Some of the core reasons for working with groups are detailed in the following sections.

Groups Can Bring About Change

By working with groups, changes in the culture can be facilitated (Dumay, 2009; Leithwood & Mascall, 2008; Printy, 2008; Vescio, Ross, & Adams, 2008). Coaches can spur change by leading efforts to develop an organizational environment—a learning community—that promotes social interaction focused on improving both teacher and student learning. Moreover, when the culture is such that teachers *as a group* share a similar vision and a sense of responsibility for all students, believe that students can learn, hold high expectations, and are committed to school improvement, it is much more likely that there will be overall improvement in student literacy learning (Leana & Pil, 2006).

A toxic environment diminishes the possibility of larger school change. Think about the need for enough effort, enthusiasm, and belief in an initiative to make a difference, what Gladwell (2000) calls a "tipping point." We have seen this in schools where reform or remodeling efforts have resulted in overall change in the school's literacy environment. When teachers are collectively excited about an initiative, they talk about it and share their ideas with others in ways that support coaching work.

Group Coaching Is Connected to Targeted Coaching With Individuals

By working effectively with groups of teachers, coaches can enhance and differentiate the coaching of individual teachers. Grierson (2011), in her study of coaching, discusses the value of group coaching as a means of identifying which follow-up coaching activities would be best for individual teachers. She found that group coaching was necessary but not sufficient. Follow-up individual coaching was an essential aspect for improving teacher practices. During group meetings, individual teachers may share their instructional experiences, positive and problematic, with group members. Follow-up individual coaching, using ideas discussed in chapter 6, can then be differentiated to better meet the needs of individual teachers. Moreover, some coaches begin with individual coaching, but then find it critical to bring a group together to share what is being learned across classrooms.

The exact order of individual and group coaching may be less important than the notion that the two activities feed into each other. Importantly, teachers in small groups begin to see each other as rich resources and supports, instead of simply looking to the coach for advice. This can potentially free the coach a bit to focus more specifically on those individuals who might want or need more intensive individual coaching.

Working With Groups Increases Efficiency

Coaches can reach more teachers when they work with groups, and there is a greater probability of large-scale or school-wide change when most teachers are involved in a specific initiative. (Yet, too often, coaches work with only a small percentage of the teachers in a school, sometimes with only those who volunteer to be coached or with those who have been identified as "needing support.") Also, working in small groups can allow coaches to harness the power of the group to encourage shy or reluctant colleagues. Where an individual teacher might balk at a suggestion from a coach in a one-on-one meeting, sometimes that same teacher may be more willing to try something new when an entire group of colleagues is taking on the same challenge. Working with groups results in a much more efficient route toward adopting and adapting new practices than does persuading and cajoling one-by-one.

In other words, while individual coaching is critical, literacy coaches need to be able to work with groups in ways that help teachers learn from and with each other. By working effectively with groups, literacy leaders who coach can build on the notion of social capacity to increase the capacity as a means of improving instructional practices and student learning in the school as a whole. When working with groups, thinking like a facilitator is key.

General Guidelines for Working With Groups of All Sizes

As literacy leaders, especially those new to their roles like Melinda, work with groups of colleagues, there are a handful of basic principles that can guide that facilitative coaching work. In the sections that follow, we outline what we consider to be essential ways of thinking about and working with groups of various sizes.

Set Norms for Participation Early and Review Them Periodically

As one of our coaching colleagues says often, "All groups have norms. It's just that some groups name them, and thereby take ownership and control of them!" Taking a few minutes to talk about and set norms for participation, either when a group first forms or when a coach begins working with an already established group, can allow a facilitator to avoid pitfalls later in the group's working life. They also provide a starting point for the facilitator (and group members) to then revisit the norms and address any group dynamic issues that may arise over time.

Some norms will likely be logistical—such as arriving on time, limiting cell phone and laptop use, and so on—while others may touch on productive ways to collaborate—posing suggestions as "I wonder . . . " statements, assuming positive intent whenever teachers talk, and so on. Finally, some norms may touch on cultural aspects of the work such as remembering to connect instructional suggestions to student learning outcomes, remembering to consider students with different learning needs, and so on. In figure 7.1, we identify a few steps a facilitator might use when working with a group to establish norms.

- Ask group members individually to make a T-chart identifying characteristics of "effective groups" and "ineffective groups."

- Share with the entire group the results of the individual work, listing characteristics of effective groups on chart paper or a SMART Board. Discuss the need to establish norms for working together so that the group can effectively accomplish its goals.

- After all the items have been listed, ask the group for help in synthesizing and combining items, or collectively making decisions about the top five characteristics that the group believes will be essential to their work. Whittling the list down to a manageable number of norms helps the group hold onto, apply, and reflect on them.

- Let the group know that these norms will be revisited in the near future, with the goal of creating a space for reflection on group process and progress. This allows the group to correct course and further revise the norms.

Figure 7.1: Coach-designed process for developing norms for small-group work.

Other suggested protocols that can assist in the establishment of strong group norms include:

▶ *Compass Points* (good for larger groups): http://schoolreforminitiative.org/doc/compass_points.pdf

▶ *Forming Ground Rules* (good for smaller groups): http://schoolreforminitiative.org/doc/forming_ground_rules.pdf

▶ *Norms Construction* (good for smaller groups): http://schoolreforminitiative.org/doc/norms_construction.pdf

Be the "Guide on the Side"

Although group facilitators may need to convey specific bits of knowledge at times, one of the major goals of group facilitation is to elicit the knowledge, beliefs, and perspectives of group members. Be a facilitator, a co-learner. You want teachers to see you as a colleague—a "lead learner" whose focus is student success. Provide opportunities for group members to share their expertise, raise questions, and participate in design thinking and problem solving.

Coaches who spend more time talking (or lecturing) than they do listening are not building the capacity of group members. Such behavior lessens teacher ownership and may generate resentment or resistance from colleagues who feel as though they are being talked at or that their beliefs and knowledge have little value. Here are three quick ways to ensure that you don't monopolize the conversation and that you're building facilitative capacity in teachers:

1. Establish a clear agenda or use a discussion-based protocol with rounds of noticing, questioning, and interpretation wherein all voices can be heard.

2. Solicit suggestions for agenda items before each meeting, perhaps over e-mail or in person depending on participants' preferences, so that the agenda is never *entirely* coach-driven.

3. Rotate the facilitation of the group meetings, so that you are not the only one leading the group meetings.

Remember That Engagement Is Important

Group leaders understand that not all members are engaged in the same way or ready for the same kinds of learning experiences (see figure 2.1 and figure 2.2, pages 24 and 25). Some group members take an active role, raising questions and making comments. Other participants are less vocal but may be mentally involved. Effective facilitators aim to hear from all members of the group in each meeting. The following points contain effective strategies for increasing participation, along with example statements and questions:

▸ Ask those who haven't said anything to respond. For example, "I'd like to hear from those who haven't said anything yet about this issue to make sure that all views are heard."

▸ Initiate a "whip-around," either written or oral, urging everyone to reply to a specific question or statement. For example, "Let's begin with Laurie. What one challenge might you experience if we decided to use more close reading in our core program?"

▸ Call for a simple thumbs-up or thumbs-down. For example, "Do you agree or disagree with this statement?"

The insights and suggestions made by those who have been silent often contribute greatly to the conversation, and the facilitator has a responsibility to encourage their participation. A facilitator might increase engagement by asking teachers to share classroom success stories as well as specific difficulties or problems. For example, each teacher can be asked to share work samples from a specific student who has made great progress and describe factors contributing to that success. Other group

members can then follow up by asking questions or making comments. For specific ideas about using this type of procedure, see the *Success Analysis Protocol for Individuals* (http://schoolreforminitiative .org/doc/success_ana_individuals.pdf) or the *Gap Analysis Protocol* (http://schoolreforminitiative.org/doc/gap_analysis.pdf).

Balance Routine and Repertoire

Wasley, Hampel, and Clark (1997) talk about the importance of balancing routine and repertoire in teaching students, and we recommend the same advice to literacy leaders who coach groups. Coaches can introduce groups to powerful *routines* for collaborative learning, mechanisms that will be used in each and every meeting, such as a five-minute whip-around asking everyone to check in and talk about one successful teaching moment in the past week, a weekly checkout where everyone states one thing they're going to try in their classrooms before meeting again, and so on. However, excellent facilitators also have a wide *repertoire* of facilitative moves that they employ, so that groups do not sink into a slump, always feeling as if they are using the same protocol or structure to learn together. The book *Facilitator's Guide to Participatory Decision-Making* (Kaner, 2014) is filled with additional suggestions for facilitating group learning and decision-making processes.

PUT INTO PRACTICE

1. Record a portion of a group session that you are leading (or one in which you are participating). Listen to the recording to answer the following questions: Did all members of the group have an opportunity to talk? How much of the conversation was directed by the leader? To what extent were all members of the group positively involved in the conversation?

2. Visit the Teaching Channel's website and watch the following video clip about a math coach working with middle school teachers on disciplinary literacy skills: www.teachingchannel.org/videos/inquiry-protocol-nvps. What is the coach doing to support group learning? What norms seem to already be in place? How would you characterize the levels of engagement and active listening?

Small-Group Coaching

There are many reasons for working with teachers in small groups. These meetings can include teachers from one school, or, at times, teachers who work across several schools in a district, such as teacher representatives across schools who are developing a common unit guide that addresses integrated language arts curriculum at a specific grade level. At times, small-group meetings may follow a large-scale presentation given at the district level. In such cases, a literacy coach assigned to a school may meet with the teachers to get a better idea of what follow-up steps are needed: Would teachers appreciate seeing a specific strategy modeled in the classroom? Do they need clarification about specific ideas? What have they attempted in terms of implementation? Most importantly, how can the literacy leader be helpful?

Working with small groups is different from giving large-group presentations in several important ways. Although it requires some of the same skills (connecting with participants and acknowledging and respecting your audience), generally the small group will be meeting on an ongoing basis and will require a clearer set of norms, goals, and routines. Therefore, small-group work requires the literacy leader to learn more about each group member, to facilitate in ways that promote active engagement of members over time, and to craft (or co-craft) each agenda in order to accomplish goals. Hersey and Blanchard (1977) call for attention to both "task actions" (how can goals be achieved?) and what they call "maintenance actions" (in what ways can relationships be built to facilitate member involvement?). In figure 7.2, we identify examples of how group leaders and participants contribute to the functioning of a group by assuming these actions.

Task Roles

Presenting or Seeking Information

- "I read an article that gives great ideas for how to help students use the Internet more effectively. It mentions the importance of checking for authenticity."

- "I'd like to hear more from Susan about using project-based learning."

Elaborating on the Contributions of Others

- "In the article that Carlos mentioned about using the Internet, there are also great ideas for specific lessons; for example . . . "

Presenting the Opinions or Seeking the Opinions of Others

- "I think the notion of sharing our learning center materials is an excellent one. I'd really appreciate getting some new ideas about writing instruction."

- "What do you think, Helena, about forming a committee to begin looking at how we can integrate English goals and assignments with those expected in social studies?"

Synthesizing the Contributions of Others

- "It's really exciting when you think about how the ideas expressed by Frank and Alicia fit together. It seems as though we could move quickly if we . . . "

Maintenance or Relationship-Building Roles

Encouraging Others to Participate

- "Zach, what do you think? You ask your students to work in small groups a lot; so, what strategies do you use to help them learn how to do that? To keep them focused on the task?"

Providing Ideas for Compromise

- "It seems as though we have two ideas, each of which requires lots of work. I wonder whether we could divide into two smaller groups, and each group could address issues related to one of the ideas."

Gate-Keeping

- "Whoa! It seems as though we are straying away from the topic. Why don't we finish discussing this topic and then move on to the new topic? We could use our 'parking lot' to hold onto the new idea for later. We are so close to a decision; let's not lose the opportunity to finish our work."

Use of Humor to Move the Agenda

- "Speaking of students and their ability to work in small groups, let me share with you a story about how Lucille got her group to work together."

Figure 7.2: Roles of group members.

Source: Adapted from P. Hersey & K. Blanchard, 1977; D. W. Johnson & F. P. Johnson, 2003.

All the actions described in figure 7.2 are important ones, but some become more important than others in specific group situations. When a group is excited and motivated by its task, there may be less need for maintenance activities, as group relationships appear to be positive and members are eager to work on the task. Or conversely, when group members don't understand the goal or are unhappy about being in this setting, relationship or maintenance actions are extremely important. All of the actions in figure 7.2 are positive ones that can be developed and practiced by both leaders and participants in the group.

PUT INTO PRACTICE

Think about each of the aforementioned actions of literacy leaders who coach small groups and those you have used in the past. Following are options that may help you observe more closely how individuals behave in groups, see which roles they assume, note their positive and negative behaviors, and how they influence the work of the group. Which actions do you engage in regularly? Which may you want to try next?

- Observe a group (either by yourself or with coaching peers) and identify the actions taken by individuals in the group. You might be able to attend a grade-level or team meeting at the school or even a school board meeting.

- Ask one of your coaching peers to observe you as you lead a group; have her look for examples of positive actions exhibited by various group members—including you!

- Find examples of small-group meetings on the Internet (e.g., the Teaching Channel and YouTube); view these meetings for examples of group members' behaviors. Your interest in viewing these videos is not in the content, but in the processes used to facilitate group work.

Other Strategies for Facilitating Small Groups

Small-group dynamics can be complex, evolving over time in ways that require literacy leaders to continually take stock and change direction. Facilitating small groups requires certain skills and strategies to ensure efficiency, progress, and a healthy group culture. Key ideas for facilitating the work of small groups are discussed in the following sections.

Establish Group Norms

In initial meetings of a small group, ask the group to establish norms that can be used to guide their work. Although we mentioned this earlier under guidelines for groups of all sizes, it is important to quickly reiterate this point here. In small groups, norms are especially useful for having an initial discussion about group goals, working habits, and potential points of conflict. Whether the coach uses a more elaborate protocol for setting norms (such as *Norms Construction* mentioned earlier) or a very simple, coach-designed process like the one in figure 7.1 (page 117), the key is to help the group identify what is important to participating members. Coaches should not shy away from helping groups bring to the surface the fact that differences in perceptions and viewpoints are inevitable; the goal is to recognize this and minimize their effects on the group.

Create an Agenda for the Group

Develop (or co-develop) an agenda for each meeting, and slowly transfer agenda creation and facilitation responsibilities to group members. Plan in ways that designate a specific amount of time for each topic to be addressed, with important topics or essential questions at the top of the agenda. The final item on the agenda should be a summary of what has occurred, assignments to be accomplished before the next meeting, and identification of who is responsible for what. It is also helpful to take time to reflect on what went well and what might be improved. Ask, "What did the group appreciate about the meeting today? How did we do with our norms? What can be done to improve the functioning of the group?" Finally, the more that literacy leaders can invite participating teachers into the work of co-creating and co-facilitating agendas, the more the group's capacity to facilitate its own collaborative inquiry work will grow. As Marsha Turner suggested in Voices From the Field, think about whether your words and actions promote teacher "dependence" or "independence."

Make Decisions in a Group-Appropriate Way

Groups can make decisions in different ways, and the literacy leader's approach to decision making depends on many factors including but not limited to school culture, the content of the decision, and the time available to make the decision. Questions that coaches may want to consider as they guide group decision making might include:

- To what extent do teachers have the authority to make policy decisions?

- Is this particular decision about classroom practices, policies, or procedures?

- Is this an important decision that can be made over time with careful study, or one that needs to be made immediately with the best information available?

When decisions are important ones affecting the direction or goals of the group, use approaches that involve all members, both for improving the quality of the decision and enhancing the commitment of the group to the decision. Groups can come to a consensus (everyone agrees) or they can vote (either in writing or by hand). At times, the group leader or an expert member of the committee may make a decision, especially about the process, and then simply ask the group to respond and/or support the decision. Alternatively, if the group has talked extensively about a specific issue without a resolution, the facilitator may suggest that the group table that issue and move to the next item on the agenda. All group members should have the information they need to make specific decisions. A series of decision-making steps should be identified so that the group members, at any given point in time, understand the extent to which they are involved in decision making and the amount of time and input they have.

The leader has an important role in facilitating decision making and can build collective capacity by not rushing groups into technical, superficial responses to complex questions. An interesting approach to decision making that builds groups' reflective and decision-making skills is called 10-10-10, outlined by Suzy Welch in a book by the same title (Welch, 2010). Group members are asked to think about the impact a specific decision might have on the school or literacy program in ten minutes, ten months, and ten years. Such a process enables the group to get some emotional distance from the question and to think of its long-term impact. Individual group members can jot down their ideas, and then the group can share, or participants can work in pairs or trios before a full group discussion. A similar process can be found in the *Future Protocol* (http://schoolreforminitiative.org/doc/future.pdf), which allows groups to discuss an ideal vision of their work five years from now and then backward-plan steps to reach that more ideal future.

Working With Difficult Members

Life would be grand if all groups were composed of positive, supportive individuals focused on achieving the same goal. But many groups have one member (or perhaps a few!) whose participation is not positive. These individuals may monopolize the conversation, make negative comments, or even attempt to shift the direction of the group through confrontational comments about the topic or about other group members. How should you deal with them?

First, think about reasons for the negativism of these members. Is it a difference in how they view the topic, a misunderstanding, or even some personal or personality issues between or among members? Taking time to think about why individuals behave as they do will help coaches manage their own frustrations and better consider how to address the problem. Sometimes, the literacy leader needs to have the skills to redirect a conversation so that the same member is not always talking, such as simply suggesting: "Okay, let's hear what others think!" Using some of the statements in figure 7.2 (page 120) will help literacy leaders facilitate group interactions. Also, at times, the coach may need to speak to an individual privately to discuss specific behaviors. You may not always be successful, but with the help of other group members, you can often minimize the negative effects of specific members.

Remember That Differences Are Inevitable

Kaner (2014) describes how groups proceed from divergent thinking—through a "groan zone"—to convergent thinking. Part of the excitement of working with groups is observing and facilitating their progress as they learn to work together, learn more about the tasks at hand, and determine how to reach their final goals. Excitement about their final product (e.g., a curriculum guide, modifications in literacy instruction for struggling readers, a video for the community that describes literacy instruction) can also motivate group members to work well together. Supporting groups as they make their own decisions builds the capacity of the group to engage independently in collaborative inquiry work and, ultimately, is the key to forming long-lasting collegial relationships.

In sum, small-group decision making and facilitative work takes time—much longer than it might take for a literacy leader to make a decision on his or her own and insist on compliance. However, on the other hand, groups that are invited, as professionals, into literacy-focused decision making and inquiry work can accomplish so much more than an individual. Moreover, as previously stated, the results decided upon by a group are far more likely to find life in the classroom or the school than decisions that are simply handed down or assigned. In the next Voices From the Field, we provide an example of how coach Linda DiMartino worked with teacher leaders in group settings to implement their coaching initiative.

VOICES FROM THE FIELD

Our school has a coaching model that is unique and similar to moving a barge: *slowly* but consistently forward. We have seventy-three teachers from kindergarten through grade four, across four buildings. There is one tugboat moving this barge of amazing teachers, and that would be the fearless coach (or captain). With the support of administration, we have one teacher leader at each grade level within each building. Additionally, we have a Reading Recovery teacher who joins the grade one team.

The coach meets with each teacher-leader team once a month by grade level. One month the meetings are held after school for two hours, and the next month for a half-day during school with a substitute provided for the classroom teacher. After-school meetings are for looking at data, discussing a book we are using, examining curriculum maps for pacing and revision, reflecting on strategies, or problem solving. The half-day meetings are more direct training sessions; for example, a workshop on a particular topic. The coach has provided in-depth training on a topic (i.e., poetry workshops) and then launched it in a classroom where others observed. The coach supported the leaders through modeling and coaching, and then the teacher leaders presented this topic during professional development for their grade-level colleagues.

This professional development model has grown because we have maintained the same teacher leaders over the past five years. They support moving the barge forward, because they participate in goal setting and share the vision of the district and coach.

—Linda DiMartino, literacy supervisor

Large-Group Presentations

In addition to small-group facilitation, literacy leaders who coach are also often asked to make presentations to large groups of teachers, administrators, or even the school board. They may introduce a curriculum plan or the state standards to an entire school or even to the district. Such large-group presentations have their place. They provide an opportunity for all to hear the same message at the same time—they are efficient. However, they also have limitations. Teacher participants are nearly always at different stages of learning—some know a lot about the topic and others do not. They may have different perspectives about the importance of the topic. Further, as is evident in studies of professional learning initiatives (Guskey & Yoon, 2009), such introductory presentations alone are rarely sufficient to guarantee effective implementation in classrooms. Ideas for how to make these large-group presentations more efficient and effective follow:

▶ Making a presentation to a large group requires close attention to both content and process. Make certain that the presentation is focused, addresses the needs of the group, and flows in a coherent and consistent manner. At the same time, include opportunities for active group participation as a means of maintaining attention and engagement. A simple "turn-and-talk" (perhaps after ten minutes of speaking or after a specific topic has been discussed) can greatly increase the power of a large-group presentation. This is also an opportunity for a coach to model group facilitation moves, which can be replicated by teachers in their PLCs, or in classrooms with students.

▶ To the extent possible, make certain that large-group presentations are planned in ways that anticipate and honor the learning needs of adults. As we expanded on in chapter 2, building on adult development theory, educators have different ways of knowing and learning. Considering potential differences between instrumental, socializing, and self-authoring ways of knowing and learning can help a coach better plan for a large-group presentation. The following questions may help you think about planning large-group presentations:

    ▷ Is the environment one that is conducive to active learning? (For example, are round tables available, which increase the possibility of small-group interaction?) Carefully plan for and set up the physical learning environment so it facilitates interaction between peers or small groups.

    ▷ Will participants have some opportunity for choice of learning activities, such as small-group breakout sessions, stations, or flexible pairings? Plan for some variety in the presentation so that individuals are involved and able to collaborate. Even a brief turn-and-talk or opportunity to chat with colleagues can help break up lengthier large-group presentations.

▷   Is there a "hook" that captures the attention of the participants? That is, is there a rationale for the session, and how it can help teachers improve student learning? Recognize the importance of the first few minutes spent with the audience. Consider how you can generate interest and "buy-in" to your topic. First, think about ways to connect with the audience—share common experiences or interest in the topic. If you are the second speaker, think of ways you can relate your remarks to what has been said before; that is, show relationships between the previous presentation and yours. Second, be sure to identify your purpose and your agenda.

▶   Provide opportunities for feedback. Such feedback can serve as a means of helping group members identify what is important to each of them and of helping you think about whether you were successful in achieving your goals. One useful strategy is the 3-2-1 exit card, in which participants are asked to identify three points to remember, two ideas they can use in their work, and one question they have.

▶   Use the right tools for delivering the presentation. Presenters may use videos that they have developed or obtained from the Internet to show examples of specific instructional strategies or approaches. Many develop PowerPoint slides to organize their remarks. We all know that when technology works, it is great; if not, it can be a disaster. Having a plan B is essential; if the video doesn't work, what options do you have? Note that PowerPoint presentations, although popular, can be extremely problematic if they are poorly done. See figure 7.3 for ideas about how to develop effective PowerPoint presentations.

- Use only a few words to make a point—keep text to a minimum, just to remind you and your audience of the key points.

- Keep the overall number of slides to a minimum.

- Make sure the font is large enough for the group to read (size twenty-four, at least).

- Combine text with visuals to hold the attention of the audience.

- If accessing the Internet, sound, or videos during your presentation, test your multimedia components as you are setting up, and be prepared to skip them or use local copies on your computer (as opposed to streaming or clicking on embedded multimedia in your presentation).

- If presenting to a large audience in a well-lit space, consider using a dark background and lighter text, as this is often better for viewing in such cases.

Figure 7.3: Tips for creating PowerPoint slides.

*Visit **www.learningsciences.com/bookresources** to download a reproducible version of this figure.*

As a test of whether you are ready to make a large presentation, practice summarizing your major points to determine if they flow well and are consistent with your goal or purpose. Too often, speakers try to put too much into a presentation. Remember, focus on your goal and the ideas and activities that will help you accomplish it.

Ideas for Follow-Up

What plans can be established as a means of following up with small groups or individuals as needed after a large-group presentation? Garmston (2005) suggests that presentations end with a call to action rather than a summary. In other words, what can participants do or how can they use the information. For example, participants might be invited to select specific instructional strategies from the presentation to try in their classrooms.

Also, the presenter can plan for small-group meetings in each school to address questions identified by teachers and provide essential support in that context. Presenters can provide contact information, so that participants can get in touch if they have questions. Providing participants with handouts (or a link to an online repository of files) to which they can refer is also helpful, as it is easy to forget or misinterpret what has been heard.

Group Activities That Support the Development of Professional Learning Communities

Recently, there has been an emphasis on establishing schools, and groups within schools, as PLCs. Such a term has been used to identify grade-level teams, department teams, study groups, or even an entire school. In fact, the term "PLC" has been used so ubiquitously that, as stated by DuFour (2004), "it is in danger of losing all meaning" (p. 6). As DuFour explains, there are three big ideas that represent the core principles of PLCs: ensuring that students learn (teachers focusing on student learning), a culture of collaboration (teachers working together to improve classroom practices), and a focus on results (assessing whether professional learning is improving teaching and learning).

We think of PLCs as "initiatives by schools for all staff members to work collaboratively as learners to achieve a common goal, that of improving student learning" (Bean & Swan Dagen, 2012, p. 360). Therefore, many different group activities can be useful in promoting such collaboration.

Although literacy leaders have an important role in facilitating collaboration, the effort requires principal support and leadership; in other words, as expanded upon in chapter 4, the literacy coach must work with principals to establish such collegial environments. Vescio et al. (2008) provide evidence that when schools function as learning communities, there is a positive impact on teacher classroom practices and student learning. They identify five key notions critical for establishing such efforts in schools: shared values and norms, a focus on student learning, reflective dialogue among teachers, teaching made public, and collaboration. For those interested in assessing the degree to which PLCs exist in their school or district, consult the two collaborative environment assessment tools reviewed in chapter 4 (the NCLE Asset Inventory and the School Reform Initiative PLC Survey).

VOICES FROM THE FIELD

A large part of our journey in becoming a true professional learning community (as a school) has to do with establishing a culture of trust where teachers feel safe saying what they're good at, where they need help, and where they also feel safe watching each other teach. This trust exists in pockets but is certainly not the norm.

—Shauna Magee, literacy coach

Many literacy leaders who coach are thoughtful about which group formats and processes will best serve teachers' needs at particular junctures. For a quick review of some of the most common options, we turn to *Best Practices of Literacy Leaders: Keys to School Improvement*, in which Bean and Swan Dagen (2012) describe various activities that are effective in promoting collaborative work in schools. We highlight a few of these activities in the following sections and provide additional suggestions.

Book Clubs or Study Groups

These can build teacher knowledge about a topic and, at the same time, help teachers become more reflective in their work. Walpole and Beauchat (2008) discuss criteria for instituting such study groups. They emphasize the importance of choice and making connections to classroom practice. We have recently worked with groups reading Doug Buehl's *Developing Readers in the Academic Disciplines*, Freeman and Freeman's *English Language Learners*, and Fountas and Pinnell's *Teaching for Comprehension and Fluency*. All worked well because the *groups* chose the texts—each book was read strategically for high-leverage strategies and routines to implement, and each could serve as a reference guide later once the formal study group had ended.

Lesson Studies

The lesson study format outlined by Stigler and Hiebert (1999) is a process that enables teachers to collectively and systematically study their own work. Teachers, as a group, plan a lesson and then one teacher volunteers to teach that lesson, which is observed by others or videotaped. The group then holds a follow-up discussion of the lesson and its effects on student learning. The lesson is revised and re-taught, and the process continues. In one school, the principal agreed to teach a lesson that was videotaped for follow-up discussion. Anxiety about videotaping was reduced and, as you can imagine, teachers enjoyed providing feedback to the principal.

Data Meetings

These meetings are held to discuss the results of assessment measures (both formal and informal) and can serve as a source of learning for teachers. In such meetings, the focus should be twofold. First, what do the data tell members about the strengths and needs of students? Second, what do the data suggest in terms of instructional changes in classrooms? (More about assessment and coaching work can be found in chapter 8.)

Grade-Level Meetings

Productive grade-level meetings provide opportunities for discussion about substantive issues in addition to addressing more logistical items, such as scheduling or test administration details. Teachers can sign up in advance to make brief presentations on a student about whom they have concerns or a strategy or approach that has or hasn't worked well. Teachers can be asked to bring documentation (student work or assessment data) for the group to see and discuss. Discussion-based protocols are often an effective means in situations such as this for helping teachers work effectively and efficiently.

Classroom Learning Walks

Another useful approach is for coaches and teachers to establish learning walks as a means of teacher learning. (Note that different districts talk about these activities and engage in them in slightly different ways. You might hear these referred to as "data walks," "instructional rounds," or "walk-throughs." While there are differences in terminology and procedures, the key is to make sure that everyone in your community knows both the purposes and rules of engagement *before* beginning.) In figure 7.4, we identify key steps for literacy leaders involved in facilitating learning walks in their school. (See appendix B for related resources.)

- Discuss the purpose of the learning walk (e.g., improvement of instruction), the nature of the activity (e.g., descriptive, not evaluative), and the content focus (e.g., observing student engagement, teacher levels of questioning).

- Decide on who will be observed (ask for volunteers or ask teachers with specific expertise or experience to volunteer).

- Develop a learning walk guide with specific questions or look-fors that address the focus of the observation (e.g., high-level teacher questioning, student grouping options, and so on). Sample overarching questions that might guide observations include: What is the literacy environment in the room (e.g., evidence of student work, books and other material)? What are students doing, and can they talk about their work (e.g., do they understand the task and reason for it)? What is the teacher doing to implement effective literacy instruction?

- Establish procedures for the learning walk. Observers should stand to the side, but if students are working at seats, observers can talk informally with them. Observers should not talk with each other as they observe. The learning walk is not for evaluative purposes.

- Schedule walks. Generally, teachers may be able to observe in at least two classrooms during one of their planning periods. The literacy leader and at least two or more teachers should observe, so a team of teachers can learn from each other.

- Spend ten minutes or so in the classroom and then debrief in the hallway. If possible, include the classroom teacher in this debriefing. Address the focus of the learning walk. What questions do you have of the teacher?

- In a later group or grade-level meeting, there can be more extensive discussion of the observation with the focus on application. What can teachers take back to their classrooms?

- Send a thank-you note to each teacher who was observed.

Figure 7.4: Steps in initiating learning walks.

*Visit **www.learningsciences.com/bookresources** to download a reproducible version of this figure.*

Collaborative Cycles of Inquiry

Finally, one of the most sophisticated yet powerful activities for small groups to undertake is that of collaborative inquiry (Cochran-Smith & Lytle, 2009). A coach can support small teams as they first identify their own inquiry goals, such as learning more about teaching peer revision processes, academic language, or close reading. Then the coach supports the team members as they find resources, read about their intended areas of interest, synthesize findings, and begin to adopt and adapt new classroom practices. When each member is ready, teachers volunteer to try new practices in their respective classrooms and then bring the results back to the group for discussion and reflection. Ultimately, the group assesses the effects of the new work and begins the cycle of inquiry over again, sometimes digging deeper into the same topic and sometimes deciding to leave a topic for a while and begin a new cycle of inquiry focused on a related or entirely new topic. We find that the School Reform Initiative's two graphics about collaborative cycles of inquiry are helpful in presenting this idea to teams of teachers: Cycle of Inquiry (http://schoolreforminitiative.org/doc /smp_cycle_inquiry.pdf) and Cycle of Inquiry for PLCs (http://schoolreforminitiative .org/doc/smp_cycle_inquiry_plc.pdf).

Although scheduling collaborative work often requires creativity (e.g., during shared planning periods, before-school breakfasts or coffees, after-school study groups) and support from administrators (e.g., flexible scheduling, professional learning days, use of substitutes), these activities can take place for short amounts of time, such as one class period, or for more extended stretches, such as two-hour blocks or one afternoon every other week. The key to any of these formats is forming ground rules when you start, and sustaining the work long enough for teachers to see the effects of their collaborative efforts such that they will see collaboration as important and will want to continue.

Summary

In this chapter, we have outlined some of the major ways of working with teachers in groups, both small and large, including the importance of setting norms, carefully selecting collaboration formats, and balancing routine and repertoire. We then offered a few suggestions for presenting to large groups of teachers. Finally, we highlighted several specifics of what group coaching typically entails, including an array of PLC collaborative inquiry formats.

Activities

1. Using the chart found in appendix A, identify ways that literacy leaders can support teachers through small-group and large-group work. How do you as a literacy leader serve as facilitator, leader, designer, and advocate when working with teachers in groups? Which activities might you consider adopting that would further these ways of thinking and working?

2. Read Kaner and Berger's (n.d.) "The Role of Facilitator" (http:// enrapkscurriculum.pbworks.com/f/Role+of+Facilitator+-+Sam+Kaner .pdf), also found in Kaner's book (2014). In what ways does Kaner and

Berger's description of the facilitator's role match ours? Any differences? What are the implications for literacy leaders who coach and adopt the role of facilitator for both small and large groups?

3. Review the tools for coaching found on the Literacy Coaching Clearinghouse (www.literacycoachingonline.org/tools.html). Which of these tools might best support the small-group activities you are planning or already facilitating (e.g., PLC meetings, data meetings, inquiry cycles, and so on)? What tools are missing that you have already created or are committed to creating?

4. Observe two different team meetings, and note the following: role of the facilitator, distribution of work and participation across the group, focus of the work, and agenda and protocol usage. As you compare the two observations, what did you learn that you would like to use in your own work? What might you offer as suggestions?

CHAPTER 8

Assessment as a Guide for Student Literacy Learning and School Improvement

GUIDING QUESTIONS

1. What are the major purposes of assessment, and what sources of data are available to assess student literacy learning?

2. In what ways can large-scale assessment measures be used effectively, and what are their limitations?

3. In what ways can literacy leaders work with teachers to help them use data effectively for informing classroom instruction?

4. What are key considerations for schools and districts in developing comprehensive assessment systems, and how can literacy leaders facilitate the development of such a system?

The title of Nater and Gallimore's (2006) book about the life of John Wooden (a great basketball coach and teacher), *You Haven't Taught Until They Have Learned: John Wooden's Teaching Principles and Practices*, summarizes well Melinda's beliefs about the importance of assessment as a means of determining whether students have learned. She and her team of teachers wanted to improve their use of data to make decisions about instruction. Specifically, what could data tell them about student needs and strengths? How might they group and regroup students? Are there ways of grouping across classrooms to take advantage of teacher strengths and interests? For example, Harold, the school's reading specialist, was especially skilled in working with students who were experiencing decoding difficulties.

These teachers recognized the importance of assessment as a means of determining whether learning goals have been achieved, and, if not, what adjustments might need to be made to reach those goals. But how could Melinda ensure that the group was thinking about assessment at different levels (student, classroom, grade, and school)? What could Melinda do to ensure a coherent and manageable approach to data collection, analysis, reporting, and instructional actions?

We begin this chapter by providing a definition of assessment and describing sources of data important for making decisions about student, classroom, and school performance. We then provide foundational information about large-scale measures used to make judgments about the school or system as a whole, identifying the potential uses and limitations of these measures. This is followed by a discussion of processes for working with teachers at the classroom level, helping them to understand how to work with data to improve instructional practices and literacy learning. We conclude by discussing the need for a well-conceived assessment system as a means of analyzing and improving whole-school performance.

The dual mindset of working at the individual and the system levels simultaneously is especially important when thinking about data use and assessment, which have the potential to inform change for individuals, classrooms, and systems. Given that our focus is on the process and use of assessment, rather than on specific measures, in appendix B we suggest several references for literacy leaders to consult for more detailed information about specific literacy assessments, their applicability, and their usefulness in assessing literacy development and learning.

Assessment of Student Learning: What and Why

When individuals are asked to define or describe "assessment," they respond with various terms: "testing," "tests," "examinations," "evaluation," "judging," or "measuring." We define "assessment" as the "task of gathering data on which to base evaluative or judgment-oriented decisions" (Bean, 2015, p. 222). Such decisions can be made about individuals or groups of students, as well as schools, districts, states, and countries. Data can be retrieved from many different sources, from tests to actual observations of students in classrooms (see figure 8.1 for examples of data sources).

Assessment serves two broad purposes. First, assessment results can be used for accountability; that is, to determine whether schools or districts are achieving their goals and where they might need to improve. These outcome measures are known as summative measures and evaluate whether students have learned what they were expected to learn. They can be used for grading purposes (of a student or school), and results can be shared with various stakeholders (e.g., parents and the school board). Summative assessments, in the form of large-scale, high-stakes measures (standardized tests given by the school district or state), are often controversial in many ways; at the same time, summative measures, as designed or selected by teachers (e.g., end-of-term examinations, end-of-unit tests, and student-developed portfolios) can be useful in determining whether students have achieved specific classroom goals.

- Tests

  - Standardized tests (statewide or district) given annually

  - Interim assessment measures or benchmark tests administered at multiple times during the school year

  - Teacher-developed tests for groups of students (end-of-unit or course)

  - Teacher-administered tests for individual students (running records or an informal reading inventory)

- Student assignments or work samples (class projects or writing samples)

- Classroom observations

- Portfolios

- Interviews with individuals or groups of students (focus groups)

- Teacher conferences

- Attendance records

- Surveys of parents, teachers, and students

- Videos of lessons taught by teachers

Figure 8.1: Sources of data.

A second purpose of assessment is to provide formative information about how to improve learning for students. Formative measures are useful for planning instructional activities, screening student performance, monitoring student progress, diagnosing learning problems, and providing feedback to students about their performance. Often, these measures are considered to be "process" strategies or approaches used during instruction (e.g., oral questioning, think-alouds, every-pupil-response techniques such as "thumbs-up" or "thumbs-down," or student-developed graphic organizers or conceptual maps). Measurement tools, such as benchmark or progress monitoring tests, can also provide formative information to teachers, useful for modifying instruction. Assessment results provide valuable information for making judgments about the learning *of* students as well as learning *for* students (Black & Wiliam, 1998; Stiggins & Chappuis, 2005); that is, we can learn much about what students know and can do from data, and we can use data to support student learning.

Assessment in today's schools is undergoing a transformation, with increased use of technology, the integration of reading with the other language arts in assessment measures, and a greater focus on formative and performance assessment for improving student learning (Kapinus, 2014). Given the importance of assessment in instructional decision making, teachers must be "assessment literate" (Stiggins, 2014, p. 67); that is, they must have an understanding of assessment, what it is, its limitations, and how student performance on these measures might affect teaching and learning. Thus, one of the important roles of literacy leaders is to support school personnel in gaining the knowledge and understanding to be able to use assessment results to inform instruction and, ultimately, to improve school literacy performance overall. In the following section, we provide some background information about the potential and pitfalls of large-scale, high-stakes assessment measures.

Large-Scale, High-Stakes Measures: Potential and Pitfalls

We have all heard tales of schools preparing for the large-scale assessments that take place each year, with time spent motivating students to do well, helping them to become familiar with various test formats or answering specific types of questions. Some schools hold motivational "testing parties" or "assemblies," or they provide incentives for those classrooms with 100 percent attendance on testing day. Parents are sent flyers or e-mails in which they are given suggestions for how they can best prepare their children for test days (e.g., make certain they get enough sleep and eat a good breakfast).

Often, the content of these large-scale measures affects the curriculum; that is, there is a focus on teaching to the test, which can narrow the curriculum and reduce time spent on subjects such as social studies, science, or the arts. Parents and teachers have raised concerns about the amount of time spent on testing and have criticized these time-consuming measures for the stress they generate. Some parents across the country are even "opting-out" of testing for their children, indicating their displeasure with these large-scale measures. Regardless, large-scale assessment measures are part of the fabric of life in today's schools, although there appears to be more recognition that the overemphasis on large-scale testing, accountability, and punitive measures of schools and teachers have not been productive in improving student learning (Darling-Hammond, 2010). In fact, the Elementary and Secondary Education Act (ESEA) law—passed in 2015 and titled the Every Student Succeeds Act (ESSA)— explicitly reduces the emphasis on over-testing. States will still be required to test students annually in reading and math in grades three and eight and once in high school; they will also be required to report achievement by subgroups. However, states will also now have more discretion in how they hold schools accountable, measure success, and collect information about student performance over time (Klein, 2015). While it is still too early to say what the end results of ESSA will be, initial responses nationwide seem positive, particularly with regard to reducing the over-testing that many communities have opposed.

Large-scale measures are generally standardized instruments which, if selected carefully for their technical robustness, provide results that enable comparisons among schools and, if data are disaggregated, generate information about the performance of various subgroups being tested. Certainly, the results have made clear the educational gaps in the performance of various subgroups (e.g., ELs, students with learning differences, those who are economically disadvantaged, racial and ethnic subgroups, and so on) and led to a more focused attempt to provide equal educational opportunities for all students (Darling-Hammond, 2010). Also, results can be useful at the school level for identifying various areas of strength or weakness in curricular areas. In other words, instruments that provide summative data can be useful for taking an overall look at the school or district as a whole. They can provide information about groups of students that can be shared with various stakeholders, including families, school boards, or legislators responsible for funding schools.

However, there are several problems that arise when these tests and their results are used inappropriately. First, results of a single measure are too often used to make high-stakes decisions (retention and graduation) that affect the lives of students. Yet, as indicated in the International Literacy Association's position statement on using high-stakes assessments (International Reading Association, 2014), a single measure does not adequately assess the literacy competencies of an individual. In the position statement, it is recommended that high-stakes decisions be based on multiple assessments that include teacher judgment as well as student and family input, in addition to test results, when making decisions about grade retention or graduation. This is especially important given that a single test result may misrepresent the learning of the diverse students in schools (e.g., ELs, those with learning differences, or those who come from economically disadvantaged homes).

Second, these tests do not provide much useful information for the classroom teacher. In fact, Buly and Valencia (2002) compared results of students' scores on a high-stakes measure with results of additional diagnostic testing and found several distinctive and different patterns of reading ability that were not evident on the large-scale measure. In other words, two students receiving the same score (e.g., reading at the third stanine or at the forty-fifth percentile) on a standardized large-scale measure may have different literacy strengths and needs. Moreover, these tests are generally given infrequently or at the end of the year and don't provide results at a useful time to guide instruction, nor are the results specific enough to set instructional learning targets for classroom instruction.

Third, given the format of most of these high-stake measures, there tends to be more of an emphasis on recall and recognition rather than on more high-level skills such as problem solving, evaluation, and drawing inferences. However, as a result of the CCSS and similar rigorous, high-level expectations for student learning, large-scale assessment tools are being designed to measure whether students are reaching these expectations and being prepared for college and careers. In fact, two consortia, the Partnership for Assessing Readiness for College and Careers and the Smarter Balanced Assessment Consortium, were awarded federal funds to develop such measures that, according to developers, are capable of providing both summative and formative information to schools. In other words, results can be used to measure program effectiveness (summative data) and, in addition, provide information for improving instruction or programming (formative data). Although it was expected that most states would use one of these two sets of measures for assessing student achievement, controversy about content and cost have led some states to develop their own large-scale measures for use in measuring student learning. It appears likely that, regardless of which new tests are used by states to measure student learning, there will be much more emphasis on problem solving and higher level thinking rather than recall and recognition on 21st century large-scale assessments.

Fourth, high-stakes measures have influenced instruction in negative ways; as mentioned previously, the curriculum has been narrowed to focus on topics addressed in the tests, and too much time has also been devoted to preparing students for the tests. In some schools, pressures to do well have influenced educators to ignore students who score the highest and the lowest on these high-stakes measures. Teachers are asked to concentrate their instructional efforts on students labeled as "bubble children," those who score just below the proficiency cutoff, with the expectation that it is more likely that these students will improve and the overall scores for the school will be higher. High-stakes testing can also affect the work of coaches (see the following Voices From the Field), taking them away from essential coaching responsibilities.

VOICES FROM THE FIELD

Another challenge for many of our coaches is the administration of standardized tests. In several schools, coaches are the test coordinators, monitors, make-up administrators, and general proctors when teachers are absent. Some are also charged with pulling out the "bubble" students and tutoring them in effective test-taking strategies, so they can help raise the school's scores and positively impact the school's report card, taking them away from their coaching responsibilities.

—Ellen Eisenberg, executive director, PA Institute for Instructional Coaching

Another concern about the misuse of large-scale measures has to do with efforts to use results of these high-stakes measures of student learning to assess teacher performance. Currently, there is much emphasis in states and districts on developing systems for assessing teacher performance, and often these systems include student test scores as one of the criteria for judging teacher quality. Although state and district educators recognize the potential of teacher-performance measures as a means of identifying teachers who might need additional professional learning experiences to improve their teaching, educators also recognize the difficulties of designing and implementing such systems. Various statistical and technical problems exist in using results of student learning for this purpose; we refer readers to the 2014 ASA statement on using value-added models for educational assessment (www.amstat.org /policy/pdfs/ASA_VAM_Statement.pdf) or the entire issue of the *American Educator* (2014, volume 38, issue 1).

The bottom line is that literacy leaders, to be effective, must understand what these large-scale measures can and cannot provide. They need to *facilitate* reflective discussions with their teacher colleagues about data from these measures and assist them in making decisions about what those data suggest about changes in literacy instruction. Further, literacy leaders can be *advocates* for teachers and for students by providing school boards, parents, and the community with accurate, up-to-date information about these measures and what the results really mean. In the following section, we discuss the use of data to improve classroom instruction.

Ideas for Literacy Leaders: Using Data to Improve Classroom Instruction

Literacy leaders responsible for coaching teachers can have an enormous influence on instruction in the classroom if they help teachers use data to identify specific needs and strengths of the students with whom they work and use those results to inform instruction. Such data can be used to make decisions about how to prioritize instructional time, to identify individual students' strengths and needs, to identify specific instructional interventions, to target supplemental instruction for students who are struggling, to judge the instructional effectiveness of specific lessons, and to refine instructional methods (Hamilton et al., 2009). Yet, often teachers who are responsible for using such data do not believe that they have the necessary professional skills that enable them to interpret and then apply the results (Beresik & Bean, 2002; US Department of Education, 2011). Thus the need for literacy leaders to help develop teacher capacity to understand and use the data available to them.

As Melinda thinks about how best to support her team in addressing assessment issues, she might do well to start with figure 8.2 (page 142). The figure contains a checklist adapted from the aforementioned report (Hamilton et al., 2009, p. 9) that identifies recommendations for using data for classroom, school, and district decision making. In this section, we discuss Recommendations 1 and 2, which highlight data use by teachers in their classrooms, and ways that literacy leaders can work with teachers to put these recommendations into practice.

Recommendation 1: Make data part of an ongoing cycle of instructional improvement.

_____ Collect and prepare a variety of data about student learning.

_____ Interpret data and develop hypotheses about how to improve student learning.

_____ Modify instruction to test hypotheses and increase student learning.

Recommendation 2: Teach students to examine their own data and set learning goals.

_____ Explain expectations and assessment criteria.

_____ Provide feedback to students that is timely, specific, well formatted, and constructive.

_____ Provide tools that help students learn from feedback.

_____ Use students' data analyses to guide instructional change.

Recommendation 3: Establish a clear vision for school-wide data use.

_____ Establish a school-wide data team that sets the tone for ongoing data use.

_____ Define critical teaching and learning concepts.

_____ Develop a written plan that articulates activities, roles, and responsibilities.

_____ Provide ongoing data leadership.

Recommendation 4: Provide supports that foster a data-driven culture within the school.

_____ Designate a school-based facilitator who meets with teacher teams to discuss data.

_____ Dedicate structured time for staff collaboration.

_____ Provide targeted professional development regularly.

Figure 8.2: Using data for decision making.

Source: Adapted from Using Student Achievement Data to Support Instructional Decision Making *(NCEE 2009-4067) by L. Hamilton, R. Halverson, S. Jackson, E. Mandinach, J. Supovitz, and J. Wayman, 2009, Washington, DC: National Center for Education Evaluation and Regional Assistance, Institute of Education Sciences, Department of Education. Retrieved from http://ies.ed.gov/ncee/wwc/pubications/practiceguides.*

*Visit **www.learningsciences.com/bookresources** to download a reproducible version of this figure.*

Make Data Part of the Cycle of Instructional Improvement

Too often, schools are inundated with data that are not used or useful. Teachers complain about having too much data and little time to do anything with it, and, as mentioned previously, lack the expertise to understand what the data mean for instruction. Other teachers are concerned that although they can analyze the data, they aren't sure how to use the results in making instructional decisions. We suggest that literacy leaders implement an assessment cycle as described in figure 8.3. This cycle is iterative and requires the team working with data to reflect on whether decisions made were useful in promoting student learning. Meetings about data should be focused with the most time spent on interpretation and development of instructional plans.

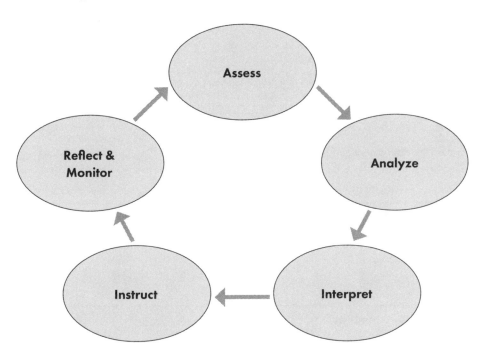

Figure 8.3: Assessment cycle.

Source: Adapted from the Pennsylvania Comprehensive Literacy Plan, CDT Core Team Assessment Cycle *(Pennsylvania Department of Education, 2012, p. 147).*

*Visit **www.learningsciences.com/bookresources** to download a reproducible version of this figure.*

As mentioned in figure 8.2, Recommendation 1, data must be collected, organized, interpreted, and then used in making instructional decisions. Data-team meetings (sometimes called problem-solving teams) have become commonplace in schools today, especially since the implementation of RTI as well as research evidence (Taylor, 2011), which indicates the value of making instructional decisions based on data. Generally, literacy leaders such as principals, reading specialists, and coaches are given the task of collecting and organizing the data for discussion by grade level or academic department teams; frequently, they also lead the meetings. Often, these meetings are focused on the results of interim or benchmark assessment measures, but in some schools, teachers are asked to analyze the results of performance measures, such as writing samples, or class assignments that provide direct evidence of students' skills, knowledge, or understanding. One of the greatest teaching and learning tools for teachers is the analysis of the work of their students and others in their school at the same grade level or in the same academic department. (See figure 8.4 for a protocol that could be used for a thirty-minute data meeting; timing can be adjusted depending on the length of the meeting.)

Steps	Comments/Questions
Guiding questions (4–5 minutes) What are the key points to consider today?	
Data analysis (8–10 minutes) What do the data say or suggest?	
Group interpretation (10–15 minutes) What do the data mean for instruction, grouping, additional assessments?	
Next steps (5–8 minutes) Who will do what and when? How? How can the coach/literacy leader be helpful?	
Follow-up for next meeting (2–4 minutes) Expectations for following meeting?	

Figure 8.4: Protocol for a thirty-minute data meeting.

Source: Adapted from the Pennsylvania Comprehensive Literacy Plan *(Pennsylvania Department of Education, pp. 147–149).*

Visit **www.learningsciences.com/bookresources** *to download a reproducible version of this figure.*

The Specifics of Data-Team Meetings

Often, results from benchmark or progress monitoring tests are an important focus of discussion in data-team or problem-solving team meetings, and generally, the goals of the meetings are to decide upon changes in instruction, grouping, or even which teachers might have responsibilities for working with specific students. These meetings, which call for collaborative problem solving, may occur frequently, perhaps once a week; however, in some schools, such data meetings are scheduled once a month or even four to six times a year. One of the major hurdles to be addressed by schools is scheduling the time for these meetings. Next, we identify some possible approaches for scheduling meetings for such collaborative problem solving (schools have become ingenious in developing schedules that enable teachers to meet together in meaningful groups):

- ▶ Include discussion of data into the weekly or bi-weekly planning meetings that teachers have as part of their schedules.

- ▶ Begin or end a school day one or two hours later, perhaps twice a month.

- ▶ Hire substitutes to cover the classes of teachers at a specific grade level for a forty-five- to sixty-minute period (e.g., four substitutes are hired to cover the classes of four teachers at a grade level and meetings of teachers from grades one to five could be held in one day). Such meetings might occur once each grading period.

- ▶ Have teachers meet after school for one or two hours every six weeks and receive compensation for these meetings.

Generally, in a data meeting, teachers are presented with a data sheet with up-to-date information about students from their grade level, generally compiled by a coach or literacy leader, and, with leader facilitation, discuss the strengths and needs of individual students and make recommendations for instruction. Teachers are asked to generate an analysis of students' strengths and needs, and then make recommendations for changes in instructional approach, grouping, or even teacher assignment. Discussion results can be summarized on a chart or computer spreadsheet for distribution to the group. Recommendations should be specific and indicate who is going to do what, how, and when. For example, the classroom teacher might focus on vocabulary development for all students while the Title I teacher might provide supplemental instruction to a small group of students (Tier 2 in an RTI program) that focuses on fluency while reading text. The literacy leader or coach might agree to obtain additional resources or materials for teachers. These collaborative meetings not only facilitate the interpretation of data but also promote a greater degree of understanding among teachers about the need to consider changes in expectations, assessment, or instructional practices.

This same approach can be used to analyze student work. For example, teachers could examine sixth-grade student writing samples in which they have been asked to write a persuasive essay. At a grade-level team meeting, focused on team understanding of writing expectations and students' current strengths and weaknesses, a coach might facilitate an ATLAS protocol (see http://schoolreforminitiative.org/doc/atlas_lfsw.pdf more for information about the ATLAS protocol). The group would first be asked to describe the student work: "What do you see?" Next, the group would be asked to make preliminary interpretations: "From the student's perspective, what is the student working on?" Finally, after describing and interpreting the work, the group is asked to reflect on implications for practice: "What are the implications of this work for teaching and assessment?"

Many student-work and data-focused protocols follow a similar pattern, supporting educators as they continually refine their skills in describing and interpreting student work and data sets and then translate their observations into implications and actions for classroom instruction.

Teach Students to Self-Assess and Set Their Own Learning Goals

Students have an important role in evaluating their own work (Afflerbach, Kim, Crassas, & Cho, 2011; Torgeson & Miller, 2009). As Stiggins (2014) indicates, students should be players, not victims or beneficiaries, in the testing game. Being able to assess one's own work is a hallmark of independent learners, strongly emphasized as an important trait in today's state standards. Stiggins (2014) identified what he calls a student's Bill of Assessment Rights that calls for students to understand the following: the purpose of each assessment and how it will be used, the learning target of a learning exercise and the scoring guides to be used, and how to self-assess their progress. He also indicates that students are entitled to dependable assessment of their achievement, which highlights the importance of high-quality assessment measures. Finally, he notes the importance of effective communication of assessment results to students, families, or other stakeholders. When teachers adhere to these recommendations, students are provided with a sense of control over their own outcomes. The notions in this Bill of Assessment Rights can be shared with teachers and used as a discussion tool for promoting better use of data by teachers.

PUT INTO PRACTICE

Discuss the students' Bill of Assessment Rights (Stiggins, 2014) with teachers, asking them to consider which of these are evident in their classrooms or school practices or how such ideas can be implemented in the school. Discuss ways that data results are shared with families and what the roles of each educator, including the literacy leader, are.

Teachers working in teams can develop common rubrics that can be given to students when an assignment is introduced (e.g., writing a persuasive essay or conducting a science experiment) and then used to provide feedback when the assignment has been completed. Students can also use the rubric to reflect on their work themselves or participate in a peer-assessment process. Providing specific, timely, and constructive feedback to students is an important means of helping students learn how to improve. Involving students from elementary through high school grades in the assessment process can help them develop independence and self-assessment strategies. Even in the early grades, students can be asked to self-assess their work, with a simple scale (e.g., "Circle one of the following: This is my very best work ☺; I know I can do better ☹; I'm not sure ☺").

Using Data for School and District Improvement

In this section, we look at data and its usefulness in school improvement and remodeling. In too many districts, decisions about the assessment tools used to measure literacy learning are made idiosyncratically. Often, there are overlaps in these measures (i.e., several measures assess the same skills) or some elements of literacy may not be measured at all. In some grades, there are many different assessment measures, and in other grades, perhaps not enough. At the time of this writing, end-of-year testing is required by the federal government in grades 3–8 and once at the high school level. However, the focus is on providing summative information; individual districts will need to develop or select measures that can provide data for formative use. In the points that follow, we identify what we consider to be important questions for literacy leaders and teams to consider when developing a systemic assessment system for a district or school:

> ▶ Are the assessments at the various grade levels consistent with the goals and outcomes identified as most critical for literacy development at those stages? Is there redundancy in measures, and if so, which can be eliminated? Are important components of literacy learning represented (e.g., reading, writing, and communications)?

▶ What purposes do each of these assessment measures serve? Do they serve accountability purposes (summative assessment)? Or do they assist teachers in planning for student learning (formative assessment)? Do teachers view the formative measures as useful for making instructional decisions?

▶ Do the measures provide a longitudinal look at student literacy learning? In other words, can educators track the growth of students over time?

Building an Assessment Culture

Afflerbach (2014), who has written extensively about literacy assessment, provides useful information for those responsible for developing a comprehensive assessment system. He describes the need for balance between the following:

- Assessment of skills and how students apply those skills (measuring specific decoding skills and students' ability to use those skills when reading text)

- Measurement of basic skills and higher order thinking

- Reading from a single text and reading from many sources, including the Internet

- Cognitive and affective reading outcomes

- Summative and formative assessments

PUT INTO PRACTICE

Discuss the need for balance in the five dimensions identified by Afflerbach (2014) with a group of teacher leaders. In what ways has your school attempted to provide for assessment as described earlier? Is there a need for improvement, and if so, where?

The goal in schools should be to develop an *assessment culture*, in which educators understand the basic principles of sound assessment practices; that is, how to gather reliable and valid evidence of student learning and then use the process and results appropriately (Stiggins, 2014). Recommendation 3 in figure 8.2 (page 142) highlights the importance of establishing a clear vision for school-wide data use and identifies the importance of a data team that provides input about which data are to be gathered and used in the school. In some schools, the literacy leadership team may have the responsibility of setting the tone for ongoing data use and supporting teachers in using data for improvement in literacy learning at the individual, classroom, and school levels. This team can assist in several ways: identifying and clarifying the school's data vision, providing teachers with a written plan that articulates the ways in which data are to be used, detailing the desired goals of such use, and helping teachers gain a better understanding of what is meant by "data" and how it can be useful. For example, the data team can help teachers in a specific school develop a common language so that there is a shared understanding of the various and varied terms related to assessment.

Another responsibility of the data or literacy leadership team may be to develop a systemic, comprehensive assessment system using the notions just described. The literacy leader might use a matrix such as the one in appendix F to lead a discussion about the various assessment tools already used in the school (or across schools), as well as identify redundancies and gaps in the system. Based on this analysis, the literacy team can make recommendations to modify the system so that there is a systemic, comprehensive approach to assessment that provides essential information but is not overwhelming to students, teachers, or parents.

Looking at Relationships Among Data for School Improvement Efforts

Schools have access to so much data beyond those provided by assessment measures, and in order to make strides toward school improvement, literacy leaders and their colleagues need to think about the interrelationships among all the data available in schools. Bernhardt (2013) in her text *Data Analysis for Continuous School Improvement* highlights the importance of data as a means of focusing the work of schools and reducing the random nature of school improvement. She identifies four categories of data that school personnel can consider as sources for improving teaching and learning (p. 17):

1. Demographics (students and their families [diversity], enrollment, attendance)

2. Student learning (formative and summative assessment measures)

3. Perceptions (attitudes, values, beliefs of teachers, families, and students)

4. School processes (programs, organizational, instructional processes)

Bernhardt also describes the importance of analyzing the interaction among the various data sources in order to make decisions about school improvement efforts. Literacy leaders, for example, can look at the relationship between demographics (e.g., ELs or high-poverty students) and performance on various student learning measures: Are specific groups doing better than others? Leaders can also look at multiple relationships; for example, do students from specific subgroups (demographics) perform better on the standardized achievement test (student learning) when they receive supplemental reading instruction from reading specialists (processes)? This type of deep analysis can provide schools with a better understanding of how to focus their energies and plan systematically to improve literacy learning in the school overall. Literacy leaders can facilitate efforts to involve teachers in analyzing data and designing curriculum and instruction that meets the learning needs of the students in the school.

> **REFLECT**
>
> Looking back at the data sources identified in figure 8.1 (page 137), consider which data sources might fit into each of Bernhardt's categories. Which of the data sources would be better for accountability purposes? Which would best serve as sources of information for instructional decision making?

Developing a Culture That Uses Data for Decision Making

Recommendation 4 in figure 8.2 highlights the importance of various supports that enable achievement of the previous goals. Literacy leaders may be responsible for serving as the data facilitators who meet with teachers individually, or, more frequently, with teacher teams. Their role is one of helping teachers interpret data and providing the professional learning experiences teachers need to make meaningful use of data. Although these literacy leaders are present to provide support, one of their important roles and goals is to build the capacity of teachers to become "assessment literate." As mentioned earlier, those responsible for developing school schedules need to provide the structured time for teachers to collaborate about assessment and instruction and to make these collaborative meetings a priority.

Providing professional learning experiences about assessment is key, and such experiences should be developed based on the specific needs in the school or district. In some instances, teachers are novices and need entry-level information about assessment. In other schools, the focus might be on interpretation and use of multiple data sources; or in some schools, the focus may be on data technology systems and how they can be useful in schools. In appendix G, we describe a series of professional learning experiences that literacy leaders can modify and use with teachers when introducing them to the notion of multiple data sources and how they can be used to improve instruction. Spending time on raising teachers' awareness and understanding of assessment and its usefulness to improving student literacy learning is time well spent.

Summary

After defining assessment as a process used for purposes of accountability, improving student learning, and overall school performance, we discussed large-scale measures, their potential uses, and their limitations. One of the major foci of the chapter was on how literacy leaders can work with classroom teachers to help them understand how to work with data to improve instructional practices and literacy learning. We concluded with a section that addresses the need for a coherent, systemic, and comprehensive literacy assessment plan that enables literacy leaders to think about the school literacy goals and vision, and how assessment can help guide efforts to achieve desired outcomes.

Activities

1. Using the chart found in appendix A, note the ways that literacy leaders function as facilitators, leaders, designers, and advocates when working on assessment tasks. List some possibilities that you might consider in your current position.

2. Using appendix F, analyze the assessment measures used in your school or district. Use the identified questions to decide whether there might be a need to make changes in the overall assessment plan for the school or district.

3. Visit the School Reform Initiative's protocol repository (www. schoolreforminitiative.org/protocols/), and click on "protocols" and then "examining data," as well as "protocols" and then "focusing on students." Review the protocols focused on data analysis and learning from student work (e.g., Data Driven Dialogue, Looking at Data Sets, the Collaborative Assessment Conference, The Slice, etc.). Which of these protocols are already part of your coaching and assessment tools? Which protocols might best serve your immediate purposes when leading your school's and system's assessment work?

CHAPTER 9

Developing, Implementing, and Sustaining School-Wide Literacy Programs

GUIDING QUESTIONS

1. What are the key roles and responsibilities of literacy leaders in the school-wide change process? In serving as members of school-wide literacy leadership teams?

2. How can literacy leaders facilitate a needs assessment process that provides comprehensive information about literacy instruction in a school or district?

3. What key notions are important for the development, implementation, and sustainability of a comprehensive literacy program for the school?

4. In what ways can literacy leaders facilitate the selection and development of materials for the literacy program?

Melinda was asked to become a member of a literacy leadership team working on the development of a comprehensive literacy plan for the district. She knew she would be responsible for sharing information with her school faculty and soliciting feedback from them. But what would the district plan mean for the school? How could they use the results to develop a school action plan? What information might she and her colleagues be asked to generate?

In this chapter, we discuss some of the potential roles of literacy leaders on school-wide literacy leadership teams and in school-wide literacy change efforts. We then describe a needs-assessment process that can lead to the development of a comprehensive literacy plan or an action plan that provides schools with a framework for developing, implementing, and sustaining the literacy program. We also include a section about a task that literacy leaders are often asked to lead: that of selecting and developing materials. We conclude with suggestions about how literacy leaders can address their dual role; that is, working at the individual and system levels simultaneously. Not all literacy leaders will be involved to the same extent in school or district efforts to remodel literacy programs. However, given the current emphasis on comprehensive literacy from birth to twelfth grade, and on the major shifts in school literacy programs, all literacy leaders should have some awareness of how they can influence school-wide change. To paraphrase Margaret Mead: "Never underestimate the power of a small group of committed people to change the world. It is the only thing that ever has."

The Role of Literacy Leaders in Improving School-Wide Literacy

A key role of literacy leaders is that of facilitating and leading efforts to develop school-wide literacy programs that provide the framework for effective literacy instruction across the board—often from prekindergarten through high school, for students of all abilities, skills, and knowledge, and across the academic disciplines. Margaret Mead's words have relevancy for the work of the literacy leader who must be able to collaborate effectively with others to make a difference, or as she says, "to change the world." In our case, the goal is facilitating organizational change for overall school literacy learning improvement.

Often, for literacy leaders, an important aspect of any school improvement program is the development of a professional learning plan that will support teachers as they work together to effect change. The results of research over the past decade have helped educators identify critical elements of effective professional learning, which include: ongoing, sustained experiences; active learning that requires inquiry and opportunities for problem solving; meaningful, authentic experiences with a focus on student learning; and ongoing support, perhaps through coaching (American Education Research Association, 2005; Bean, 2012; Learning Forward, 2010; Risko & Vogt, 2016). Learning Forward's *Standards for Professional Learning* (http://learning forward.org/docs/pdf/standardsreferenceguide.pdf) provide a useful tool for educators who want to know more about key factors that influence teacher learning.

Literacy coaches might lead or be involved in many different systematic school-wide efforts: developing a needs-assessment process at the school or district level; developing a comprehensive literacy plan that includes a logical, long-range program of professional learning; selecting or developing materials for the literacy program; leading professional learning activities to support implementation of a new literacy program or approaches; monitoring and/or evaluating implementation efforts. Following, we describe some possible school-wide projects or initiatives in which literacy leaders might be involved. Think about how you might approach each of these important and possibly urgent tasks. What are the important questions and issues to consider when responding to each of these tasks?

- The superintendent calls you into her office and indicates that the district has received money from the state to upgrade the technology resources in the middle school. Decisions have to be made about the selection of specific hardware and software by the end of next month. She is concerned about how to involve teachers in the decision-making process, but also wants to make certain that the school gets the funding. The job is yours. Congratulations! (What is your first step?)

- Elementary teachers have been concerned about the alignment between new state standards and the "old" core program used for reading instruction for the past ten years. The district has agreed to allot funds to purchase a new series. The assistant superintendent for curriculum has appointed a committee charged with selecting the new series. You have been asked to chair the committee. So, what are your first steps (other than holding a committee meeting)?

- The principal at the high school has volunteered the school to be part of a professional development effort to integrate disciplinary literacy instruction across all academic subjects. Because you are the department chair for English, he thinks you would be a great coach. Your responsibilities include helping all content-area teachers understand, accept, and become excited about participating in this endeavor in general. The project sounds exciting, ambitious, and ambiguous. What exactly will be your new responsibilities? And how will you balance your new and current roles?

- All on the district leadership team agree that the newly adopted state standards have great implications for curriculum development in the area of literacy. The team is trying to develop a well-structured series of workshops at the district level to help teachers understand the standards and then to begin revising curriculum and instruction to address the intent of the standards. As a member of the team, you will be responsible for following up with teachers at your school. You know the next step is to talk with your principal about this upcoming initiative, but how will you begin this conversation?

It's evident that at times there will be specific tasks or activities that you as a literacy leader will be asked to address. The trick, of course, when thinking like a leader, is to balance the competing commitments of urgent new requests on your time with current work efforts. Across this book, we address each of the aforementioned possible tasks (and others) in various chapters. Literacy leaders may, at times, be focused on a set of tasks (e.g., developing and then implementing a comprehensive literacy or action plan); at other times, the focus will be on a single task, such as leading professional learning for teachers (e.g., using technology in instruction) or selecting a new core series. In the following section, we discuss the importance of a literacy leadership team as a vehicle for improving the literacy program in the school. For additional resources about developing school-wide literacy programs, see appendix B.

Establishing a Literacy Leadership Team

School and district literacy teams can be useful, both for the successful, ongoing implementation of a literacy program and for more long-term efforts related to developing, implementing, and sustaining a comprehensive literacy plan. The literacy team can generate a sense of ownership of the literacy program—it can help teachers develop a common understanding and language about literacy instruction and assessment. The focus of the literacy leadership committee might be different, however, depending on where the school is in the change process. In some schools, the focus might be on the development of a literacy plan, while other schools might be involved in selecting assessment tools that provide for systematic, reliable evaluation (prekindergarten through twelfth grade); still other schools might be developing or selecting curriculum that fits the vision and goals in the plan itself. The team might also be responsible for monitoring the efforts of the school as it continues its journey to improved instruction and student literacy learning.

Several key notions for the development of such a literacy leadership team follow:

▸ The leader should be someone who has the leadership and facilitation skills that inspire and persuade others to work collaboratively. At times, a principal or another administrator serves as leader of the team, but in some schools, literacy coaches have been asked to lead such efforts. Often, the literacy coach has an important role in obtaining or providing important information about current literacy efforts and in facilitating team efforts.

▸ The team should include a representative group of teachers, including those from different grade levels, those who teach various subgroups of students (e.g., ELs, special education, Title I), and teachers of the disciplines (e.g., English language arts, history, math, science). Teachers on the team might serve for several years and then be replaced by other teachers, so that many have a chance to be involved in this in-depth work of school change. Involvement creates ownership—and ownership creates a willingness to apply what has been developed.

▶ Although the team may begin by working as a whole group, subgroups can be formed as a means of moving forward quickly and efficiently. For example, groups might meet by levels (e.g., early childhood, elementary, and so on) or even by programs (e.g., special education, Title I, and so on) to discuss current curriculum, needs, and strengths. Or each subgroup might be asked to focus on a specific component of literacy (e.g., writing, reading, and communications) or on specific demographic groups needing specific attention (e.g., ELs, special education, and so on). The groups can work separately on their tasks and then report back to the full literacy leadership team. Each can also talk with other teachers in the school to seek and share information. The leader should work with the team to establish timelines and work schedules and assume responsibility for sharing information across the entire group (see chapter 7 for ideas about working with small groups).

In the initial stages of any effort to make changes in the school literacy program, getting input from faculty is important. The literacy leader may hold a discussion with the entire faculty in a workshop setting to discuss perceptions about the status of the literacy program, its strengths and weaknesses. The following questions are examples of those that teachers might discuss, in person or first through online surveys (using tools such as SurveyMonkey or Google Forms) and then in person (see figure 9.1, page 158). These questions can be modified or supplemented in order to more accurately reflect each school's specific context.

Additionally, there can be adaptations in the structure and responsibilities of a literacy leadership team, depending on whether it is school- or district-based and also on the size of the organization. There may be a district-wide literacy leadership committee whose responsibilities are to conduct a district-wide needs assessment and develop a comprehensive literacy plan across schools. Members on the team may represent specific schools and may have responsibilities for leading efforts in their own schools, working with smaller school-based teams. Such a district-level team might also include representation from community entities (e.g., parents, libraries, or universities) and also include students. Ultimately, alignment of efforts within and across schools is key to producing school-wide and district-wide literacy plans that serve all students. And whether working with a school-based or district-based literacy leadership team, often the best starting point for both is a well-planned needs-assessment process.

Questions for All Teachers

- What are our literacy goals for the students at specific grade levels? For this school? To what extent are we accomplishing these goals? Where are we experiencing difficulties? (Each grade level can address this question.)

- Are we meeting the needs of all students, especially those identified as ELs, special education students, Title I, gifted, and so on? If not, any thoughts as to why?

- To what extent are students able to read, write, and communicate in discipline-specific and age-appropriate ways, across all grade levels, in preparation for the demands of college and the workplace?

- Are the materials we use adequate for helping us accomplish our goals? If not, what materials are needed? In what ways are we preparing students to use technology as a resource for learning?

- What assessment tools are used to inform instruction? Are they useful in planning lessons?

- In what ways do we involve families and the community in our literacy efforts? What improvements are needed?

- How can the school better support each of us as learners? What additional professional learning experiences would be useful?

Additional Questions for Content-Area Teachers Across Grade Levels

- To what extent are students in our classes able to address the literacy tasks (reading, writing, speaking, listening, representing) expected of them (e.g., lab-report writing in science classes, analyzing primary sources in social studies, translating a word problem into a figure and then into an algebraic expression in math class)?

- To what extent are we familiar with the literacy strengths and weaknesses of the students in our content-area classes?

- What assessment tools do we use to determine the literacy needs and strengths of the students in our content-area classes? To assess content knowledge and understanding?

- To what extent are we familiar with literacy strategies specific to each of our disciplines (e.g., sourcing and corroboration in a social studies class; analyzing word parts for Greek or Latin prefixes, roots, and suffixes in a biology class; analyzing multiple representations in a math class)?

- Are adequate professional learning experiences provided for us as teachers, experiences that assist us in integrating literacy in our content-area teaching? If not, what might be useful?

Figure 9.1: School-wide literacy programs—questions for discussion.

The Needs-Assessment Process

For many schools or districts, involving faculty in conducting a needs assessment of the literacy program and how it supports literacy and overall learning, is an important first step. The questions in figure 9.1 can be used to generate some in-depth thinking by groups of faculty and help the literacy leadership team think about the upcoming work. It may also be helpful to have a more comprehensive template or guide that assists in the needs-assessment process.

In 2010, the federal government funded state efforts to develop state comprehensive literacy plans and, as part of that process, required that states develop needs-assessment documents that could be used by districts to assist them in assessing the status of their own literacy programs. Given that forty-seven states and the District of Columbia responded to this opportunity, a wide range of state literacy plans and needs-assessment documents are available on the Internet and can be used as guides by schools. Some of the needs-assessment documents are quite complex, while others are much simpler. Many of the documents include protocols for assessing needs at all levels. The document *Guidelines for Developing an Effective District Literacy Action Plan* (Meltzer & Jackson, 2010), prepared for the Massachusetts Department of Elementary and Secondary Education, describes three key steps for district plan development: organizing for action, assessing current status, and developing a plan. The document is succinct and provides useful information for those involved in district-wide literacy plan development (www.doe.mass.edu/literacy/presentations /LiteracyGuidelines.pdf).

As mentioned, it may be more efficient to locate a needs- or self-assessment tool that has already been developed, especially if one has been developed for your state, and then modify it to fit the needs of your specific school or district. However, for those who want to develop their own needs-assessment tool, or a more targeted needs-assessment tool that aims at a particular grade-level or content-area department, Vogt and Shearer (2010) provide a useful list of guiding questions for gathering program data. Next, we identify steps to assist those involved in conducting a needs assessment of the literacy program in a school or district.

Identify the Goals of the Needs Assessment

Is this an effort designed for a comprehensive view of the literacy program or is it more narrow? For example, is it focused on teachers' knowledge of the standards adopted by the state? A focus on literacy at the secondary level? The professional learning experiences available for teachers?

Design or Select the Needs-Assessment Tool to Meet Your Goals

Take into consideration the questions or goals to be addressed. Again, investigate possible tools available from your state or other sources, and then modify or adapt them to meet district and school needs.

Most needs-assessment documents include the following categories for consideration: standards and curriculum, assessments, instruction, professional learning and practice, literacy leadership, and family and community partnerships. Your school should decide whether to study all, several, or just one of these, perhaps using the results of teacher discussions (see figure 9.1) to determine the major foci. Often, it is better to start small and "drill down" rather than trying to attempt too much initially and, perhaps, superficially. Conducting a needs assessment could take a substantial amount of time and effort, especially if the district or school feels as though there is a serious need to "revamp" the entire program. On the other hand, when data are available (e.g., classroom teaching practices; test data; and perceptions of teachers, parents, and students), they can be used to describe the current status, and the leadership committee can move quickly to determine "where we want to go" and "how we can get there." If specific data are missing, arrangements can be made to obtain them (e.g., data about current practices to ensure transition from elementary to middle school).

Determine Sources of Data

As described in chapter 8, the four sources of data described by Bernhardt (2013)—demographics, student learning, perceptions, and school processes—can provide critical information for decision making.

Determine How Data Will Be Collected

Three powerful data collection tools are available to help schools obtain the data they need: surveys, interviews and focus groups, and document analysis.

Surveys involve asking various audiences (e.g., parents, teachers, or students) questions to get their perspectives. Some schools use technology as a means of soliciting information from various groups. Middle and high school educators may consider using the free online needs-assessment tool the Content Area Literacy Survey (CALS), developed by the Strategic Education Research Partnership (http://adlitpd.org/category/assess/).

At Hudson High School, in Hudson, Massachusetts, the literacy leadership team decided to use the CALS as one source of data in a comprehensive needs-assessment process. The team administered the CALS during the winter of 2012 to 185 students and 88 teachers across grade levels and content areas. The leadership team was excited to receive immediate digital feedback on questions they had been wrestling with both in and out of school. Similar data were collected from teachers about their literacy instructional practices in the content areas, and, importantly, the leadership team was also able to gather data about teachers' previous professional development experiences focused on literacy. While the team supplemented the CALS data with a number of other data sources, the CALS digital reports provided a quick, free, and substantive look at both teacher and student literacy dispositions and practices. (To read more about how Hudson High School used this tool in its needs-assessment work, see the extended case in chapter 12.)

Teachers at specific grade levels or departments can be interviewed for their perspectives on literacy instruction, individually or in focus groups. Focus group sessions can provide a more systematic approach to gathering data from various stakeholders, with some similar and different questions asked of each group. For example, groups of parents representing specific grade levels—primary, intermediate, secondary—can be asked to participate in hour-long sessions to discuss specific aspects of the instruction received by their children. Reading specialists who provide interventions for struggling readers might participate in such a group to discuss their perceptions of the effectiveness of instructional approaches, grouping, scheduling, and so on. Teachers at the secondary level might be asked to discuss their perceptions of what it means to integrate literacy into their discipline, how prepared they feel, their concerns, and so on.

Document analysis—analysis of standardized test scores, lesson plans, materials used for instruction, and so on—can serve as a rich source of information. Sharing student assignments across classrooms for a specific unit of study can be revealing: How similar are these assignments, and do they all help students to think and perform at high levels? Pictures or videos of classrooms to illustrate the access that students have to literacy materials, the grouping patterns, and whether student work is displayed can be helpful in thinking about the current status of literacy in the school. Teachers can keep logs of their instruction. For example, how much time did they spend on teaching comprehension during a week? Writing? Providing opportunities for choice in reading? Results of these simple logs can be discussed; often, these results can be eye-opening for teachers and reveal differences (as well as similarities) in the emphasis given by teachers to various practices or even to specific groups of students (e.g., those who have strong reading skills compared to those who are experiencing difficulties).

Decide on the Audiences To Be Consulted

In what ways can the team conducting the needs assessment reach all intended audiences? Who will be responsible for obtaining information from classroom teachers, specialized professionals, students, parents, and so on? Strategic literacy leadership teams often divide and conquer, discussing target audiences together and then collecting data from separate audiences in small groups. Data can then be compiled, summarized, and analyzed by the small group or the larger team.

Analysis of Data

Without analyzing the collected data, little will be gained. Strengths, needs, and priorities for change must be identified. The analysis should be a team effort, and it requires excellent facilitation by the leader of the literacy team. Again, see the Hudson High School case in chapter 12 for an example of how one high school went through the needs-assessment process and used it for making decisions about instruction, professional learning, and assessment.

The Comprehensive Literacy Plan: Planning for Action

The results of a needs-assessment process, with its identified priorities, should lead to an action plan or, if conducted district-wide, an overall comprehensive literacy plan. Each individual school in the district may then develop action plans based on the district framework. Appendix H identifies a list of questions to consider when developing an action plan or a comprehensive reading plan (Bean, 2014). The  questions address issues related to curriculum, instruction, assessment, and the process for change.

In the paragraphs that follow, we identify key ideas about writing a comprehensive plan and/or an action plan.

Writing the Document

The written document should be reader friendly, accessible, and provide a useful guide for leading literacy efforts for several years. The literacy leadership team can serve an important role here: they can summarize findings from the needs assessment that lead to specific recommendations for action. There may also be a need for editing, often done by a literacy leader or multiple leaders, so that there is coherency in the document.

In our recent work with districts in the development of comprehensive plans, most were available electronically as well as in print, and teachers could access those sections most critical for them (e.g., teachers at the secondary level could focus on those sections specific to adolescent literacy). Included in any district plan should be notions about articulation from prekindergarten through twelfth grade. Components that can be included in such a plan are presented in figure 9.2; these elements can be modified for use at the school level.

- Goals and vision for literacy learning (What are the district's core beliefs about students, literacy, and literacy learning?)

- Standards as a means of identifying outcomes

- Curriculum and instruction that address standards in reading, writing, and communications; the core curriculum, approaches, and materials for differentiating instruction (e.g., the role of technology in the literacy curriculum)

- Literacy across the content areas

- Specific interventions for various subgroups

- Assessment tools

- Time allocations for literacy instruction and instructional design (What would instruction look like in a literacy block?)

- Professional learning opportunities and commitment

- Partnerships with families and communities

- Leadership responsibilities

- An action plan

- Plans for dissemination

Figure 9.2: Components of a comprehensive literacy program.

Identifying Priorities

One of the key aspects of any comprehensive literacy plan is that it identifies priorities, probably not more than two to five. Establish these priority goals and then work "full speed ahead" to accomplish them. In too many instances, schools and districts are attempting to do too much in a short amount of time. Schmoker (2011) says it well: keep in mind "the power of simplicity, clarity, and priority" (p. 12). Multiple and scattered initiatives frustrate and confuse everyone. By establishing priorities, being clear about how you are going to achieve them, and developing a simple but focused plan, there is much more likelihood that you will achieve your goals.

Processes for achieving those priority goals should be described. Who will do what, when, and how (processes and resources needed to achieve the goals)? Also, it is important to identify and collect evidence that you have accomplished your goals.

One possible way to think about this is to distinguish between short-term and long-term goals (see appendix I for a sample Action Planning Guide).

Disseminating the Information

One step, often forgotten, is "getting the word out." Even though there is a literacy leadership team and teachers have been involved, to a lesser or greater degree, some in the district or school will have little or no awareness that there is a comprehensive literacy plan designed to guide instructional literacy efforts.

Designing a dissemination plan that includes ideas for sharing the document with teachers and the wider community is key to implementation efforts. Some districts have developed videos that highlight ideas in the plan. In others, the plan serves as the professional development focus for the year; specific sections are "unpacked" and elaborated on in mini-workshops. Think about the authenticity of such workshops, where the focus is on genuinely improving literacy instruction and assessment based on the analysis of current efforts in your specific school.

Implementation and Sustainability: Keys to Change

As is all too familiar, school improvement initiatives come and go. A too-often accurate statement made by teachers is that they can wait out the current program because surely there will be another one the following year. As one participant in a study of professional change indicated, "Seems like a freight train coming through . . . last year it was math, this year it's writing, and now all of a sudden it's the six-trait writing model . . . what happened to math?" (Nielson, Barry, & Staab, 2008, p. 1294). Literacy leaders, then, need to be aware of the many factors that can influence implementation efforts in positive and negative ways. They must also be thinking—from the beginning—about ways that they can evaluate what they are doing, and make changes necessary to ensure sustainability. The action plan, with its recommended set of priorities, activities, and timeline, can assist in guiding school efforts.

Readers who want to know more about implementation can access modules and lessons that help them become more knowledgeable about this key aspect of school change from the website of the National Implementation Research Network (http://nirn.fpg.unc.edu/). The website provides in-depth information about implementation issues and how to address them, including a lesson on how coaches might be selected and prepared to assist in working with teachers. We highlight some roadblocks that may arise and identify possible ways to address these barriers in figure 9.3.

Roadblocks	Possible Solutions
Lack of understanding (knowledge) of the vision and goals Difficulty accepting notions of the initiative (not consistent with current ideas)	Communicate the vision consistently and with all. Involve teachers from the very beginning (not just to gain "buy-in"). Provide the necessary professional learning experiences, not just for building knowledge, but also for applying in classroom instruction (informational sessions plus ongoing practice and coaching). Be willing to live with "growing pains." Recognize that there will be some critics (at least at first) and a possible implementation dip. Support by monitoring and celebrating small positive steps.
Lack of support and resources for initiative (time, funding, personnel, materials)	Involve school leadership in the implementation efforts. Restructure the school schedule to provide necessary professional learning experiences. Work with district leadership to obtain necessary support and funding.
Lack of long-term effort to achieve goals Lack of a reasonable roadmap	Monitor efforts to determine any needed modifications and adaptations. Recognize the need for long-range planning and implementation.

Figure 9.3: Possible implementation roadblocks and solutions.

Source: Adapted from The Implementation Trap: Helping Schools Overcome Barriers to Change *by C. Jerald, 2005, Washington, DC: The Center for Comprehensive School Reform and Improvement.*

PUT INTO PRACTICE

Talk with teachers and other literacy leaders about a specific implementation effort at your school. Use figure 9.3 to discuss roadblocks that your school experienced and how you overcame those barriers. What might you have done differently?

Developing or creating a literacy plan is important, but "the implementation stage is the most difficult of all" (Jerald, 2005, p. 2), given it often involves transformational change and adaptive challenges. Two important points about implementation follow:

1. Teachers need to be provided with adequate support and recognition for their efforts, even small ones, as they move through the implementation process. Because teachers are faced with many demands and responsibilities, working with them so that they understand the initiative and its importance to student learning is key. Literacy leaders, often coaches, must encourage, nudge, and motivate teachers, providing them with needed resources and the professional learning experiences that enable them to implement an initiative as designed. At the same time, keep those involved in implementation accountable; literacy leaders should monitor change efforts and provide feedback that includes ideas for improvement.

2. Regardless of how prescriptive or well-defined a project initiative is (e.g., a state mandate that all districts implement RTI initiatives in their schools), implementation is complex, and local schools and educators in them will shape how the program unfolds (Coburn & Woulfin, 2012). McLaughlin (1990), in discussing implementation, describes this as "mutual adaptation"; that is, the ways in which organizations make modifications, based on "local expertise, capacity, and sophistication in project implementation, as well as local motivation and management style" (McLaughlin, 1990, p. 12). For example, in districts in Pennsylvania implementing Reading First, a large-scale initiative funded by the federal government, the ways in which reading coaches were selected and the ways in which they fulfilled their responsibilities differed from district to district (Bean et al., 2010; Zigmond, Bean, Kloo, & Brydon, 2011). Districts have a responsibility to think about their specific contexts and how a specific implementation effort might be adapted to fit the needs of that district. As an example, think about the implementation of coaching in a specific school. In some schools, with experienced and knowledgeable staff, coaches may spend more time working with groups and encouraging shared leadership by others. They may be more involved with adaptive change efforts. In schools with many novice teachers or those new to the initiative, coaches may spend more time helping teachers develop the technical skills they need to implement the program rather than focusing on problems that require adaptive thinking.

From Implementation to Sustainability

Implementation is not a short-term effort; it requires ongoing attention over a long period of time. Fixen, Naoom, Blasé, Friedman, and Wallace (2006) describe the following five stages of implementation: exploring and installing, initial implementation, full implementation, adaptations, and sustainability. Schools will need different amounts of time to go through these stages, and those who write about implementation and sustainability often talk about the need for a three- to five-year process for full implementation. In a recent study of sustainability of Reading First in two states, Bean, Dole, Nelson, Belcastro, and Zigmond (2015) found many factors that contributed to sustainability. These included: leadership of principals and their belief in and support for the initiative; ongoing professional learning experiences and support for teachers, including coaching; need for adaptations for their school context; a commitment to using data to inform instruction; and stability in students and staff. One of the notions discussed in the study was the interaction between increases in student learning and implementation. There was greater evidence of student learning in schools where there were greater degrees of implementation and acceptance of the literacy beliefs promoted in the initiative.

An essential aspect of sustainability is ongoing monitoring and evaluating to obtain evidence about the process of implementation and impact (outcomes) of the initiative. Plans for such evaluation should be part of the action plan (see appendix I) and should include both formative and summative data. Again, the four sources of data—demographics, student learning, perceptions, and school processes—and the interactions between and among them can provide schools with useful information about program effectiveness. In sum, evaluation should be an essential aspect of any programmatic initiative, addressed on an ongoing basis, so that appropriate modifications or adaptations can be made.

VOICES FROM THE FIELD

Knowing what I know now, I would have collected data on how coaching impacted not only student achievement, but also how it impacted the correlates of student achievement like collective efficacy, school culture, and social capital. Transforming low-achieving, high-risk school systems takes time, but that is no excuse for not measuring incremental growth. When it comes to evaluating coaching programs, I believe we should spend as much attention measuring the invisible impacts, such as changes in collective efficacy and social capital, as we do measuring the visible impacts like student achievement.

—Christina Steinbacher-Reed, supervisor of coaches

Developing or Selecting Materials for the Literacy Program

Previously, we outlined our views about widespread shifts in modern literacy instruction, including a discussion of standards as a driver for developing curriculum, and technology as an important learning tool (see chapter 3). Next, we build on our discussion from chapter 3, focusing on factors for literacy leaders to consider in the development or selection of materials or programs that align with and support the vision and goals of the overall comprehensive literacy program. Districts across this country vary in how they determine what curriculum to use for their core literacy program. Some rely on materials produced by publishers that seem to meet current requirements for high-level, rigorous standards. Others develop their own curriculum, involving teachers in making decisions about themes and approaches that provide for integration and project-based, inquiry-focused learning. Still others follow a middle road, often selecting a core set of materials and then asking teachers to work together to make adaptations (e.g., finding ways to embed literacy instruction within the content areas by designing various projects). The CCSS and similar standards have led many districts to this middle-road approach. Although they might use a core program, they develop themes, search for other resources (both print and digital) from various content areas, and design appropriate learning experiences and specific assessment tools to measure student learning. (For an example of an integrated framework of literacy and sample units, see the Massachusetts Model Curriculum Units [www.doe.mass.edu/candi/model/default.html].)

In the next section, we address three issues about materials development and selection: first, defining what we mean by "materials" and identifying guidelines for selecting or developing them; second, discussing processes for developing or selecting materials; and third, discussing literacy leaders as advocates for specific programs or materials.

Guidelines for Selecting or Developing Materials and Programs

Materials are key resources for those who teach literacy, including teachers in the disciplines, and must be chosen wisely. By "materials," we mean all resources, digital and print, used by teachers to support effective literacy instruction, including those used for whole classes, small groups, and individual instruction. We identify two guidelines for selecting or developing materials (a key resource for the following statements was Guidelines for Selection of Materials in English Language Arts [www.ncte.org/positions/statements/material-selection-ela]):

1. Criteria for selection of materials may be dictated by state policies and, at times, even the process for selection is prescribed. At the same time,

districts should identify their own policy for materials selection: first, by identifying their goals and vision for literacy learning as a lens through which to evaluate whether materials under consideration are aligned with them, and second, to determine whether the materials address the needs of students in that district. The CCSS and other similar standards have created a shift in how districts think about literacy and the materials they need to address these standards, with a call for materials that address the integrated nature of the language arts, a need for more informational text and nonprint materials. Districts are grappling with the demand to include more complex text in the curriculum and what that means for instruction. The document *Literacy Implementation Guidance for the ELA Common Core State Standards* (International Reading Association, 2012) provides practical information for those involved in making decisions about text. Districts must also take into consideration the students they serve: Does the curriculum include materials that meet the needs of EL students, those who experience difficulty with reading and writing, and those students identified as proficient or advanced?

2. Districts should identify or develop their own criteria for materials selection or development. There are many resources that can aid districts in this process, including the book by Dewitz, Leahy, Jones, and Sullivan (2010), *The Essential Guide to Selecting and Using Core Reading Programs.* Some of the checklists they identify are available from the International Literacy Association's website (www.literacyworldwide.org). These checklists provide information about how to review the teachers' manual, the content, skill development, assessment tools, and supplemental materials.

Processes for Selecting or Developing Materials

As we have written throughout this book, involvement in decision making will increase the probability of teacher understanding, ownership, and implementation. Further, when districts are considering major changes in materials (e.g., selection of a new core program), community involvement is an imperative. Well-qualified teachers who can represent various grade levels and schools should be invited to serve on the selection committee. Such teachers should have knowledge of the current standards in the state and district and also a strong background in literacy. In some districts, teachers apply to serve on such committees, describing in writing their qualifications and reasons for applying. The same criteria should apply when selecting a committee to work on the development of materials.

Those districts choosing to involve teachers in developing curriculum or in modifying the core program can use such a process as a professional learning tool for teachers involved in these efforts. Teachers can work together to develop a curriculum that reflects the vision and goals they have for the students in their school and their beliefs about literacy learning.

Advocating for Programs or Materials

As mentioned in chapter 2, we view literacy leaders, given their literacy expertise, as having a role in advocating for specific programs or materials. Changing materials can become a controversial issue, with teachers taking sides, some of them defending current programs while others criticize them. It can also become a political issue, especially if the process for materials selection is not well-defined or described. Therefore, any advocacy work must be undertaken collaboratively and cautiously, with administrators and teachers fully engaged in the conversation and decision-making process. While not all stakeholders may see eye-to-eye at first, creating a shared understanding of students' needs and what particular literacy programs or models can (and cannot) offer students is an important step toward aligning practices with needs.

Maintaining the Dual Focus on Individuals and the System

As a quick review, at the end of this chapter on thinking about school-wide literacy programs, we provide a few possible moves that support the dual focus of literacy leaders on individuals and the system simultaneously:

- Hold regular conversations with school and district leadership about the larger vision for school and district instructional change, focusing on change goals and action steps along the way. When formal and informal leaders develop a shared understanding of desired literacy instructional goals and reasonable action steps to achieve those goals, then coaches and teacher leaders are better positioned to see and communicate how individual work aligns (or doesn't) with the larger vision.

- Keep individuals in mind during larger vision conversations to mentally test the validity of larger school change policies and procedures. As a thought exercise and validity check, coaches might spend a few minutes during regularly scheduled conversations with school and district leaders, asking, "How does this vision of change map onto my experiences working with teachers?" Coaches might raise concerns if there appears to be too big of a gap between administrators' and teachers' expectations of change. In other words, how prepared are teachers to adjust to proposed changes? Do they have the resources and support they need to move forward? Have they been involved in discussions about the proposed changes? Literacy leaders can be very helpful in *bridging* the gap between administrators and teachers.

- Link individual practice and dilemmas to larger change initiatives, so that conversations with individual teachers are never *just* about that particular teacher's students or classroom. Effective literacy leaders are able to frame and reframe individual classroom dilemmas as part of larger school- and district-wide efforts to support students. If a teacher is concerned about ensuring that students' academic discussions are truly supporting content-area reading and writing, then a coach might use this as an opportunity to connect the teacher's concerns to larger school-wide initiatives about productive classroom talk. If such a larger initiative doesn't currently exist in the school (or the school-wide focus is slightly different), then this might be an opportunity to test whether other individuals are wondering about the same instructional moves. We are not suggesting that coaches twist every conversation to suit larger school or district goals; however, we invite coaches to consider the power of helping teachers connect individual efforts to larger group initiatives and existing supports.

- Plan carefully for meetings and conversations with teachers and leaders, so that these interactions with large groups, administrators, and individual teachers each touch briefly on the concerns of the system and the concerns of individuals. This does not mean the rigid or lockstep use of formal written agendas or discussion-based protocols as scripts; instead, just a bit of planning ahead for meetings can help coaches ensure that both system and individual concerns are represented in decision-making conversations.

Summary

In this chapter, we discussed the key roles and responsibilities of literacy leaders in the school-wide change process and the important role of the literacy leadership team. We then described the processes for leading various school-wide efforts (e.g., conducting a needs assessment, building a comprehensive literacy plan, and crafting an action plan). After describing important notions about implementation issues and sustainability, we provided information about the selection or development of instructional materials. We concluded with a brief review of the importance of the dual focus of literacy leaders: working with individuals and the system simultaneously.

Activities

1. Using the chart found in appendix A, note the ways that literacy leaders function as facilitators, leaders, designers, and advocates when involved in school-wide literacy initiatives. List some possibilities that you might consider adopting in your current position.

2. Using the Internet, locate two different needs-assessment documents (if possible, one from your own state). Compare and contrast the documents: In what ways are they similar and different? Which would be more helpful to you and your school?

3. Use figure 9.1 (page 158) and facilitate a discussion with teachers about the literacy program in your school and their perceptions of it. Use the results of the discussion to analyze the current strengths and needs of the program, as perceived by teachers. Talk with colleagues about these results and possible next steps.

4. Discuss with a colleague one of the scenarios at the beginning of chapter 9 (section titled The Role of Literacy Leaders in Improving School-Wide Literacy [page 154]) that describes a task that may be assigned to a literacy leader as an important responsibility. How would you address this leadership task? (Think about possible steps or a process.)

CHAPTER 10

Working With Families and Communities

GUIDING QUESTIONS

1. Why should literacy leaders promote family and community involvement?

2. In what ways can literacy leaders work with teachers to promote family and community involvement?

3. In what ways can funded grants support the school's literacy program? What are some key guidelines for writing grants?

As part of their needs-assessment process and newly drafted school-wide literacy action plan, Melinda and her teaching colleagues identified a great need to improve their involvement with the community, not only with families but with the agencies and organizations in the local region. The team wanted to include a number of concrete steps in their school-wide literacy action plan focused on improving school-community relationships. As the team looked to Melinda for suggestions, she felt the need to learn more about productive school-community partnering strategies. What might she recommend? Where might she turn to learn more?

In this chapter, we focus on the importance of developing strong links to the external community—families, community agencies, businesses, libraries, universities, and so on—for improving literacy learning. We address several ways that literacy leaders can facilitate efforts to build meaningful relationships with these entities. We also describe ideas for how literacy leaders can obtain external funding to support important literacy initiatives. This chapter highlights the many ways that literacy leaders who coach think as leaders, designers, facilitators, and especially advocates when working with families and communities.

The Importance of Engaging Families and Community

Research points to the positive relationships that exist between higher levels of family involvement and student achievement, motivation to learn, higher rates of graduation, and even higher secondary school grade point averages (Bryk et al., 2010; Burton, 2013; Henderson & Mapp, 2002; Leana & Pil; 2006; Paratore, Steiner, & Dougherty, 2014). This engagement is important for all students, yet, at times, family situations prohibit or limit involvement. Such factors may include language or cultural barriers, financial constraints (parents working multiple jobs or single-parent households), or negative experiences with schooling that affect families' willingness to participate in school activities (Edwards, Paratore, & Sweeney, 2014). Moreover, too frequently, traditional models of family involvement, such as volunteering at the school, chaperoning field trips, or attending PTA meetings, excludes parents who don't have the resources or time for such activities. We encourage literacy leaders to think broadly about parental involvement. Epstein et al. (2009), for example, identify six general categories of parental involvement:

1. **Parenting.** Working with parents in ways that help them establish effective home environments for learning (e.g., opportunities for conversation, availability of reading materials).

2. **Communicating with families.** Designing effective modes of home-school communication that include the use of technology.

3. **Volunteers.** Providing opportunities for volunteers in the school. Such volunteers can include family members, senior citizens, members of local service organizations, university students, and so on.

4. **Learning at home.** Developing families' ability to support student learning at home (e.g., helping with homework, reading to and with children).

5. **Decision making.** Involving families in decision making at the school (e.g., how and when to schedule events, deciding the best ways to communicate).

6. **Collaborating with the community.** Developing partnerships with various community organizations and providing services to the community (e.g., adult literacy, family literacy programs).

PUT INTO PRACTICE

Discuss with teachers the six types of family involvement just described. How does your school enact each of these? What are its strengths in this area? Weaknesses? Needs? Develop an action plan for improving family involvement by identifying two or three priority items that could serve as goals for your school over the next two years.

Next, we identify three major points to be considered in the development of effective school-community relationships and describe suggestions for implementation. We focus on strategies that can be used by literacy leaders to support teachers in their efforts to work effectively with these external communities. Many of the ideas are adapted from several sources, including the Henderson and Mapp report (2002) and the PTA's (2008) *National Standards, Goals, and Indicators for Family-School Partnerships*. For resources that provide additional and more in-depth information, see appendix B.

VOICES FROM THE FIELD

The district and community are striving to battle poverty's effects. In the district, it is a challenge to give some students a vision or goal, build relationships with the child and family system, and highlight the special skills and talents of all students. Many parents living in poverty have had negative school experiences. With generational poverty, there is a lack of exposure to the outside world. The parental and community filters of the area affect school experiences, background knowledge, and the curriculum.

—Annette Vietmeier, Director of Curriculum, Instruction, and Technology

—Tracy Toothman, Reading Recovery teacher/literacy coach

—Fran Hardisty, Reading Recovery teacher

Ideas for Developing a School Culture That Understands, Values, and Celebrates the Diversity of Its Communities

Building school capacity so all staff members in the school (e.g., teachers, administrators, clerical staff, custodians, and so on) work effectively with families and community members is a first, and challenging, step. Individual teachers in the school may work well with families, but the goal of this book is to promote both individual *and* systems-level change; that is, to create a school-wide or district-wide climate that respects, values, and appreciates cultural diversity. Literacy leaders have many opportunities to think as leaders as they work with others to develop such a culture. Suggested ideas follow:

▶ Develop awareness of the existing school culture as related to family engagement. Staff can respond to the questions in figure 10.1 individually and then, as a group, discuss responses. They can describe ways that teachers individually and as a group provide for active engagement of families. All staff members, from those who sit in the reception area to those responsible for maintaining the environment in and around the school, can be asked to participate in this activity. Based on the results, ideas for improving faculty and staff receptivity to family and community involvement can be generated.

_____ Do we welcome families into our school by greeting them with enthusiasm and providing an atmosphere that shows our support of their presence?

_____ Do we treat families with respect?

_____ Do we use the expertise of families to help us do our job more effectively?

_____ Do we use many different ways to engage families in helping their children learn?

_____ Do we as staff believe that we can improve student learning by engaging families?

Figure 10.1: Discussing family and community involvement.

Source: Adapted from 101 Ways to Create Real Family Engagement *by S. M. Constantino, 2008, Galax, VA: ENGAGE! Press.*

▶ Create a welcoming environment for those who enter the school. Possible ways of doing this include posting welcome signs, invitations to visit classrooms, and designated parking spots for guests (all in multiple languages to reflect the native languages of families and community members). The front office makes an important first impression—family members should feel welcome (e.g., pictures of student work can be posted and staff can quickly and pleasantly welcome those who enter).

▶ Provide staff with related professional learning experiences. Such learning experiences can focus on the importance of developing a school community that respects and values the diversity of the families. Such experiences can involve staff in understanding their own backgrounds and in recognizing how bias and perceptions can influence the ways in which they treat individuals. They can be asked to read and discuss materials related to working effectively with students and their families. (A possible text is Constantino's [2008] book *101 Ways to Create Real Family Engagement*.)

▶ Celebrate the diversity that exists in the school (among the staff as well as in the community). Students and teachers can design posters that identify traits of their respective cultures (e.g., foods, traditions, and activities). Family members can be invited to talk to students about their heritage, their jobs, and so on. Students at the secondary level can interview family members or write their biographies.

▶ Assist teachers in selecting materials (print and nonprint). Classroom and library materials should reflect the diversity that exists in the school and community.

As Annette, Tracy, and Fran mention in the upcoming Voices From the Field, literacy leaders have a responsibility for working with teachers to help them recognize what students *can* do, to have high expectations for all students, and to plan instruction that enhances literacy learning through recognizing and celebrating diversity in the school and community.

VOICES FROM THE FIELD

As a coach, I was challenged by all the teachers . . . [who] felt the children could not perform at the level mentioned, and we could not come to a consensus for an end-of-year grade-level proficiency expectation. We held in-depth grade-level meetings with them throughout the year, followed by individual coaching sessions with each teacher in their own room. I provided modeling experiences, team teaching, observation opportunities, and assessment training. At the end of the year, the students excelled beyond all expectations, much to the teachers' surprise. We have seen a great change in the way our teachers see the students and envision success. We still would like to see the classroom teachers have high expectations for the low-achieving students. While these children may not meet end-of-year proficiency goals, we need to expect growth and acceleration from these children. They can perform!

—Annette Vietmeier, Director of Curriculum, Instruction, and Technology

—Tracy Toothman, Reading Recovery teacher/literacy coach

—Fran Hardisty, Reading Recovery teacher

Build Two-Way Communication Channels to Enhance Family Understanding and Involvement

Make efforts to inform families and seek information from them; that is, obtain feedback that can influence various decisions about curriculum, school events, scheduling, and so on.

Find Ways to Communicate With Families

Design, with teachers, simple practices for reaching out to parents. In one school, teachers were asked to make four phone calls a month: two positive ones and two addressing needs about students about whom they have concerns. In another school, teachers selected three or four students per month and sent written certificates to families that identified these students as honor students. Each certificate had one or two sentences describing the accomplishments of that student.

Develop and use multiple means of communication to increase family involvement. Electronic communication can be especially helpful for working parents who might have limited time to visit the school. Consider the following: develop a means of using e-mail addresses for communication (with realistic expectations about responding); develop and maintain a school or district website; write and distribute electronic newsletters (secondary students could be responsible for writing these newsletters or updating classroom blogs with student work or reports of class activities); provide online access to student data (using password-protected websites). Use a classroom management app that enables parents to obtain access to feedback about the behavior of their children (e.g., ClassDojo).

Send surveys seeking family opinions about various school events or activities, to inform parents about upcoming events, and to provide information about ways that parents can support their child's learning.

Provide Activities and Programs That Support Families in Their Efforts to Guide Their Children's Learning

Continue efforts for family involvement throughout the grades. Although secondary students may not need direct assistance with their school work, proactive communication between home and school and a focus on helping students and their families think about academic achievement (and its relationship to future success) are important.

Hold sessions for families to explain important initiatives or instructional efforts and explain how they can be of assistance to schools in achieving specific goals. For example, literacy leaders might explain the standards-based curriculum that requires students to engage in high-level, critical reading and writing. However, explanations should be audience friendly, and families should be provided with specific examples that illustrate what is meant. To the degree possible, don't use educational jargon and make sure to explain what a specific term means. Parents may even be asked to participate in an activity (e.g., they can experience close reading or view examples of how students responded to writing a response to the book they read in class, with the literacy leader showing examples of good work).

Remember that open houses and parent-teacher conferences are informal learning opportunities for parents to not only engage with faculty and staff but to also engage with materials and content that their children are learning. Parents who learn something during an open house are often better prepared to help their children at home. Student-led conferences are another mechanism for connecting teachers, students, and families in meaningful ways. Read more about student-led conferences on the Teaching Channel (https://www.teachingchannel.org/blog/2013/03/20/student-led-conferences/).

Be specific with parents about educational requirements for students: How long should a homework assignment take? How can parents best support their children? How can families contact teachers? Requirements differ for various levels, of course. At the preschool level, parents may be provided with information about how they can develop the oral language of their children by holding dinnertime conversations or reading to them. At the elementary level, parents may be given suggestions for what they need to do when they listen to their child read. At the middle school level, parents may be asked to collaborate with their children on homework assignments. At the high school level, parents may attend meetings or receive information electronically about various program options and graduation requirements.

Create a family resource center where families can find information about student learning or supporting students at home. Such a place can also provide opportunities for adult learning (e.g., learning English). For example, parents in the Springfield, Massachusetts, school system who want to help their children with the college-application process, figure out how to balance the family budget, learn to knit, or even become a certified lifeguard can take a class through the district's Parent Academy (http://springfieldparentacademy.com/). The Parent Academy, a collaborative effort of community agencies, businesses, and schools, focuses its work on helping parents understand their important role as models for their children. Also, leaders of the Academy design workshops that address needs identified by parents.

Seek volunteers from the community to work in the schools. Such volunteers may tutor children, perform clerical tasks that assist teachers in their work (duplicate necessary materials, make materials for learning centers, and so on) or work informally with the teacher to manage classroom activities (e.g., putting on a classroom play or going on a field trip). In all cases, volunteers need to be prepared for the tasks they are being asked to do. For example, those tutoring students should be given specific instructions about how to use instructional materials and how to address any specific behavioral issues. Volunteer tutors often need help in understanding the culture of the school (the "dos and don'ts" for each classroom and for the school in general). In the America Reads program (Bean, Turner, & Belski, 2002), in which college students tutored students in inner city schools, we had to address questions related to the clothing tutors wore to school, teachers' approach to discipline, and ways tutors could effectively manage students who exhibited behavioral problems.

Involve Families in Decision Making and Encourage Their Participation as Partners in Efforts to Educate Their Children

Families can be partners in the educational enterprise in many different ways. Educators can consider how to involve families in decision making, so that agendas are mutually determined and beneficial (Pushor & Ruitenberg, 2005). In other words, families can be empowered to work *with* schools to develop programs that meet the needs of students. Some ideas follow:

▶ Support the development of various parent organizations or advisory councils (e.g., PTAs and PTOs, safety committees, or curriculum committees).

▶ Offer training that assists parents in learning how to serve as representatives of the school, including how to reach out to other families in the school.

▶ Provide information about school processes and events to all families, so that they are informed about school programs, challenges, and concerns.

▶ Consider involving parents in decisions about homework assignments, school priorities, and so on.

▶ Ask parents to lead informal after-school clubs or to work with teachers on such clubs (e.g., a book discussion group only for boys or girls, a Shakespeare club, or a science club).

Help Develop Teachers' Understanding of How to Talk With and Support Families

It's common for teachers to reach out to their colleagues or to literacy leaders about individual students who may be experiencing difficulties, either with behavior or with academic subjects, not only to seek advice about how to help that student, but also for advice about how to talk with the family about the student's difficulties.

In addition to providing specific advice, literacy leaders can also develop mini-workshops that focus on this topic. When meeting with families, use examples of student work to illustrate what the child can and cannot do; sit at a table next to the parent rather than behind a desk; talk only about the specific child rather than making comparisons with others in the classroom; listen more than you talk; refrain from using jargon; *show* more than you *tell* what may be difficult for the child (Bean, 2015). Various scenarios, based on actual events in the school, might be used in these mini-workshops to generate discussion. Some examples include: a parent is concerned about the instruction that her child in first grade, who knows how to read, is receiving; the science teacher is meeting with the parent of a middle school student who has not been turning in assignments and has serious difficulties responding to writing tasks.

One way to develop teachers' ability to communicate effectively with families is to work internally in ways that establish connections among all professionals in the school. Although literacy leaders might have awareness of the academic or literacy needs of specific students or families, collaborating with other school professionals, such as social workers, guidance counselors, and teachers, can be helpful in identifying more specifically the reasons students might be experiencing difficulties and the type of support needed. For example, although the literacy leader or a teacher may notice that a student has been sleeping in English class, it may take a conversation with the social worker to identify the cause (e.g., the father is unemployed, and the family is now living with cousins in an overcrowded apartment). Schools that have leadership teams, with representation of specialists from various fields, are better able to communicate with each other about specific students and their needs.

Capitalizing on Community Resources by Establishing Relationships

Educators are well aware that "student success requires attention to the needs of the whole child" (National Education Association, n.d., p. 1). Thus, we see a recent emphasis in some underserved communities on the establishment of full-service schools that provide comprehensive "wraparound" services. Such services often include health care, family engagement and learning experiences, expanded after-school learning and summer programming, and even opportunities to discuss post-secondary education and career options. Literacy leaders may find themselves advocating such services and leading efforts to develop them. (See the Coalition for Community Schools [http://www.communityschools.org] for additional information.)

Even if a district is not involved in a comprehensive effort to establish a full-service school, it must consider ways that it can involve community partners in an effort to educate the students it serves. Schools are affected by, and affect, the organizations around them. Businesses expect schools to produce employees who can communicate effectively, are able to work well with others, and have well-established work habits. Libraries can support the work of the school by housing books and resources that align with the curriculum of the school. They can also provide summer (as well as year-round) programming that supports the work of the school. Universities can learn from schools, getting a better idea of how research is affecting practice; at the same time, they can help enhance educational programs in the school by their involvement. Another important partnership is that of schools with preschool providers in the district. Given the emphasis on early childhood education, schools will need to learn more about what is provided in these contexts and, just as important, share what they are doing with their preschool partners. In the paragraphs that follow, we provide some examples of our work with schools in establishing school-community relationships. At the same time, the local context and availability of specific partners should guide school efforts to develop, maintain, and sustain such partnerships.

Working With Local Preschool Providers

Given the current emphasis on early childhood education and research evidence that points to its importance in increasing student learning (McGill-Franzen, Lanford, & Adams, 2002), schools would be well advised to partner with preschools that exist within their community. Some possible efforts follow:

▶ Literacy leaders, such as coaches or reading specialists, can meet and collaborate regularly with preschool educators and administrators (e.g., meeting with them to discuss school initiatives, expectations, and so on).

▶ Schools can invite early childhood educators to attend workshops at the school that are relevant to beginning literacy instruction. Even if only a few can attend, those who do participate can share information with their colleagues when they return to their schools.

▶ Schools can provide opportunities for early childhood teachers, kindergarten, and first-grade teachers to meet and discuss questions: What are the expectations and goals for each level? How can we make certain that students entering kindergarten or first grade are prepared to succeed? What are the goals and programs in preschools that are important to students' developmental literacy growth?

▶ Literacy leaders can volunteer to talk with parents of preschool children to describe expectations and assist early childhood teachers in discussing how parents can help support literacy and language learning.

Working With Local Libraries

As Bean (2015) describes, there are many different ways that schools can partner with the community library:

▸ Given that students, especially those from low-income families, may suffer from the lack of learning experiences during the summer (Alexander, Entwisle, & Olson, 2001), encouraging students to participate in community library offerings during the summer is important. Meeting with librarians to discuss offerings and collaboratively brainstorm ideas can also be helpful.

▸ In my community (Bean), the library, in partnership with the local Lions Club, a service organization, provides programming that encourages students to read actively (e.g., Book Walks, Read to the Dogs, Book Bingos, and Reading with the Stars, where local celebrities, including the mayor, read to children). Programs that build parents' and children's enthusiasm for reading are important to the work of the school and are even more helpful when schools encourage students to attend.

▸ In this same community, the library and the school district participate in an adult literacy program for refugee adults from Nepal who live there. The adults are transported to the library on a bus called the "Learn Bus," supplied by the school district. They attend classes at the library to improve their ability to speak and read English.

▸ In a large urban school district, the community library developed a program in which librarians went into the school to read and discuss books with third-grade children. The students learned more about the community library and its resources, and enjoyed listening to librarians read from quality books—informational and fiction. Teachers appreciated the opportunity to learn about new trade books. In fact, the books were then given to the teachers to use in their classrooms (Genest & Bean, 2007; Genest, 2014).

Working With Local Universities

School-university partnerships are win-win situations. Schools benefit from the infusion of additional personnel and ideas from university students and faculty. Universities benefit because they can place their teacher candidates or graduate students in real-life situations where they have authentic problems to solve. Further, such partnerships enable university faculty to test their ideas and beliefs and keep them apprised of current school efforts and initiatives. How often do we hear that university faculty have an "ivory-tower" mentality? Working in school settings prevents that sort of thinking and provides ongoing learning for all involved in teacher education or educational research.

For the past twenty-five years, the Reading Department at the University of Pittsburgh has placed candidates for the reading specialist certification program in local school districts. These graduate students serve as reading specialist interns who work with struggling readers and writers, with the guidance of district reading specialists and classroom teachers. This year-long internship has been invaluable: it provides support to young readers and writers, energizes classroom teachers who are exposed to new ideas from university students, and provides the university intern with a real-life experience as a reading specialist. The longevity of the program speaks to its value, and even given funding or other difficulties with implementation, it has stayed the course. We encourage school districts to seek out interested university or college partners as they move forward with various literacy initiatives.

Grant Writing: Accessing Resources From External Sources

Although some literacy leaders may not view grant writing as one of their primary responsibilities, most will have the opportunity or need to write a proposal at some point. Community organizations or foundations, for example, often provide teachers with opportunities to write mini-proposals to fund special projects (e.g., writing oral histories of senior citizens, purchasing books related to a special theme, or purchasing digital tools, such as iPads or digital cameras). The state may have special initiatives that require proposals; for example, upgrading school technology resources or hiring technology coaches to help teachers integrate technology into their instruction). Lastly, a local foundation may be eager to fund special summer programs to support young students' literacy learning. In other words, external funding can often provide the impetus for a school to implement initiatives that it can't fund itself.

Funding can jump-start important initiatives. In large school districts, there may be a dedicated district-level grant writer who can help with this sort of task; in smaller districts, school-based literacy leaders, with help from colleagues, may need to write the proposal. We provide some key ideas for proposal writing and recommend several resources that may be helpful to those involved in such efforts:

▸ Take the risk! There is a trite but true expression that says, "If you don't put your foot in the water, you won't get wet." Be willing to write and submit a proposal. Even a rejection can provide feedback that can be helpful for the next submission. And contact the funder *before* you begin writing if you have questions. Funders *want* to give away monies and, generally, they are very willing to answer questions you may have about writing the proposal, its appropriateness for your program, and so on.

▸ Work collaboratively with others in your school. Develop ideas together and share the proposal with others to get feedback about its clarity. (Is it convincing? Do you have a good idea that will intrigue the funder?)

Funders also appreciate (and sometimes require) group involvement in and support of proposals. Such proposals are much more likely to be granted funds, implemented, and sustained in schools.

▶ Find the right match for your proposal. At times, you may be writing to the state or responding to a call for proposals, but at other times you may be looking for an agency interested in your specific idea or program. Find an agency interested in that specific problem. Make your case with a local nonprofit as to why this particular idea is critical now. Create a sense of urgency, and connect your ideas clearly to teacher- and student-level outcomes.

▶ Write clearly and succinctly. A well-written proposal is a must. A proposal that contains grammatical errors, or one that is difficult to understand, will not likely be funded. It sounds simple, yet so many proposals are compiled quickly, by multiple authors, that they aren't coherent or polished. Take the extra time to polish your proposal.

▶ Follow the guidelines. Be certain that you address all elements required by the funder. Almost all funders ask for goals or objectives, a description of project activities, personnel to be involved, how the project will be evaluated, a timeline, and a budget. Some larger and lengthier processes will also include space for you to write a summary of related research or evidence supporting the idea.

One final caveat about grant-writing: while literacy leaders can play key roles in seeking and securing grant funding to jump-start literacy-focused initiatives, we want to add a cautionary note about actually funding literacy leadership work itself with grant monies. All too often, we have seen excellent literacy leadership and coaching initiatives begin with grant seed money, only to disappear completely two years later when the grant money has been spent. If grants are being sought and secured to begin a literacy coaching or literacy leadership project, we suggest that sustainability and long-term feasibility be considered up-front. One recommendation, in cases like this, is for a school or district to reevaluate and edit its current budget to create a literacy leadership or coaching role from sustainable funds (e.g., creating a coaching line item), and then seek and secure grant money to pay for other aspects of a literacy-focused initiative (e.g., books, technology, and teacher stipends for participation in literacy-focused professional development). This allows for the school or district to directly manage the literacy leadership and coaching work, assess ongoing success of the project, and not be suddenly "surprised" when grant funds come to an end and a key leader (i.e., the coach) disappears! In appendix B, we suggest additional resources for those involved in grant writing.

Summary

In this chapter, we discussed the importance and responsibilities of parents in promoting children's learning (including being a cheerleader, teacher, enforcer, and advocate). We also described ways that schools can support parents—and parents can support schools. We also highlighted the importance of local service organizations, businesses, and universities as key partners in educating students and in facilitating whole school improvement. We concluded with a section on grant writing as a source of additional and needed funds. Finally, we encouraged literacy leaders to use their creative and problem-solving skills to collaboratively write grants that address special literacy goals or initiatives.

Activities

1. Using the chart found in appendix A, note the ways that literacy leaders function as facilitators, leaders, designers, and advocates when working to establish relationships between the school and community. List some possibilities that you might consider adopting in your current position.

2. Hold meetings with other specialized professionals, such as the school psychologist, librarian, guidance counselor, or special educator to discuss ways in which they develop and establish connections between families and school. Ask these professionals to share their ideas with classroom teachers and administrators.

3. Ask teachers to write a brief scenario describing a dilemma or problem related to family-school relationships. Use these scenarios as the basis for a larger discussion, asking participants to discuss possible solutions to the identified dilemmas. Hold workshops with teachers about how to facilitate effective parent-teacher conferences. Role-play various scenarios, with teachers and literacy specialists assuming the specific roles of parents or teachers. See Bean (2015, p. 258) for several examples.

CHAPTER 11

The Literacy Leader as Lifelong Learner

GUIDING QUESTIONS

1. In what ways can literacy leaders maintain a focus on lifelong learning, while simultaneously maintaining their focus on *leading* learning for colleagues?

2. What is the knowledge base for those seeking to become literacy leaders?

3. What are some possible ways for literacy leaders to continue their journey as lifelong learners?

Melinda was settling into her new role as a literacy teacher leader, and finding it quite rewarding. At the same time, she recognized the need to learn more about the various nuances of literacy assessment, instruction, and intervention and about how to be effective in working with other adults. What should she read? With whom could she share confidences and concerns? How might she even begin determining her own areas of professional strength and areas of growth?

In this chapter, we review some of the broad categories of knowledge that literacy leaders and coaches often possess and acquire slowly over the course of their careers. While there are certain areas that even the most novice of coaches and literacy leaders should gain familiarity with, our argument throughout the chapter is that working as a literacy leader requires adopting the stance of lifelong learner. In fact, we have found that the best coaches are often those *leaders* that position themselves alongside colleagues as *co-learners*, and we expand on this notion of *leaders as learners* throughout this chapter. Finally, we end with a list of concrete strategies for maintaining a focus on learning and leading simultaneously.

A Quick Caveat About "Expertise"

If you're anything like us when we worked as teachers and coaches in schools, you probably think to yourself on a regular basis, "I'm not so sure I'm expert enough to *really* help my colleagues transform their practice and meet all students' needs." In fact, anyone who is paying attention to the growing number and range of student needs today might be living in a constant state of low-level panic, because the needs are many and the research-based answers are relatively few. In the midst of the maelstrom of standards, accountability (for students, teachers, and leaders), and day-to-day dilemmas, you as a literacy leader or coach might be singled out by colleagues as the lone hero (or sometimes villain), because, after all, *you're the expert*, right? And if you're anything like us, there is a small part of you that takes great pride in being the literacy expert. Then there is likely a larger part that might be quite nervous that all of your colleagues have gotten it wrong—you might wonder, "How can *I* really be the expert? What exactly is expected of me, after all?"

When we look across relevant books, articles, and national policy documents, we find a wide variety and large number of areas in which literacy leaders are often expected to be expert. For example, Elish-Piper and L'Allier (2011), in their study of literacy coaching, found a relationship between advanced literacy preparation of coaches and student reading performance. Documents of various professional organizations (Frost & Bean, 2006; International Reading Association, 2004; International Literacy Association, 2015) recommend that coaches have specialized knowledge about literacy learning, assessment, adult learning, leadership, and school change. At the same time, those who coach need to know how to use their expertise in ways that honor and value what others bring to the table: the principal with special leadership skills, the teachers with their knowledge of classroom instruction, the psychologist, special educator, librarian and so on. Although your knowledge of literacy, leadership skills, and experience will guide and influence you in your work with others, *how* you use your expertise will make a difference in whether there are changes in teaching and in overall school literacy learning.

The notion of expertise can sometimes create a dynamic where teachers, administrators, and parents will turn to you—the *expert*—for a quick and authoritative (perhaps technical) answer to whatever might be the most pressing literacy-related issue at hand. Of course, this can create some tension and is sometimes dangerous, for if we give in to the temptation to always provide a quick, technical answer, we run the risk of never reaching those deeper, adaptive, transformative solutions that are successful in part because they were crafted by a larger group and thus have earned widespread support. This is yet another version of the myth of "heroic leadership" that we see operating in schools, where we pin all of our hopes on a savior (a new leader, a new program, a new building) and then attribute any subsequent successes or failures to the appearance of that hero (Bradford & Cohen, 1997, 1998).

Schools rarely transform in positive, sustainable ways as the result of single heroic acts; instead, they transform slowly as a result of concerted group efforts, or what Bradford and Cohen (1997, 1998) term "post-heroic leadership," in which leaders operate as developers who support shared-responsibility teams. When faced with the expert label ourselves, we often try to reframe the conversation by saying something like, "Well, remember that true expertise resides in us as a group. Our ideas, strategies, and plans are always better when we create them together, because each of you knows your students and classrooms best." The more carefully you manage your own and your community's understanding of literacy expertise by distributing that expertise across groups of teachers, administrators, and leaders, the better positioned you will be to actually build widespread, shared understandings of what it means to effectively teach and learn literacy skills.

As we wrote in chapter 2, we strongly urge literacy leaders to adopt the mindset of advocate, wielding the expertise you have in order to improve literacy teaching and learning methods in your school. However, literacy leaders and coaches rarely make great changes in schools by leading with the "I'm the expert, so follow my advice" stance. Instead, the most powerful models we have witnessed all share a common principle: the literacy leader works as a facilitator, leading groups and teams to review, discover, adopt, adapt, and invent the practices that will work best for their particular population of students. When operating with the mindset of a leader (who, instead of dictating, is interested in building capacity and creating community) and the mindset of a facilitator (concerned with helping others have rich conversations and reflect deeply on their own work), literacy leaders are able to wield their expertise deftly. It is in this delicate space that literacy leaders are able to connect individual adult learning, to larger group learning, to the learning of the school as an organization. It is this kind of relational and facilitative expertise that we end up prizing in literacy leaders just as much as any particular literacy-content knowledge. With this caveat out of the way, we now turn to some of the other domains of knowledge necessary for literacy leaders and coaches to acquire over time in order to be truly effective.

VOICES FROM THE FIELD

Last year was a new experience for me. I was hired as a district literacy coach / state and federal programs coordinator for a rural school district. Instead of being part of a team of coaches, I was *the* coach for the district. . . . I was also responsible for their Title program, an area I had zero experience in, so I had a steep learning curve. Both parts of my position required new learning and adjustments to what I knew before. With that being said, I wouldn't trade it for the world. I love the challenges that being the district coach offers, including how to be a more effective and efficient coach, and I have learned so much about federal programming. Both positions have allowed me a district-level view into providing on-the-job professional development and federal support.

—Marsha Turner, literacy coach

Knowledge That Supports Literacy Leadership Work

As Marsha states in the preceding Voices From the Field, her role as literacy coach has changed over the years and has required a great deal of "new learning" along the way. As we have written about elsewhere (Ippolito, 2012), one way to think about the lifelong learning of an effective literacy leader is to consider the different domains of knowledge that directly relate to the work of literacy leadership and school change. We have identified seven domains of knowledge that seem most relevant for both those preparing to become reading specialists and literacy coaches (e.g., in graduate coursework) as well as for literacy leaders engaging in ongoing learning while in their professional roles. These domains certainly do not represent the totality of what a coach may want or need to know, but we would argue that a literacy leader who has a working knowledge of these seven domains is well positioned to operate as a lead-learner within almost any school setting. The seven identified domains are outlined in figure 11.1, with a few suggested resources for further study in each domain.

Domain	What It Means	Related Resources
Literacy content knowledge	Knowledge of research and practices related to reading, writing, and oral language instruction and assessment for all students prekindergarten to age sixteen, including ELs and students with learning differences (e.g., language-based disabilities, gifted students, and so on)	*The Continuum of Literacy Learning, Grades K–8: A Guide to Teaching* by I. Fountas and G. S. Pinnell, 2007, Portsmouth, NH: Heinemann *Developing Readers in the Academic Disciplines* by D. Buehl, 2011, Newark, DE: International Reading Association *Best Practices* book series by Guilford Press (search for "literacy best practices" at www.guilford.com)
Adult learning theories	Knowledge of research and practices related to how adults develop cognitively and socially over the adult life span, including constructive-developmental stages of development and how this applies to individuals and groups	*Leading Adult Learning: Supporting Adult Development in Our Schools* by E. Drago-Severson, 2009, Thousand Oaks, CA: Corwin Press *In Over Our Heads: The Mental Demands of Modern Life* (4th ed.) by R. Kegan, 1998, Cambridge, MA: Harvard University Press *Immunity to Change: How to Overcome It and Unlock the Potential in Yourself and Your Organization* by R. Kegan and L. Lahey, 2009, Boston, MA: Harvard Business School Press *An Everyone Culture: Becoming a Deliberately Developmental Organization* by R. Kegan and L. Lahey, 2016, Boston, MA: Harvard Business Review Press
School reform	Knowledge of research and practices related to how schools behave (and misbehave) as organizations, including major theories of school change and transformation	*School Reform from the Inside Out: Policy, Practice, and Performance* by R. F. Elmore, 2004, Cambridge, MA: Harvard Education Press *The Human Side of School Change: Reform, Resistance, and the Real-Life Problems of Innovation* by R. Evans, 1996, San Francisco, CA: Jossey-Bass *The Practice of Adaptive Leadership: Tools and Tactics for Changing Your Organization and the World* by R. Heifetz, A. Grashow, and M. Linsky, 2009, Boston, MA: Harvard Business Press

Figure 11.1: Seven domains of literacy leadership knowledge and skill.

continued ⟶

| Professional learning theories and practices | Knowledge of the major mechanisms, research, and practices related to effective professional development (e.g., embedded nature, effective dosage, evaluating professional development, and so on) | *Preparing Teachers for a Changing World: What Teachers Should Learn and Be Able to Do* by L. Darling-Hammond and J. Bransford, 2007, San Francisco, CA: Jossey-Bass

Leading Adult Learning: Supporting Adult Development in Our Schools by E. Drago-Severson, 2009, Thousand Oaks, CA: Corwin Press

Evaluating Professional Development by T. Guskey, 2000, Thousand Oaks, CA: Corwin Press

"What Works in Professional Development?" by T. Guskey and K. S. Yoon, 2009, *Phi Delta Kappan*, 90(7), pp. 495–500

Professional Learning in Action: Inquiry for Teachers of Literacy by V. Risko and M. E. Vogt, 2016. New York, NY: Teachers College Press |
| Facilitative leadership and group mentoring | Knowledge of research and practices related to facilitative leadership, mentoring groups, and the design and use of discussion-based protocols and learning routines | *The Facilitator's Book of Questions: Tools for Looking Together at Student and Teacher Work* by D. Allen and T. Blythe, 2004, New York, NY: Teachers College Press

Facilitating for Learning: Tools for Teacher Groups of All Kinds by D. Allen and T. Blythe, 2015, New York, NY: Teachers College Press

Leadership for Powerful Learning: A Guide for Instructional Leaders by A. Breidenstein, K. Fahey, C. Glickman, and F. Hensley, 2012, New York, NY: Teachers College Press

Facilitator's Guide to Participatory Decision-Making (3rd ed.) by S. Kaner, 2014, San Francisco, CA: Jossey-Bass

The Power of Protocols: An Educator's Guide to Better Practice (3rd ed.) by J. P. McDonald, N. Mohr, A. Dichter, and E. C. McDonald, 2003, New York, NY: Teachers College Press |

The roles of specialized literacy professionals	Knowledge of research, roles, and responsibilities among different specialized literacy professionals (e.g., reading specialists, literacy coaches, literacy coordinators or supervisors, and so on)	*The Reading Specialist: Leadership and Coaching for the Classroom, School, and Community* (3rd ed.) by R. M. Bean, 2015, New York, NY: Guilford Press *Best Practices of Literacy Leaders: Keys to School Improvement* by R. M. Bean and A. S. Dagen, 2012, New York, NY: Guilford Press *Student Achievement Through Staff Development* (3rd ed.) by B. Joyce and B. Showers, 2002, Alexandria, VA: ASCD *Research Brief: The Multiple Roles of Specialized Literacy Professionals* by International Literary Association, 2015, Newark, DE: Author
Coaching methods	Knowledge of research and practices that support literacy coaches' direct work with teachers (e.g., individual coaching, group coaching, data coaching, cognitive coaching, establishing cycles of inquiry, and so on)	*The Reading Specialist: Leadership and Coaching for the Classroom, School, and Community* (3rd ed.) by R. M. Bean, 2015, New York, NY: Guilford Press *The Common Core Coaching Book: Strategies to Help Teachers Address the K–5 ELA Standards* by L. Elish-Piper and S. L'Allier, 2014, New York, NY: Guilford Press *Collaborative Coaching for Disciplinary Literacy: Strategies to Support Teachers in Grades 6–12* by L. Elish-Piper, S. L'Allier, M. Manderino, and P. D. Domenico, 2016, New York, NY: Guilford Press *The Literacy Coach's Handbook: A Guide to Research-Based Practice* (2nd ed.) by S. Walpole and M. C. McKenna, 2012, New York, NY: Guilford Press *Differentiated Literacy Coaching: Scaffolding for Student and Teacher Success* by M. C. Moran, 2007, Alexandria, VA: ASCD

Source: Adapted from Ippolito (2012). These resources are just a few that we have used over time, and the list is by no means exhaustive.

*Visit **www.learningsciences.com/bookresources** to download a reproducible version of this figure.*

While at first it might seem overwhelming to read over these domains and consider your own degree of familiarity and comfort with each, remember that these domains represent a wide range of knowledge and skills that are best acquired over the length of a professional career. A graduate preparation program or coaching endorsement program might do well to touch on each of these domains lightly, but deep expertise in each will only come from practice in a professional role over time and adoption of the lifelong learner stance. Perhaps the four domains that have most relevance to those early in their careers are literacy content knowledge, the roles of reading professionals, coaching methods, and facilitative leadership. As literacy leaders continue their own personal and professional plan for growth, we would recommend delving deeper into adult learning, professional development, group mentoring, and school reform theories and practices. However, we fully acknowledge that each literacy leader will likely

 walk a slightly different path. The key, ultimately, is to continually identify professional learning goals and then spend some time each academic year investigating (ideally as part of a network of teachers or literacy leaders) the targeted domain. We highlight a few practical ways to manage the professional learning process in the paragraphs that follow.

Keep Appraised of National and State Standards for Reading Professionals and Literacy Instruction

This includes position statements on the work of reading specialists and literacy coaches (International Literacy Association, 2015), recent surveys of professionals holding these positions, and instructional standards around which literacy leadership work will focus.

Form a Network of Colleagues With Whom You Set and Explore Professional Learning Goals

In the national survey of specialized literacy professionals (Bean et al., 2015), respondents indicated that networking with those who held similar positions was most beneficial as a means of ongoing learning. Whether talking with a few colleagues once a month as part of an after-school study group, connecting with colleagues with similar roles across the district on a monthly basis, or meeting with colleagues farther afield on a monthly online webinar or participating in blogs, it is important to be able to reflect on and discuss professional dilemmas and successes with colleagues (see Messina [2013] for a rich description of just such a network of coaches and secondary teachers across a district that formed a "disciplinary literacy network").

Some literacy leaders have indicated that they appreciated being assigned to a mentor coach who would work with them as they began their role in the school. In the upcoming Voices From the Field, Christina Steinbacher-Reed discusses how important an external coach or consultant was to her development as a coach.

VOICES FROM THE FIELD

During our consultant's first visits, I would shadow her while she coached teachers. This included observing her doing in-class demos, co-planning, and building relationships. Eventually, I would engage in coaching activities while the consultant observed me and provided feedback. This type of job-embedded support was the single most important layer of support that I received as a coach. Not only did it provide me with essential coaching strategies, it also allowed me to understand what it felt like to be coached. It was important for me to feel the same anxiety, vulnerability, trust, and success that many teachers would experience when working with a coach.

—Christina Steinbacher-Reed, literacy coach

Keep a Professional Reflective Log, Journal, or Blog

Although this is one of the toughest pieces of advice to follow (at least for us), those literacy leaders who take the time to regularly write about and reflect on their work, dilemmas, insights, and successes find themselves better equipped to respond effectively to future professional challenges. The brief Voices From the Field excerpts scattered throughout this book, as well as the case examples in chapter 12, highlight the insights of literacy leaders in schools as they reflect on their own evolution as literacy leaders. One of the primary paths to improvement is self-reflection, and we find that regular reflective writing about your own work helps enormously. Consider reading the work of literacy leaders who blog, such as Dave Stuart Jr. (www.davestuartjr.com), Kasey Kiehl (middleschoolteacherto literacycoach.blogspot.com), Tim Shanahan (www.shanahanonliteracy.com), or Jan Burkins and Kim Yaris (www.burkinsandyaris.com/blog/). Each of these literacy leaders works at different levels, but each shares wonderful strategies and research while modeling self-reflection through regular blogging.

Join Literacy-Focused and Professional Learning–Focused Professional Organizations

One of the easiest and most effective ways to stay up-to-date regarding emerging literacy research and practices is to join a national and/or state professional organization and read their regular publications as well as attend their conferences. Suggestions of such professional organizations follow:

- The International Literacy Association (formerly the International Reading Association) produces several highly respected journals that many literacy leaders have come to rely on: *The Reading Teacher*, *The Journal of Adolescent and Adult Literacy*, and *Reading Research Quarterly*.

- State-level affiliates (e.g., Keystone State Reading Association, the Massachusetts Reading Association, and so on) offer regular publications and conferences. Both provide opportunities for colleagues in schools or districts to learn together.

- The National Council of Teachers of English is a one-stop shopping center for everything from lesson plans and journals (such as *Language Arts*) to research summaries, standards, position statements, and timely policy analyses.

- Other professional learning–focused organizations, such as the School Reform Initiative (with its excellent annual "Winter Meeting"), and Learning Forward, which focuses exclusively on supporting high-quality professional learning for educators, are excellent choices for broadening and deepening your professional knowledge and network.

Read a Variety of Materials

Balance your investigations of popular press, research journals, and online offerings, perhaps seeking to read—or skim—one from each category every month (or at whatever interval makes sense for you). Just as students need to consume a "balanced diet" of literary and informational text, along with easy readers and more complex text, we suggest that literacy leaders balance their diet of professional texts (Dave Stuart Jr. has several good tips about how to do this: www.davestuartjr.com/professional -reading and www.davestuartjr.com/how-to-read).

Don't double-down on dense research articles and then grow quickly jaded about how to implement research findings. Try to find one or two research pieces that fit your targeted professional learning goals, then branch out to shorter, digestible pieces from sources such as *Phi Delta Kappan*, *Ed Leadership*, *Ed Week*, or Edutopia.com. Many of these publications can be read digitally, which is often our preference for skimming and saving our favorite articles quickly into folders associated with different literacy domains (e.g., beginning reading, writing, discussion, comprehension strategies, and so on).

Stay Informed of Policy Changes on All Levels

Keep apprised of local, state, and national policies that affect curriculum, instruction, and school programming. Such policies may also affect your current position!

The webinars and papers of the National Alliance for Excellent Education (http://all4ed.org) are quite helpful, as they address national topics of importance (e.g., CCSS, reforming high school instruction, and digital learning). They often host webinars with nationally known speakers addressing these various topics. These webinars provide literacy leaders with an opportunity to obtain up-to-date information about topics that may affect their schools. One of their major foci is addressing ways to improve high school instruction, often through the integration of disciplinary literacy strategies into content-area instruction.

Most importantly, remember the "lifelong" component of the lifelong learner recommendation. We cannot overstate the point that it could take a lifetime to master just one of the aforementioned domains in figure 11.1 (page 191), let alone all seven! Focus on becoming an *expert learner*, and the content expertise will naturally follow.

Self-Assessments: Possibilities and Pitfalls

As a lifelong learner in the realm of literacy leadership, it can be invaluable to look at a few different rubrics and frameworks that might serve as self-assessments. Note that this isn't about conducting a formal evaluation; rather, this is about literacy leaders and those who coach better understanding where they are in their own work and career paths and determining what they want or need to learn next. The challenge here, of course, is that because the roles of literacy professionals are often debated and in flux (Bean, et al., 2015; Dole, 2004; ILA, 2015; Quatroche, Bean, & Hamilton, 2001), existing self-assessments may or may not directly apply to your specific role. Moreover, much like the seven domains of knowledge presented in figure 11.1, existing self-assessments might simply overwhelm or intimidate those new to their roles.

Thus, we have created a quick self-assessment rubric that we call Adopting a Coaching Mindset (see figure 11.2, page 198). The tool is designed as a quick screening tool to help coaches think about their strengths in the various domains shared across this book, with the eighteen items "mapped" onto those domains. Responses to the items can help those who coach think about areas of strength as well as future needs. The tool can also be useful as a means of developing learning experiences for groups of coaches in a district or school.

Domain	Emerging	Developing	Proficient
Literacy Content Knowledge 1. Advanced, strong knowledge of literacy instruction (e.g., reading specialist certification, coaching program endorsement, and so on) 2. Advanced, intensive knowledge of literacy assessment 3. Ability to work with teachers to solve design problems related to instruction for students			
Adult Learning 4. Understanding of how adults learn (e.g., need for meaningful, authentic experiences) 5. Understand that adults differ in how they make meaning and learn (e.g., instrumental, socializing, and self-authoring ways of knowing) 6. Ability to apply knowledge of adult learning to develop professional learning experiences			
School Reform 7. Understanding of school reform models that indicate the need for both top-down and bottom-up efforts 8. Understanding of the importance of collaborative efforts to reform or remodel schools 9. Understanding of how to assist in developing conditions so the school is a place of learning for students and teachers			

Professional Learning			
10. Understanding of research findings about effective professional learning (e.g., authentic, job-embedded, and long-term)			
11. Ability to use knowledge to lead, facilitate, and evaluate effective professional learning experiences in schools			
Facilitative Leadership			
12. Understanding of research findings about importance of shared leadership in schools			
13. Ability to facilitate in ways that develop capacity of others to lead and participate collaboratively in individual and school change efforts			
Roles of Literacy Professionals			
14. Understanding of the various ways to support student learning (e.g., assisting with analyzing assessment, suggesting instructional strategies, serving as an advocate, and so on)			
15. Understanding of the various ways to support teacher learning (e.g., serving as a resource, coaching, facilitating teacher leadership, being an advocate, and so on)			
16. Understanding of and ability to work effectively in developing school-community partnerships			

Figure 11.2: Adopting a coaching mindset—self-assessment of coaching skills, knowledge, and dispositions.

continued →

Coaching Methods			
17. Understanding of how to work effectively with individual teachers			
18. Understanding of how to work effectively with groups of teachers (small and large)			
Overall assessment of myself as a coach:			
Based on this self-assessment, what are my current strengths?			
Current needs?			
What are my short-term improvement goals? How can I best achieve these goals?			
What are my long-term goals? How can I best achieve these goals?			

*Visit **www.learningsciences.com/bookresources** to download a reproducible version of this figure.*

In addition to our self-assessment tool in figure 11.2, we share a few additional self-assessment tools in the following list. We have used each of these tools with literacy leaders and coaches, and each has its own strengths and weaknesses. Often, such assessments can be used by groups of literacy leaders who can complete them individually and then discuss with others (in pairs or small groups) their responses to specific items, addressing the questions: What do I see as my strengths? My needs? What are my goals for improvement, and what can I do to achieve them? Any collective goals that we would like to focus on? The following resources can help coaches begin to answer these questions:

- **Literacy coach self-assessment tools from the Literacy Coaching Clearinghouse.** Two self-assessment tools, one for elementary coaches and one for secondary coaches, were sponsored by the Carnegie Foundation and the Literacy Coaching Clearinghouse, which in turn was created through a partnership of the then International Reading Association and the National Council of Teachers of English (NCTE). Full disclosure, we had a small hand in the creation of the tools, and they are not only quite lengthy and comprehensive, but they can also seem a bit overwhelming (with regard to the number of areas of mastery assumed). Yet, we have used these with pre-service and in-service literacy leaders, simply as a quick way of mapping the territory of literacy leadership knowledge and setting some personal and professional learning goals. If you are able to look past the sheer number of expected outcomes and focus more on the broad categories of knowledge, you may find these quite helpful. The tools are available (respectively) at:

  - Self-Assessment for Elementary Literacy Coaches—www .literacycoachingonline.org/briefs/tools/self_assessment_for _elem_lit_coaches.pdf

  - Self-Assessment for Middle and High School Literacy Coaches—www.literacycoachingonline.org/library/resources /self-assessmentformshsliteracycoaches.attachment/attachment /selfassessmentPrint.pdf

- **Teacher Leader Self-Assessment from the Center for Strengthening the Teaching Profession.** The self-assessment tool developed by this group for assessing skills, knowledge, and dispositions of teacher leaders is organized into five categories: working with adult learners, collaborative work, communication, knowledge of content and pedagogy, and systems thinking. The tool identifies key questions related to teacher leadership and would provide literacy leaders with a comprehensive assessment of their own competencies. The tool could be used at the beginning of a coaching initiative and then again at the middle and end of the year. While we are not suggesting formal evaluations, if one is required, this tool could also be used as the beginning template for designing a coaching evaluation system. A coach- and principal-modified self-assessment could be completed individually by both the literacy leader and principal and results discussed. The original tool can be found at http://cstp-wa.org/cstp2013/wp-content /uploads/2013/11/CSTP_self_assessment.pdf.

- **Standards for Reading Professionals (revised 2010).** These standards, revised and re-released every handful of years, are a good source of information about expectations for those serving as reading specialists, literacy coaches, or principals. The standards are available at www. literacyworldwide.org/get-resources/standards/standards-for-reading -professionals.

- **Standards for Middle and High School Literacy Coaches.** These standards were created in 2006 to help guide the preparation and support of secondary literacy coaches, a relatively new role at the time. While the document was designed as a set of standards and not explicitly as a self-assessment tool, the document does provide another way for literacy leaders at secondary levels to consider the scope and efficacy of their work. Again, just as with the self-assessment tools noted previously, readers should not let themselves get overwhelmed by the number of roles and areas of expertise suggested by these standards. If you find yourself reading them and asking, "Who are the superhumans who can actually fulfill these roles?" then you're not alone. Just remember that these were written with an ideal coach in mind, and they do not always (or even often) reflect the reality of the training or current roles coaches play. The standards are available at www.ncte.org/library/NCTEFiles /Resources/Positions/coaching_standards.pdf.

- **Disciplinary Literacy Professional Learning and Coaching Standards.** These standards were originally created for the Orange County, California, Department of Education, as a way of describing the professional learning work of coaches, teacher leaders, and groups of teachers in Orange County schools who were undertaking disciplinary literacy professional learning work. The premise of these standards is that coaching toward disciplinary literacy instruction may require a slightly different set of literacy leadership moves. Thus, the resulting document describes what disciplinary literacy coaching and professional learning work might look like at three different points in time, with notes about the roles of coaches and the roles of groups of teachers at each time point. The standards were influenced heavily by the Teacher Leader Model Standards (www.teacherleaderstandards.org/), the Standards for Reading Professionals (see preceding bullet), the Standards for Middle and High School Literacy Coaches (see the preceding bullet), and *Continuum of Mentoring Practice* (www.scsvntp.com/uploads/3/7/3/5/37354959 /complete_mentor_continuum.pdf). Again, like the other sets of standards noted here, these are not meant to be used in an evaluative manner; however, they could be used effectively by coaches at the secondary level to define goals and target next steps. The *Disciplinary Literacy Professional Learning and Coaching Standards* are available at http://adlitpd.org/2011-2.

Each of these documents and tools are merely beginning places for literacy leaders to consider their current knowledge and skill base as well as which domains might be the focus of targeted future inquiry. The real power in any of this work is in the selection of a focus area for personal and professional growth and the adherence to a system (e.g., monthly study groups, discussions with a coaching network, weekly journaling, and so on) by which you plan to grow your literacy leadership toolbox.

A Quick Reminder About the Many Pathways to Becoming an Effective Coach

As mentioned in chapter 1, although reading specialist certification is a key pathway to coaching, and we encourage all those becoming or working as literacy leaders to enroll in such a program, we recognize there are other roads to becoming an effective coach. This is especially true at the secondary level, where literacy leaders most frequently work with content-area teachers who have different responsibilities and backgrounds from teachers at the elementary level. In some schools, excellent content-area teachers can be identified as potential coaches and then provided with experiences that build their literacy knowledge as well as coaching expertise. Note that literacy, in our view, is still at the core of improving student learning in the academic disciplines. For a description of a state-wide coaching initiative and the professional learning experiences provided for coaches, see the Pennsylvania Institute for Instructional Coaching (PIIC) case in chapter 12. Coaches in this initiative receive rich, in-depth experiences with literacy based on the Penn Literacy Framework (www. gse.upenn.edu/pln).

A Final Note About Our Own Coaching Habits of Mind

As we conclude this chapter about coaches and literacy leaders as lifelong learners, we return to the four major habits of mind that we introduced in chapter 2: thinking like a leader, facilitator, designer, and advocate. Again, as a literacy leader (regardless of your specific role), the degree to which you can balance thinking and working like a leader, facilitator, designer, and advocate could determine both your professional success and job satisfaction. In closing, we list a few guiding questions for self-reflection related to these habits of mind, which literacy leaders might use as a quick self-check:

- ▸ In what ways have you served as a *leader*, working collaboratively with others to develop a comprehensive vision of literacy and a plan that enhances quality teaching and student literacy learning?

- ▸ In what ways have you, as a *facilitator*, provided colleagues with low-risk opportunities to be co-learners, to reflect on their practices with you and others? What might you do in the future?

- ▸ In what ways have you served as a *designer*, helping teachers adopt a design mindset and recognize that there are few "right" answers and that productive problem solving requires technical and adaptive thinking?

- ▸ In what ways have you served as an *advocate* for students, teachers, community partnerships, specific practices, models, and programs?

Summary

In this chapter, we discussed ways that literacy leaders can maintain a focus on life-long learning, reflected on the term "expert," and the danger of being viewed as the "superhero" in the school. We described seven domains that serve as a knowledge-base framework for those who are literacy leaders. In the next section, we described activities for ongoing learning and reiterated our stance that all literacy leaders, regardless of their pathways into coaching, must have the skills, knowledge, and dispositions described in the seven domains of our knowledge-base framework if they are to be effective in their roles.

Activities

1. Review the reflective chart in appendix A that you have been referring to throughout this book. Use the four aforementioned questions as a self-reflective tool. In what ways have you changed as you have read

and thought about the chapters in this book? In what ways are you thinking differently? Perhaps do a bit of self-reflective writing, using one of our favorite end-of-session prompts: "I used to think . . . And now I think . . . "

2. Complete the self-assessment screening tool in figure 11.2 (page 199), and answer the questions at the bottom of the protocol. Think about how you might be able to obtain the professional learning experiences that would help you become better at your role.

3. Check out one of the blogs, identified in the Keep a Professional Reflective Log, Journal, or Blog (page 195) section of this chapter. How do these literacy leaders reflect on their work and the larger field of literacy teaching and learning? Any implications for your own work, or your own reflective writing about your roles?

4. Read the case in chapter 12 about the Pennsylvania Institute for Instructional Coaching. What questions does it bring to mind about the preparation of coaches? About the coaching model? The framework used to develop literacy knowledge and understanding?

CHAPTER 12

Coaching Cases: Stories of Coaches and Coaching

GUIDING QUESTIONS

1. In what ways do the stories in this chapter connect to the work you do? What lessons can you learn from the stories?

2. What similarities and differences are there in these stories (e.g., the way that coaching was operationalized, preparation of coaches)?

3. In what ways are all those who tell their stories "literacy leaders"?

We have met many successful coaches who have talked with us about their work and the ways in which they have supported and coached educators in their schools. Their voices are heard in the short snippets provided throughout the book. Now, in this chapter, we include four longer stories of coaches and coaching initiatives, each one demonstrating a different aspect of literacy leadership, but none "finished"—they are all ongoing and continually evolving. Like the Voices From the Field segments, the stories that follow are either told in the literacy leaders' own words or as related to us by the coaches themselves. By providing these stories, we hope readers will again note the many different pathways into coaching, the various ways in which coaches function, and the evolution of coaching over time. Before each case narrative, we provide several questions to help readers consider what they can learn by reading these stories.

Case 1: The Evolution of a Coach

Source: Christina Steinbacher-Reed, coordinator of professional learning and curriculum development, Intermediate Unit 17, Williamsport, Pennsylvania

In the first case, Christina Steinbacher-Reed talks about her journey, beginning as a new coach in a single school and moving to a supervisory role in which she supported the work of multiple coaches. Currently, she serves as an external coach for a technical support unit responsible for providing resources and professional learning to schools in the northeastern region of Pennsylvania.

QUESTIONS TO PONDER

1. What were the greatest challenges for Christina in her first coaching position?

2. Why does Christina think that external coaches can be helpful to school districts or schools?

3. After reading about Christina and her views about coaching, what do you see as three important take-aways?

During the past fifteen years, I have served as a literacy leader responsible for coaching, but in different contexts. In the paragraphs that follow, I describe my journey, what I have learned, and how I have evolved as a coach.

School-Based Coach (2003–2005)

I became an instructional coach in 2003 in a school district plagued by generational poverty and labeled as a "failing school district." Prior to becoming an instructional coach, I had been an elementary classroom teacher in a high-performing, suburban school district. Going into this new position, I only had five years of successful teaching experience under my belt coupled with graduate work in school leadership. I tried to convince myself that I was ready for such a position—but to be honest, I was not. I was terrified and consumed with self-doubt. The work awaiting me as a coach in a high-needs district was in stark contrast to my teaching experience.

I will never forget the lump in my throat on my first day. The school was nestled in the center of the most violent community housing development in the city. When I pulled into the parking lot, I noticed the tall metal fence that enclosed the lot and wondered if it would eventually make me feel safe—because at that moment, I felt vulnerable. I was scared of the uncertainty that lay ahead of me. The uncertainty of not knowing simple things like where to find the bathroom or how to find that secret stash of chart paper when you need it. The uncertainty of not knowing the important things, like a single student or a single teacher—or how to be a successful coach in one of the lowest-performing schools in the state.

When I walked through those doors and saw the students, I was quickly reminded that I did know some important things. I knew how to immediately connect with kids, and I knew how to build relationships with teachers. So that's what I did, and it got me through week one. Then I wondered, "What should I do for the next forty-four weeks?" Here's what I learned *not* to do:

- Do not give a teacher who expresses frustration with classroom management an article titled "Classroom Management for Balanced Literacy." (That resulted in tears.)

- Do not say, "I'm here to help you." (That resulted in a flood of copy requests.)

- Do not have your office anywhere near the principal's office. (That resulted in many thinking I was an administrator and the administrator constantly asking me to proof his parent letters.)

- Do not assume that teachers are waiting for you with open arms, eager and ready to expose all of their vulnerabilities. (That results in delusional thinking.)

While I was quickly learning what *not* to do, the fact remained that I needed to know what *to* do. Thankfully, I had a network of internal and external support. Our district team of ten coaches met once a month to work with an external consultant on developing coaching skills and knowledge. This was also a time to build strong partnerships with other internal coaches who understood the complexities and challenges of working in a high-needs district. Our external consultants worked individually with coaches at our school two to four times a month for the specific purpose of "coaching" coaches.

A Change in Direction

Having survived my first year, I started feeling like I was finally figuring out this coaching thing. I was building trusting relationships and designing my coaching based on teachers' individual needs. Then I was anointed a Reading First coach, and it seemed like everything changed. This transition was first described to me by my administration as "no big deal; just need to change the title for funding purposes." I quickly learned that, as a recipient of over six million dollars in federal funding, Reading First was *indeed* a big deal.

In that first year of Reading First, I was supposed to become an expert in DIBELS (the Dynamic Indicators of Basic Early Literacy Skills assessment), uninterrupted ninety-minute reading blocks, the five essential elements of reading, researched-based core reading programs, progress monitoring, and effective interventions. There was no longer time to work with our external consultants, as they did not meet the Reading First criteria of being "scientifically based," so out went my job-embedded coaching support. Instead, I was assigned a "technical assistant," who asked to see my logs and wanted to visit classrooms with me to complete "fidelity checklists." During that year, my role significantly shifted from that of a confidential coach to a Reading First compliance officer. I was frustrated with my new role, and so were our teachers. They were used to me meeting them where they were at, and now my approach prioritized the grant's needs over their needs.

Looking back on those two years, I now realize that my first year of coaching was based on a purely responsive model, while my second year as a coach I was asked to assume a very directive approach to coaching. My first year of responsive coaching provided me with an opportunity to really get to know the individual needs of teachers. The challenge of that first year was that while I felt like I met the individual needs of some teachers, I didn't feel like I was impacting the system. For example, some teachers improved in their guided reading instruction while others enhanced their writing workshop. But I was left wondering how random acts of improvement would ever result in systemic reform.

By the end of my second year, I started to notice that my most successful coaching experiences were when I was intentional about my coaching. Knowing when to use which approach, and being aware of why I was using that approach, made all the difference. Oftentimes, it wasn't one approach over the other but rather a balance of both responsive and directive coaching. My first two years of coaching were the most difficult years of my career, but I embraced those challenges as opportunities to deepen my understanding and craft of coaching. And as a result, those two years were filled with some of the most rewarding experiences to date.

I often think back to my first day when I was sitting in the fenced-in parking lot, scared of the uncertainties. I now have over ten years of coaching experience to draw from, and this is what I know—there will be uncertainties. The truth is, coaching is filled with uncertainties—we never quite know what approach will work with any given teacher at any given time. Skilled coaches have a repertoire of skills and strategies that can balance the needs of individuals with the needs of the system.

Supervisor of Coaches (2006–2010)

In 2006, I transitioned from a coaching role into an administrative role, where I was responsible for supervising a team of ten district coaches. Supervising coaches came with its own set of challenges and rewards. One of the first challenges that I experienced was that our team was not "walking the walk" when it came to coaching. We focused so much attention on coaching our teachers that we neglected our own coaching needs. One of my first challenges of supervising coaches was to build a system in which coaches would have opportunities to coach each other.

When entering into a "coach-the-coach" partnership, I quickly realized that coaches felt the same level of vulnerability as our teachers. This process also uncovered some hard truths about our coaching model—we didn't all share the same beliefs about effective coaching. I committed to creating a system of professional learning for our coaches that was responsive to their individual needs while also trying to adhere to established criteria of best practices for coaches. Although we were still in the midst of our Reading First grant, the coaching guidelines of the grant did not align with our district philosophy on coaching. We believed that our coaching should reflect a balanced approach that would provide us with opportunities to be both directive and responsive. I focused much of my work that year in working with coaches to develop self-assessment tools, a differentiated supervision model, lab classrooms, and criteria for effective coaching. I felt that as a team, we were building a shared mental model of effective coaching.

In my last year as supervisor, our grant had expired, and the district did not have the funding to sustain full-time coaches. I desperately wished that I had some solid evidence to demonstrate the impact that coaches had on our system. I wanted the board to have tangible evidence, so it could know what would be eliminated. I doubt it would have saved coaching positions, but it would have at least provided evidence of their impact.

My experiences as a coaching supervisor provided me with a systems perspective on coaching. Over time, I realized the value of a more systemic approach to coaching. I began understanding that a strategic approach to coaching could yield a greater return to a system. One of my mentors often reminded me, "If you put a good person in a bad system, the system will win every time." The work I do now focuses on building good systems and allowing that system to develop the capacity of the individual.

External Coach (2010–2015)

Currently, I work as a coordinator for professional learning and curriculum development. In this role, I have the opportunity to serve as an external coach to a number of districts across our state. School districts contract with me for a specific number of days to provide job-embedded instructional coaching in a very specific strategy. At first I found this coaching model to be incredibly challenging, because I was walking into a coaching partnership "cold." I did not have preexisting relationships with the teachers or administrators, and I had very limited experience with their school system. I wondered how I could possibly be effective without having time to build trusting relationships. To my surprise, I discovered that many of the challenges faced by external coaches may also contribute to successful coaching partnerships:

- **Objectivity.** Not having preexisting relationships with staff makes it easier for me to enter partnerships with total objectivity. My only focus is to work with that teacher in that moment. I am removed from the school politics that can pose challenges for school-based coaches.

- **Credibility.** Because we do not have any shared history, teachers need to know quickly that I have something of value to offer. Teachers do not care about my degrees and certifications, and rightly so. We do not have any shared history, so I need to build instant credibility. To do this, I build modeling or demonstration lessons into one of my first school visits.

- **Focus.** Administrators and teachers hold our time together sacred. Schedules are made months in advance, substitutes are secured, and there are no interruptions. I have the luxury of participating in highly focused and engaging coaching activities.

External coaching can add value to a system only if the purpose is to create sustainable school improvement. With this goal in mind, districts should not be dependent on external coaches. Instead, external coaches and school teams need to work together to determine how the coach's impact will improve the system, not just individuals. The ultimate goal of external coaching is that the district has the internal capacity to sustain the improvements over time.

Case 2: Learning, Leading Learning, and Enacting Disciplinary Literacy at Brookline High School

Source: Jenee Ramos, Kate Leslie, and Astrid Allen, Brookline High School, Brookline, Massachusetts

In this second case, Jenee Ramos, Kate Leslie, and Astrid Allen, teacher leaders at Brookline High School in Brookline, Massachusetts, discuss their literacy leadership efforts to equip teachers across departments with the knowledge and skills needed to help students read more effectively in their content-area subjects. They focus on their role as "lead learners."

QUESTIONS TO PONDER

1. In what ways does the development of this specific initiative align well with research findings about effective professional learning?

2. What do you view as the strengths of this initiative to implement disciplinary literacy instruction at the high school level?

3. In what ways do these teacher leaders exhibit the mindsets of thinking like a leader, a facilitator, a designer, and an advocate?

In 2011, a small group of teachers at Brookline High School in Brookline, Massachusetts, came together to craft a new literacy plan to support our most struggling students. We had found that a sizable number of students were struggling to read the textbooks, manuals, primary sources, and literature that formed the basis of the curriculum at the high school. Efforts to improve reading and comprehension skills in English classes were not sufficient. The skills students needed to read a novel for American literature class were not the same as the skills needed to understand a physics textbook. We realized that what was needed was a multipronged approach in which teachers would teach literacy skills in every content-area classroom, so that students could learn the specific tools that they needed to tackle discipline-specific texts. This need resulted in the creation of Brookline's CRI (Content-area Reading Initiative)—a disciplinary literacy project aimed at equipping teachers in all departments with the knowledge and skills needed to help students read more effectively in our classes. This initiative currently involves thirty-six teachers from seven specific departments: world languages, social studies, English, math, science, the library, and special education.

This project was conceived of as a joint venture, a collaboration among teachers, teacher leaders (i.e., literacy leaders and coaches), administrators, and outside university consultants to better support the roughly 150 Brookline High School teachers in improving disciplinary literacy teaching and learning. From the very beginning, however, the heart of the project has been the work of elected teacher leaders. With the financial support of three independent funders—the Brookline High School 21st Century Fund, the Brookline Education Foundation, and the public schools of Brookline—we were able to provide small stipends and a one-course release for six teacher leaders across the four years of the project. In the first two years of the project, Jenee Ramos, Kate Leslie, and Astrid Allen served as teacher leaders working respectively with English, social studies, and world languages colleagues. In years three and four of the project, new teacher leaders were elected to work with math, science, and special education teachers. In this brief case, we (Jenee, Kate, and Astrid) share some of the successes and challenges we have faced working as facilitators and coaches within a high school disciplinary literacy project. Our hope is that other schools will be inspired by our story and implement similar programs.

A Disciplinary Literacy Program Led by Teacher Leaders

We started the CRI project in the spring of 2012. Department heads, our university partners, and our project design group then worked together to recruit teams of teachers from the English, social studies, and world languages departments to be the first groups to participate in CRI. Six teachers were selected for each departmental team, including us as team leaders. Because of the critical nature of literacy leadership to the success of the project, the teacher leader positions were created to facilitate the work of each departmental team, with one position designed also as a project director to oversee the whole initiative.

Our colleagues selected the three of us as team leaders for our departments because we initiated the team-forming efforts; we also expressed great enthusiasm about disciplinary literacy learning, and we each had taken on various leadership roles in the past. The team leader was to effectively and efficiently manage, lead, and inspire the team, in addition to recording and disseminating curricula, assessments, and instructional techniques designed by the departmental team to the departments, school, and school community. Importantly, everyone involved believed that we, as content-area classroom teachers, would serve best as teacher leaders and coaches within the project because of our deep background knowledge in our disciplines. With varying amounts of experience in the field of literacy, we would also serve as "lead learners" in the project, not literacy experts positioned to tell our colleagues what to do. Instead, we would be positioned as facilitators of collaborative inquiry.

Since so many of us lacked background in foundational and disciplinary literacy, the first step of CRI was to hold a five-day summer institute designed to help teachers and us learn more about vocabulary acquisition, reading comprehension, reading assessment, and also content-specific literacy skills. Our university partners, Jacy Ippolito (Salem State University) and Christina Dobbs (Boston University), conducted this institute. By the end of the five days, all departmental teams had chosen a literacy focus area to begin the academic year and had a basic plan for skills teachers hoped to incorporate into their lessons, starting in September.

CRI work continued during the school year, because the three teams made use of one hour of paid time each week to meet and collaborate, facilitated by the team leader. We found it critical that CRI meeting time was dedicated only to our content literacy work in and outside of the classroom; the meetings were not part of broader collaboration efforts at the high school. This promise ensured that team leaders could direct the course of meetings without worrying about other obligations or agendas and team members could dedicate themselves completely to the CRI work.

Departmental teams also had opportunities to collaborate with each other during "days away" throughout the school year. Four times a year, teachers received coverage for their classes and attended day-long workshops away from the school campus. These days gave departmental teams a chance to take strategic stock of new learning, synthesize student data, and recommend adjustments to instruction. It also allowed teams the vital practice of participating in cross-disciplinary conversations and activities.

The structure of the CRI program is part of what made this initiative so successful. Teachers had adequate time to dedicate to new learning, collaborating with colleagues, and sharing the work. Therefore, CRI has led to big changes in the way that the English, social studies, and world languages departments at Brookline High School teach literacy skills. In the next section, we outline more specifically our evolving roles as teacher leaders in disciplinary literacy.

The Evolution of Our Roles as Teacher Leaders

We have been particularly amazed by the ways in which our comfort and proficiency as teacher leaders has grown over the course of CRI. All three of us initially experienced some anxiety and apprehension about our roles: Would our colleagues expect us to be experts at teaching literacy? How would we simultaneously manage our teams and make changes in our respective teaching practices? What would be the best way to facilitate team meetings? What would collaboration between the three teams look like? And how would we measure the overall success of the project?

While we all felt that our team members had confidence in our leadership, we were acutely aware of our lack of knowledge about what our collaborative work could and should look like. This way of working together was completely new to Brookline High School, and we did not have a model to follow.

Luckily, our team members enjoyed the experimental nature of CRI and did not need team leaders to have all of the answers. They appreciated being able to explore *for themselves* different techniques to address literacy issues among their students—instead of just being told what to do. Furthermore, they remarked that CRI felt unique, because it trusted teachers to provide professional development for each other instead of relying on department heads or outside experts.

We believe that our dual roles as teachers and teacher leaders created the positive team dynamic crucial for the success of CRI. Because we are primarily classroom teachers, our colleagues did not expect us to always direct new learning. This belief meant that the team could truly engage in an inquiry process together, in which we identified our students' weaknesses and then experimented with different strategies to tackle literacy issues. If administrators or consultants had led each team, it might have made it easier for teachers to defer to their authority, but group members might not have ever really owned their students' literacy problems.

Placing a classroom teacher in the team leader role also allowed team members to feel safe when experimenting with new teaching methods in their classrooms. In order for CRI to work, team members needed to be willing to change their teaching practice and start incorporating new methods and strategies to address literacy without fear of judgment or evaluation. In other words, team members needed to feel free to mess up, make mistakes, and have new lessons fail. If administrators had been team leaders, group members might not have dared to be as experimental. With classroom teachers as teacher leaders, the groups did not feel any of this outside pressure.

Additionally, our dual roles as teachers and leaders made it easier, at times, to convince colleagues to incorporate more disciplinary literacy instruction into their practice. As classroom teachers, we recognize the heavy demands and time constraints our peers face. We also understand their hesitancy to try new things—especially literacy strategies that are not familiar. But, by test driving new techniques in our own classrooms first, we can turn to colleagues and provide evidence of strategies' successes, as well as give our peers tips and tricks for smooth implementation. This trust and collaboration has increased fellow content-area teachers' willingness to experiment with literacy instruction. And finally, the CRI structure of a teacher team leader allowed for growth in learning as true professional *teams* in ways we had not experienced previously. Everyone grew—as educators, as leaders, as collaborators, as confidantes. The position of team leader necessitated that we capture and disseminate the shareable aspects of the work and also—quite wonderfully—find ways to champion the meaningful bonding moments that occurred within our groups. As we complete the third year of CRI work together, we are convinced that teacher-facilitated PLCs are the most effective form of professional development. We doubt that CRI would have been as successful under a different format for team leadership.

Final Thoughts

In reflecting back on the first two years of the project, one of our most powerful outcomes has been teacher testimonials of their experiences. For example, the following CRI members praise their participation in the project:

- "CRI has been very invigorating intellectually. My classroom has been very alive. My students and I have been in it together—learning, exploring. . . . I heart CRI!"

- "I wanted to try and break reading down into its component skills then teach them to my students, but then I realized that reading is far too complex for that. Since the CRI institute, there are many concrete strategies that I have tried in my teaching. I have introduced new reading assignments (observation-inference charts, annotating the text), tried small group discussions, held reading conferences, offered greater choice of texts, and each of these things has impacted my instruction. I have been thinking a lot more about why reading is hard for my students and how I can support them through those challenges, and I have worked to engage and motivate my students more. Overall, I learned that there are advantages and disadvantages to every strategy, and that ultimately you have to choose a purpose and choose your strategy to fit that purpose."

- "I feel that my thinking has been transformed. I feel myself, just in conversations with colleagues and in my own thinking, going back to research pieces that came up in the CRI summer and that we encountered as a team. I'm building a new lens for myself."

- "CRI has dramatically changed how I teach my class, changed my focus to more skills based while realizing that I don't really have to sacrifice content. Whether in my daily instruction and discussion or pushing me to establish purpose for activities, it has made me a better teacher."

- "I think that this has really been everything that a professional development experience should be. I like that it's really flexible depending on my needs as a teacher. It's immediately applicable to what I do in the classroom. I think the best part about it is the collaboration. It's not about us receiving information. It's about us talking to one another and learning from one another."

What is clearly evident from all of these quotes is that CRI is something transformative, invaluable, and special. It has inspired new teachers and re-energized veteran teachers to make changes in their teaching practice. It has ignited a new spirit of collaboration in departments that had been very unilateral before. Finally, it has caused content-area teachers to view literacy instruction as a crucial component of their classes.

Moving forward, one of our greatest hopes is that other high schools start professional learning teams similar to CRI that tackle issues of content-area literacy for all students. We hope that other districts are inspired by CRI's story—both to prioritize disciplinary literacy in their schools and to put teachers in the pilot seat, leading future professional development opportunities. This initiative is slowly revolutionizing our school, and it can do the same elsewhere.

Case 3: Conducting a Needs Assessment: An Example of the CALS in Action

Source: Todd Wallingford, curriculum director, Hudson, Massachusetts

In the third case, Todd Wallingford of Hudson, Massachusetts, and Jacy Ippolito describe the high school's Literacy Action Team (LAT) as they engaged in an overarching self-assessment process focused on students' literacy skills and achievement. As part of their work, the LAT made use of a free, online needs-assessment tool (the Content-Area Literacy Survey, available at http://adlitpd.org/category/assess/) to identify literacy strengths and needs of students at the high school level.

QUESTIONS TO PONDER

1. In what ways did the results of the Content-Area Literacy Survey (CALS) assist the leadership team in making decisions for improving literacy instruction at the high school level?

2. What were the advantages of this particular needs-assessment tool for the high school level?

3. Why might it have been important for the leadership team to use a discussion-based protocol to analyze the data they collected?

4. Which parts of this story mirror work happening in your school setting? What ideas might you adopt after reading the case?

To illustrate how school leadership teams are beginning to use dynamic, online diagnostic tools, we turn to a case example from Hudson, Massachusetts. Hudson is a semirural town, home to over seventeen thousand people, and is a metropolitan suburb forty miles west of Boston. The town supports three elementary schools (prekindergarten through fourth grade), one middle school (fifth to through seventh grades), and one high school (eighth through twelfth grades).

District and school leadership began their investigation of literacy diagnostic tools for teachers and students in 2011, knowing that their teachers and students might need additional support in meeting the challenges of CCSS. As a first step toward increasing students' literacy achievement across the board, a team of seventeen educators (teachers and administrators) came together to form a Literacy Action Team (LAT), which then began reviewing existing sources of student data. The team examined state standardized test scores, SAT, PSAT, and Advanced Placement test scores for graduating students; however, these quantitative data were not helping the LAT better understand how secondary teachers in Hudson were supporting their students' deeper reading, writing, and communication skills. The team members quickly realized that they needed more information from both teachers and students about their collective understanding of literacy instruction within and across content areas. The LAT began designing a survey to administer to teachers and students, and in its search for existing templates, it found the CALS. After contacting Dr. Joshua Lawrence (one of the CALS's architects) and chatting about the possibility of using the CALS with a high school group of teachers and students (a small shift from the survey's original target population of middle school teachers and students), the Hudson LAT agreed to administer it.

LAT members reported that using the CALS was an easy decision because "it was already on the computer" and because "it actually didn't take teachers and students as long as we thought it might, because we were really sensitive to that." Todd Wallingford, the Hudson curriculum director for English language arts and social studies for sixth through twelfth grades (and one of the primary conveners of the LAT) commented further: "We didn't want anything that was going to take more than twenty minutes—and it didn't!"

The Hudson team administered the CALS during the winter of 2012 to 185 students and 88 teachers across grade levels and content areas. The LAT was excited to receive immediate feedback on questions it had been wrestling with. For example, the LAT appreciated hearing students' responses to the question, "How much and what kinds of reading and writing do you do?" both in and out of school. Similar data were collected from teachers about their literacy practices in the content areas and, importantly, the LAT was able to gather data about previous professional development experiences focused on literacy.

The results of the CALS survey data helped confirm and quantify a number of suspicions the team had already identified from other data points: that a majority of the secondary teachers had not been given access to literacy-specific professional development; meeting the literacy needs of students with special needs and low literacy levels was challenging; and students were finding it challenging to draw inferences when reading. Several new findings arose as well. Teachers reported spending a fair bit of time teaching vocabulary, but they also reported that students were not demonstrating strong understandings of academic and subject-specific vocabulary. Meanwhile, students were reporting not enjoying learning new vocabulary in the subject areas, but they recognized its importance in understanding course content. Such findings created opportunities for faculty to talk and collaborate with one another as part of district-designed, targeted professional development.

Perhaps more important than any one piece of data or particular finding was the process that the LAT underwent in analyzing and reporting the data. The team engaged in multiple data analysis sessions, meeting as a large group and then as small subgroups to explore different aspects. Notably, the team created a discussion-based protocol (see appendix J), adapted from the School Reform Initiative's Data Driven Dialogue protocol (available at http://schoolreforminitiative.org/doc/data_driven _dialogue.pdf). The protocol allowed the team to explore their own assumptions about teachers' and students' literacy practices, make nonjudgmental observations about the resulting CALS data, and then craft evidence-based inferences.

The power of working in such a collaborative and deliberate manner is clear years later. The school and district have used these data to spur several waves of district-designed professional development addressing areas such as drawing inferences, vocabulary instruction, and refinement of disciplinary literacy practices. Study groups and summer institutes have been formed and led by LAT members and other expert content-area teachers and leaders. The study groups have been reading Doug Buehl's excellent book, *Developing Readers in the Academic Disciplines*. In response, teachers have been collaboratively designing instruction within and across content areas to address achievement gaps.

Now, several years after the administration of the CALS, Todd Wallingford reports that while the LAT does not often revisit the CALS data, the process the team underwent administering and analyzing the data was pivotal in raising areas of challenge and confirming suspicions about areas of need. The idea of looking at data collaboratively built faculty's and leaders' capacity to tap local expertise and provide targeted professional development efficiently (as opposed to blindly choosing new, expensive curricular packages).

Case 4: Pennsylvania Institute for Instructional Coaching (PIIC)

Source: Ellen B. Eisenberg, executive director, Pennsylvania Institute for Instructional Coaching

In this case, Ellen Eisenberg discusses the evolution of PIIC, a state-wide initiative to implement coaching in schools throughout the Commonwealth.

QUESTIONS TO PONDER

1. What factors might account for the longevity and breadth of this coaching initiative?

2. In what ways do the leaders of this initiative assist schools in developing a readiness for coaching?

3. What are the primary beliefs and assumptions underlying coaching in this initiative?

Instructional coaching at the high school level has been part of the education landscape in Pennsylvania since 2005, when a public-private partnership was established between the Pennsylvania Department of Education and the Annenberg Foundation. That relationship produced an instructional coaching model called the Pennsylvania High School Coaching Initiative (PAHSCI) and evolved over a five-year period into PIIC. Our current model includes ongoing PIIC preparation and support to coaches through regional education agencies called Intermediate Units; as a result, approximately 400–500 instructional coaches are implementing the PIIC model of instructional coaching and professional development in their school communities (elementary and secondary) across Pennsylvania.

The PIIC Model

PIIC is a "train the trainers" model and provides ongoing professional development to instructional coaches on four core elements: working one-on-one and offering small-group support to teachers and other school leaders; focusing on data collection, analysis, and use; using evidence-based literacy practices applied across all content areas; and supporting reflective and non-evaluative practice. PIIC instructional coaches provide teachers with tools to help them improve their practice and deliver quality instruction. As part of their preparation, PIIC coaches are supported by instructional mentors, experienced professionals who help coaches improve their practice so they can work more effectively with teachers and other school leaders.

Instructional coaches team with teachers and provide one-on-one, side-by-side assistance, working together on specific needs in their classrooms. They provide professional development for teachers and school leaders with real-time support focused on changing practice, increasing student engagement, and improving student achievement.

The following "B, D, A" cycle of consultation describes how coaches work one-on-one and in small groups with teachers and other school leaders.

The B, D, A Cycle of Consultation

Central to the PIIC model is the B, D, A (**B**efore, **D**uring, and **A**fter) cycle of consultation and feedback. It is a cycle of communication, collaboration, confidentiality, and collective problem solving. In brief, the process works in the following way: In *before* class visits, coaches co-plan with teachers to create goals, determine strategies, and identify materials and resources to use. The coach and teacher identify what data to collect during the class period. This list is limited and is constructed once the coach and teacher collaborate on the expectations of that class lesson. At this time, the teacher and coach also schedule the *after* visit with the specific day and time devoted to debriefing and providing feedback for the class period visited. *During* class visits, coaches work with teachers to implement a specific literacy-based instructional approach, which emphasizes the consistency of language and practice across all content areas. Coaches concentrate on the mutually agreed-upon items from the co-designed visitation list and think about ways to help support the teacher's individual needs. This can be accomplished through co-teaching or modeling parts of the lesson.

When a coach is modeling a specific strategy or concept, the teacher should have an identified focus as well. The purpose of this time is for the teacher to watch the coach share his or her expertise and then provide feedback at the scheduled meeting time. The coach is modeling the B, D, A process with the teacher and asking the teacher to follow the cycle of consultation with roles modified for the occasion. *After* the visit, coaches and teachers discuss what goals were met and what worked effectively, focusing on their next steps to improve student performance. This is a nonevaluative process that encourages teachers to try innovative ways to engage students in a risk-free environment.

The Coach

Instructional coaches are hired by their districts and may be either full-time or part-time coaches. In the PIIC model, instructional coaches have daily release time to work with their colleagues. As skilled practitioners, they are careful to honor the teachers' voices with whom they work and do not let ego drive their assistance. That means they are not focused on being "right." They are focused on helping teachers reach their own decisions through a series of appropriate and critical questioning. In our universe of coaching and the lexicon of our model, instructional coaches establish partnerships with their teaching colleagues, guide practice, and ask essential questions to help teachers find their own voice, make their own choices, have open dialogue with colleagues, practice together in a nonthreatening environment, and reflect *in*, *on*, and *about* their action.

While skilled in selected content areas and able to provide professional development both one-on-one and in small groups, the most important qualities of an effective coach are the ability to listen fully and be respectful, nonjudgmental, able to establish effective working relationships, skilled in the art of questioning, a good communicator, responsive and receptive, a learner, reflective, and able to model effective instructional strategies in a variety of ways to a variety of students.

Sometimes, the coaches are current teachers on staff who want to explore opportunities as a school leader but are not interested in becoming a school site administrator. In these situations, coaches must understand how to renegotiate their roles. Yesterday, they were "next door neighbors" teaching the same students; today, they are senior among their peers, and that can be a bit messy if not approached with sensitivity. How an instructional coaching model is rolled out to the staff with expectations, shared visions, and clear roles will make a difference in how the instructional coaching model and coach are accepted. The goal is to reduce the possibility of resistance by being as transparent as possible from the inception through implementation.

Coaching Challenges

Coaching is situational. What works well in one environment may not work as well in another one. Coaches need to know the "lay of the land" prior to implementation and need to spend a fair amount of time preparing for their coaching roles and responsibilities. They need to know the school-wide vision for school improvement and the expectations of instructional coaching. The intersection of the two along with the shared vision of how coaching works sends a clear message that working together to increase student engagement and building teacher capacity are the main objectives.

One challenge that our coaches have shared is the lack of understanding of what coaches do. Most people understand that coaches wear many hats and not all of them at one time. What has stood out for some of our coaches is that the roles and responsibilities of the instructional coach must be shared prior to implementation. Coaches are not supervisors, substitute teachers, whistle blowers, evaluators, or tutors. There must be a shared vision that explains why coaches cannot be auxiliary substitutes or why they don't evaluate a teacher's performance. Administrators and staff members alike must understand how coaches work and that working one-on-one or in small groups in deliberate and intentional ways to help teachers change practice cannot be accomplished if coaches are pulled away to do non-coaching activities. Coaches may work in classrooms with teachers to support selected cooperative group work, but they cannot be expected to stay regularly in one teacher's classroom to provide an extra pair of hands. They cannot be "assigned" to a new teacher to maintain control in a classroom but rather need to work with the new teacher to understand student engagement and effective lesson design.

If inclement weather exists and there are several teachers unable to get to school, coaches gladly step in to help and cover classes or provide substitute coverage for the day. These occurrences should be limited, shared, and quite infrequent. Unfortunately, we recognize that some schools just don't have the human resources to create a system that allows for shared responsibilities, but in those cases, school administrations need to recognize that the coaches are not able to provide the services for which they were hired.

PIIC's Evidence-Based Literacy Practices

PIIC advocates evidence-based literacy strategies, techniques, and support so that all students are exposed to literacy practices that teach students how to engage with their text. It's not about teaching students to read and write; it's all about teaching students and their teachers how to use literacy (reading, writing, and communications) to enhance learning. Research indicates that the effective development of literacy skills influences student learning and achievement. One of the PIIC technical providers is the Penn Literacy Network, Graduate School of Education at the University of Pennsylvania. They provide a graduate-level course for our coaches and selected school teams, helping them identify effective teaching strategies appropriate for content areas. Participants complete in-class assignments, practice with their coaches and mentors, and design an end-of-year project that applies their learning. Coaches also facilitate turn-around training on the various concepts and instructional practices learned, enabling schools to provide consistency in language and practice.

Ways of Thinking and Working Like a Coach Framework

This template may be helpful to readers wishing to reflect on their own practice as they read this book.

- In what ways do literacy leaders think and act when working on specific tasks or with specific groups?

- In what ways are you already thinking and working like a "literacy leader who coaches" in your current role? Where do you see room for growth?

Thinking and Working Like a . . .

	Leader	Facilitator	Designer	Advocate	Possibilities for me as a literacy leader
Chapter 3 Coaching for Student Success: What 21st Century Literacy Leaders Need to Know					
Chapter 4 Analyzing and Shaping School Culture: All Systems Go!					

Chapter 5 Overview: Ways of Working With Teachers				
Chapter 6 Working With Individual Teachers to Analyze and Transform Instructional Practices				

continued →

Thinking and Working Like a . . .

	Leader	Facilitator	Designer	Advocate	Possibilities for me as a literacy leader
Chapter 7 Working With Groups to Establish Schools as Places of Learning					
Chapter 8 Assessment as a Guide for Student Literacy Learning and School Improvement					

Chapter 9 Developing, Implementing, and Sustaining School-Wide Literacy Programs					
Chapter 10 Working With Families and Communities					

→ continued

Thinking and Working Like a . . .

	Leader	Facilitator	Designer	Advocate	Possibilities for me as a literacy leader
Chapter 11 The Literacy Leader as Lifelong Learner					

*Visit **www.learningsciences.com/bookresources** to download a reproducible version of this figure.*

For Further Study:
Resources for Literacy Leaders

In this appendix, we have listed select additional resources that pertain to each chapter. We encourage literacy leaders to examine additional resources as they can, or if they are involved in specific areas of interest or topics of study—ideally with colleagues as part of a collaborative study group.

Chapter 1. Remodeling Schools for Effective Literacy Learning: The Case for Coaching

Blachowicz, C. L. Z., Buhle, R., Ogle, D., Frost, S., Correa, A., & Kinner, J. D. (2010). Hit the ground running: Ten ideas for preparing and supporting urban literacy coaches. *The Reading Teacher, 63*(5), 348–359.

Blamey, K. L., Meyer, C. K., & Walpole, S. (2009). Middle and high school literacy coaches: A national survey. *Journal of Adolescent and Adult Literacy, 52*(4), 310–323.

Dole, J. A. (2004). The changing role of the reading specialist in school reform. *The Reading Teacher, 57*(5), 462–471.

Neuman, S. B., & Wright, T. S. (2010). Promoting language and literacy development for early childhood educators: A mixed-methods study of coursework and coaching. *The Elementary School Journal, 111*(1), 63–86.

Skiffington, S., Washburn, S., & Elliott, K. (2011). Instructional coaching: Helping preschool teachers reach their full potential. *Young Children, 66*(3), 12–19.

Toll, C. (2004). Separating coaching from supervising. *English Leadership Quarterly, 27*(2), 5–7.

Chapter 2. Cultivating Coaching Mindsets: Ways of Thinking and Working Like a Coach

Barth, R. S. (2006). Improving relationships within the schoolhouse. *Educational Leadership, 63*(6), 8–13.

Calo, K. M., Sturtevant, E. G., Kopfman, K. M. (2015). Literacy coaches' perceptions of themselves as literacy leaders: Results from a national study of K–12 literacy coaching and leadership. *Literacy Research and Instruction, 54*(1), 1–18.

Collet, V. (2012). The gradual increase of responsibility model: Coaching for teacher change. *Literacy Research and Instruction, 54*(1), 27–47.

Drago-Severson, E. (2008). 4 practices serve as pillars for adult learning. *Journal of Staff Development, 29*(4), 60–63.

Fullan, M. (2001). *Leading in a culture of change personal action guide and workbook.* San Francisco: Jossey-Bass.

Fullan, M. (2006). Chapter 12: Understanding change. In the *Jossey-Bass Reader on Educational Leadership* (2nd ed.). San Francisco: Jossey-Bass.

Helsing, D., Howell, A., Kegan, R., & Lahey, L. (2008). Putting the "Development" in professional development: Understanding and overturning educational leaders' immunities to change. *Harvard Educational Review, 78*(3), 437–465.

Kegan, R., & Lahey, L. L. (2016). *An everyone culture: Becoming a deliberately developmental organization.* Brighton, MA: Harvard Business Review Press.

Knight, J. (2011). *Unmistakable impact: A partnership approach for dramatically improving instruction.* Thousand Oaks, CA: Corwin Press.

Steckel, B. (2009). Fulfilling the promise of literacy coaches in urban schools: What does it take to make an impact? *The Reading Teacher, 63*(1), 14–23.

Walpole, S., & Blamey, K. L. (2008). Elementary literacy coaches: The reality of dual roles. *The Reading Teacher, 62*(3), 222–231.

Chapter 3. Coaching for Student Success: What 21st Century Literacy Leaders Need to Know

Beck, I., & Sandora, C. (2016). *Illuminating comprehension and close reading.* New York: Guilford Press.

Brock et al. (2014). *Engaging students in disciplinary literacy, K–6: Reading, writing, and teaching tools for the classroom.* New York: Teachers College Press.

Brozo, W. G., Moorman, G., Meyer, C., & Stewart, T. (2013). Content area reading and disciplinary literacy: A case for the radical center. *Journal of Adolescent & Adult Literacy*, *56*(5), 353–357.

Buehl, D. (2014). *Classroom strategies for interactive learning* (4th ed.). Newark, DE: International Literacy Association.

Draper, R. J., & Broomhead, G. P. (Eds.). (2010). *(Re)imagining content-area literacy instruction*. New York: Teachers College Press.

Ellery, V., Oczkus, L., & Rasinski, T. V. (2015). *Literacy strong all year long: Powerful lessons for K–2*. Newark, DE: International Literacy Association.

Fisher, D., & Frey, N. (2015). *Improving adolescent literacy: Content area strategies at work* (4th ed.). Boston: Pearson.

Fisher D., Frey, N., & Lapp, D. (2016). *Text complexity: Stretching readers with texts and tasks* (2nd ed.). Newark, DE: International Literacy Association.

Graham, S., Harris, K. R., & Chambers, B. (2015). Evidence-based practice and writing instruction: A review of reviews. In C. A. McArthur, S. Graham, & J. Fitzgerald (Eds.) *Handbook of writing research* (2nd ed). New York, NY: Guilford Press.

Ippolito, J., Lawrence, J. F., & Zaller, C. (Eds.). (2013). *Adolescent literacy in the era of the common core: From research into practice*. Cambridge, MA: Harvard Education Press.

Jetton, T. L., & Shanahan, C. (Eds.). (2012). *Adolescent literacy in the academic disciplines: General principles and practical strategies*. New York: Guilford Press.

Kucan, L., & Palincsar, A. S. (2013). *Comprehension instruction through text-based discussion*. Newark, DE: International Literacy Association.

Lattimer, H. (2014). *Real-world literacies: Disciplinary teaching in the high school classroom*. Urbana, IL: National Council of Teachers of English.

Lent, R. C. (2015). *This is disciplinary literacy: Reading, writing, thinking, and doing . . . content area by content area*. Thousand Oaks, CA: Corwin Press.

Leu, D., Kinzer, C. K., Coiro, J., Castek, J., & Henry L. A. (2013). New literacies and the new literacies of online reading comprehension: A dual level theory. In D. E. Alvermann, N. J. Unrau, & R. B. Ruddell (Eds.), *Theoretical models and processes of reading* (6th ed., pp. 1150–1181). Newark, DE: International Reading Association.

Manderino, M., Berglund, R. L., & Johns, J. L. (2014). *Content area learning: Bridges to disciplinary literacy* (4th ed.). Dubuque, IA: Kendall Hunt Publishing.

McConachie, S. M., & Petrosky, A. R. (2010). *Content matters: A disciplinary literacy approach to improving student learning.* San Francisco, CA: Jossey-Bass Publishers.

McLaughlin, M., & Rasinski, T. V. (2015). *Struggling readers: Engaging and teaching in grades 3–8.* Newark, DE: International Literacy Association.

Roth, K., & Dabrowski, J. (2016). *Interactive writing across grades: A small practice with big results preK–5.* Newark, DE: International Literacy Association.

Chapter 4. Analyzing and Shaping School Culture: All Systems Go!

Diversity—Resources

Gay, G. (2010). *Culturally responsive teaching: Theory, research and practice* (2nd ed.). New York: Teachers College Press.

Gonzalez, N., Moll, L. C., & Amanti, C. (2006). *Funds of knowledge: Theorizing practices in households, communities, and classrooms.* New York: Routledge.

Ladson-Billings, G. (2009). *The dreamkeepers: Successful teachers of African American children.*

Milner, H. R., & Lomotey, K. (Eds.) (2014). *Handbook of urban education.* New York: Routledge.

Skerrett, A., & Hersi, A. A. (2012). Culturally responsive literacy instruction. In R. M. Bean & A. S. Dagen (Eds.), *Best practices of literacy leaders: Keys to school improvement* (pp. 230–247). New York: Guilford Press.

Websites

Children's Book Council Diversity Committee (www.cbcdiversity.com).

International Literacy Association (www.literacyworldwide.org). The ILA website provides an assortment of classroom resources. For example, the ILA's Bridges units include titles such as: Celebrating Me, Celebrating You: We Are Alike and Different (kindergarten); the Steps to Race in America: A Grade 9 Unit for Understanding the Development of the Construct of Race. The E-essentials series include articles for educators on practical classroom ideas grounded in best practices of literacy research.

ReadWriteThink (www.readwritethink.org). Sponsored by ILA and NCTE, ReadWriteThink provides resources and lesson plans on many topics (kindergarten through grade 12), including that of diversity.

Teaching Tolerance (www.teachingtolerance.org).

WIDA (www.wida.org).

Working With the Principal—Resources

Ippolito, J. (2009). Principals as partners with literacy coaches: Striking a balance between neglect and interference. *Literacy Coaching Clearinghouse*. Retrieved from www.literacycoachingonline.org/briefs/Principals_as_Partners.pdf

Kral, C. C. (2012). Principal support for literacy coaching. *Literacy Coaching Clearinghouse*. Retrieved from www.literacycoachingonline.org/briefs/PrincipalSupportFinal3-22-07.pdf

Mangin, M. M. (2007). Facilitating elementary principals' support for instructional teacher leadership. *Educational Administration Quarterly, 43*(3), 319–357.

Neumerski, C. M. (2013). Rethinking instructional leadership, a review: What do we know about principal, teacher, and coach instructional leadership, and where should we go from here? *Educational Administration Quarterly, 49*(2), 310–347.

Shanklin, N. L. (2007). What supports do literacy coaches need from administrators in order to succeed? *Literacy Coaching Clearinghouse*. Retrieved from www.literacycoachingonline.org/briefs/LCSupportsNSBrief.pdf

Toll, C. (2009). Literacy coaching: Suggestions for school leaders. *Principal Leadership, 9*(9), 24–28.

Chapter 5. Overview: Ways of Working With Teachers

Allen, D., & Blythe, T. (2004). *The facilitator's book of questions: Tools for looking together at student and teacher work* (2nd ed.). New York: Teachers College Press.

Allen, D., & Blythe, T. (2015). *Facilitating for learning: Tools for teacher groups of all kinds.* New York: Teachers College Press.

Boudett, K. P., & City, E. A. (2014). *Meeting wise: Making the most of collaborative time for educators.* Cambridge, MA: Harvard Education Press.

Harvard Business School Publication Corporation. (2016). *Difficult conversations.* Boston, MA: Author.

Kegan, R., & Lahey, L. L. (2001). *How the way we talk can change the way we work: Seven languages for transformation.* San Francisco, CA: Jossey-Bass.

McDonald, J. P., Mohr, N., Dichter, A., & McDonald, E. C. (2013). *The power of protocols: An educator's guide to better practice* (3rd ed.). New York: Teachers College Press.

Miller, S., & Miller, P. A. (1997). *Core communication: Skills and processes.* Colorado: Interpersonal Communication Programs, Inc.

Peterson, D. S., Taylor, B. M., Burnham, B., & Schock, R. (2009). Reflective coaching conversations: A missing piece. *The Reading Teacher, 62*(6), 500–509.

Pomerantz, F., & Ippolito, J. (2015). Power tools for talking: Custom protocols enrich coaching conversations. *Journal of Staff Development, 36*(1), 40–43.

Chapter 6. Working With Individual Teachers to Analyze and Transform Instructional Practices

Bean, R. M. (2011). The reading coach. In T. Rasinski (Ed.) *Rebuilding the foundation: Effective reading instruction for 21st century literacy* (pp. 315–336). Bloomington, IN: Solution Tree Press.

Inam, H. (2012). *Five C's of great coaching conversations.* Retrieved from www.transformleaders.tv/five-cs-of-great-coaching-conversations

L'Allier, S., Elish-Piper, L., & Bean, R. M. (2010). What matters for elementary literacy coaching: Guiding principles for instructional improvement and student achievement. *The Reading Teacher, 63*(7), 544–554.

Robertson, D. A., Ford-Connors, E., & Paratore, J. L. (2014). Coaching teachers' talk during vocabulary and comprehension instruction. *Language Arts, 91*(6), 416–428.

Stover, K., Kissle, B., Haag, K., & Shoniker, R. (2011). Differentiated coaching: Fostering reflection with teachers. *The Reading Teacher, 64*, 498–509.

Chapter 7. Working With Groups to Establish Schools as Places of Learning

City, E. A., Elmore, R. F., Fiarman, S. E., & Teitel, L. (2009). *Instructional rounds in education: A network approach to improving teaching and learning.* Cambridge, MA: Harvard Education Press.

Dana, N. F. (2013). *Digging deeper into action research: A teacher inquirer's field guide*. Thousand Oaks, CA: Corwin Press.

DuFour, R., DuFour, R., & Eaker, R. (2008). *Revisiting professional learning communities at work: New insights for improving schools*. Bloomington, IN: Solution Tree Press.

Easton, L. B. (2011). *Professional learning communities by design: Putting the learning back into PLCs*. Thousand Oaks, CA: Corwin.

Jolly, A. (2008). *Team to teach: A facilitator's guide to professional learning teams*. Oxford, OH: National Staff Development Council. Retrieved from http://learningforward.org/docs/default-source/docs/teamtoteach-tools.pdf

Martin, L. E., Kragler, S., Quatroche, D. J., & Bauserman, K. L. (2014). *Handbook of professional development in education: Successful models and practices, preK–12*. New York: Guilford Press.

Roberts, J. E. (2012). *Instructional rounds in action*. Cambridge, MA: Harvard Education Press.

Chapter 8. Assessment as a Guide for Student Literacy Learning and School Improvement

Afflerbach, P. (2012). *Understanding and using reading assessment K–12* (2nd ed.) Newark, DE: International Reading Association.

Afflerbach, P. (2016). Reading assessment: Looking ahead. *The Reading Teacher*, *69*(4), 413–419.

Blythe, T., Allen, D., & Powell, B. S. (2015). *Looking together at student work* (3rd ed.). New York: Teachers College Press.

Deshler, D. D., Palinscar, A. S., Biancarosa, G., & Nair, M. (2007). *Informed choices for struggling adolescent readers: A research-based guide to instructional programs and practices*. Newark, DE: International Reading Association.

McKenna, M., & Stahl, K. D. (2015). *Assessment for reading instruction K–12* (3rd ed.). New York: Guilford Press.

Mesmer, H. A. E., Mesmer, E., & Jones, J. (2014). *Reading interventions in the primary grades: A common-sense guide to RTI*. New York: Guilford Press.

Morris, D. (2014). *Diagnosis and correction of reading problems* (2nd ed.). New York: Guilford Press.

Morsy, L., Kieffer, M., & Snow, C. E. (2010). *Measure for measure: A critical consumers' guide to reading comprehension assessments for adolescents*. New York: Carnegie Corporation of New York. Retrieved from http://files.eric.ed.gov/fulltext/ED535299.pdf

Chapter 9. Developing, Implementing, and Sustaining School-Wide Literacy Programs

Irwin, J., Meltzer, J., Dean, N., & Mickler, M. J. (2010). *Taking the lead on adolescent literacy: Action steps for schoolwide success.* Thousand Oaks, CA: Corwin Press.

Lewis, W. E., Walpole, S., & McKenna, M. C. (2014). *Cracking the Common Core: Choosing and using texts in grades 6–12.* New York: Guilford Press.

Morrow, L. M., Shanahan, T., & Wixson, K. (2014). *Teaching with the Common Core standards for English language arts, preK–2.* New York: Guilford Press.

Taylor, B. M. (2011). *Catching schools: An action guide to schoolwide reading improvement.* Portsmouth, NH: Heinemann.

Wepner, S. B., Strickland, D. S., & Quatroche, D. J. (2014). *The administration and supervision of reading programs* (5th ed.). New York: Teachers College Press.

Chapter 10. Working With Families and Communities

Allen, J. (2007). *Creating welcoming schools: A practical guide to home-school partnerships with diverse families.* New York, NY: Teachers College Press.

Browning, B. A. (2014). *Grant writing for dummies* (5th ed.). Hoboken, NJ: Wiley.

Constantino, S. M. (2008). *101 ways to create real family engagement.* Galax, VA: Engage Press.

Dusmore, K., & Fisher, D. (2010). *Bringing literacy home.* Newark, DE: International Reading Association.

Sliger, B. (2009). *Grant writing for teachers and administrators.* Durham, CT: Strategic Book Group.

Websites

Grants for Teachers (www.grantwrangler.com)

Family Friendly Schools (www.familyfriendlyschools.com)

National Standards, Goals, and Indicators for Family-School Partnerships (www.pta.org/files/National_Standards_2.pdf)

Partnership Center for the Social Organization of Schools; Urban Family Engagement Network (www.pta.org/programs/content.cfm?ItemNumber=2135)

Note-Taking Organizer When Coach Is Modeling Instruction

Teacher: _____

School/Grade/Department: _____

Coach: _____

Date/Time(s): _____

Goals of Lesson: _____

Look-Fors: _____

Teacher Activities (e.g., monitoring, assisting): _____

Use the following chart to take notes during the lesson. We can address questions and comments in the post-lesson conversation.

What is the coach doing?	What are students doing?	Comments/Questions

*Visit **www.learningsciences.com/bookresources** to download a reproducible version of this figure.*

Observation Protocol for Content-Area Instruction

Teacher: _____   **Date:** _____

Content Area/Grade Level: _____

Time Begin: _____   **Time End:** _____

Number of Students Present: _____

Special Circumstances to Note: _____

Lesson Focus: _____

Materials Being Used (check all that apply):

☐ Textbook

☐ Board/Chart

☐ Computer(s)/SMART Board

☐ Worksheet(s)

☐ Student-generated work

☐ Other: _____

Grouping (check all that apply):

☐ Whole class

☐ Small groups

☐ Pairs

☐ Individuals

☐ Other: _____

Protocol to be used as a guide. Scale to be completed after the observation has been completed.

Scale:	Great Extent	Some Extent	Minimal Extent	Not Observed
	(4)	(3)	(2)	(1)
Classroom Environment				
Materials supporting literacy are available *Books, visuals, and print and nonprint materials about topic are evident*	☐	☐	☐	☐
Provides for social interaction *Areas for small-group/partner work*	☐	☐	☐	☐
Strategies for learning are displayed *Informative, positive strategies (e.g., why and how of summarizing)*	☐	☐	☐	☐
Instruction				
Before reading *Sets purpose, makes connections, develops vocabulary*	☐	☐	☐	☐
Small-group discussion	☐	☐	☐	☐
Engages in coaching/ scaffolding, teacher models strategies	☐	☐	☐	☐
During reading *Think-alouds by teacher, connects to students' experiences, points out text features*	☐	☐	☐	☐
Questioning that requires high level thinking, engages in coaching/scaffolding	☐	☐	☐	☐
After reading *Small-group discussion or writing activities that require responding to text*	☐	☐	☐	☐

Activities require high level thinking	☐	☐	☐	☐
Opportunities for differentiation to meet student needs	☐	☐	☐	☐
Teacher monitors and supports student work	☐	☐	☐	☐
Classroom Climate/Engagement of Students				
High level of student participation Students are actively engaged	☐	☐	☐	☐
Positive learning environment Interactions are respectful and supportive, encourages risk taking	☐	☐	☐	☐
Students use strategies to learn Evidence of students knowing when, how, and which strategies to use (e.g., note taking, summarizing)	☐	☐	☐	☐
Students show evidence of being able to think about their own learning Provide justification for thinking, evidence of being able to organize their own learning	☐	☐	☐	☐

Reprinted with permission from: The Reading Specialist: Leadership and Coaching for the Classroom, School, and Community *(3rd edition). New York: Guilford Press, pp. 293–294.*

Notes:

Visit ***www.learningsciences.com/bookresources*** *to download a reproducible version of this figure.*

Lesson Analysis Guide for the Post-Observation Conversation

Teacher: _____   **Coach:** _____   **Date:** _____

Focus of Lesson/Objectives: _____

In Column 1, the coach can write notes about the observed lesson. In Column 2, the coach can summarize the post-observation conversation, indicating follow-up steps. The guide then serves as a record of what the coach and teacher plan to do as a result of the observation and follow-up discussion.

Summary of Lesson Analysis	Results of Discussion With Teacher
(After Observing)	**(After Post-Observation Conversation)**
• What did you see? Think? Wonder?	• What was the conversational focus?
• Draft comments and focus questions that you may include in your post-observation conversation	• What action steps were agreed upon?
	• Who will do what? Teacher? Coach?

continued ⟶

Summary of Lesson Analysis	Results of Discussion With Teacher
Instructional Strategies/Approaches Used: Active engagement of students? Appropriate for lesson? Need for differentiation?	
Materials Used: Appropriate for this lesson? Used effectively?	
Classroom Management: Were students attentive and engaged? Grouping appropriate?	
Classroom Environment: Did the environment provide for maximum learning? Were all students involved in meaningful work?	
Other:	

*Visit **www.learningsciences.com/bookresources** to download a reproducible version of this figure.*

Developing a Comprehensive Assessment System

Identify the measures (formal and informal) used to assess students' literacy performance in your school or across schools within a district/system. This tool can also be used by multiple schools at the same time, with the intent of compiling information in a larger group meeting.

Discuss the following questions with your team:

- How are each of the identified measures currently being used (e.g., screening, diagnostic, progress monitoring, outcomes)?
- Do they provide formative or summative information?
- Are all of the assessments necessary, or are there redundancies?
- Do they provide for a well-aligned, coherent assessment system?

Do the measures have the technical validity and reliability necessary for assessing competencies of students?

Literacy Assessments	Primary (PreK–2)	Intermediate (3–5)	Middle School (6–8)	High School (9–12)
Phonemic Awareness				
Word Analysis				
Fluency				
Vocabulary/ Oral Language				

Comprehen-sion				
Writing				
Spelling				
Other **(e.g., Content-specific; Mathematical literacies; Visual literacies)**				

*Visit **www.learningsciences.com/bookresources** to download a reproducible version of this figure.*

Sample Assessment-Focused Professional Learning Experiences

We suggest that literacy leaders begin by working with teachers at the school or district level and then follow up with small groups of teachers (e.g., grade-level or academic teams) as a means of focusing their work. Although we identify a series of steps for literacy leaders, we recognize that differences in contexts may require leaders to modify these suggested procedures.

The Large-Group Meeting

The purpose of this initial meeting is to introduce teachers to the importance of using data for informing instruction (this meeting could be a school- or district-wide workshop). Following are some suggested steps to make the large-group meeting go smoothly:

- Ask teachers to identify sources of data they find useful individually and to share with others. Share figure 8.1 with participants and have them compare their suggestions with those in the figure (participants may add other sources of data).

- Ask participants to identify which sources might be better for accountability purposes or instructional decision-making purposes. Ask teachers to describe some of the advantages and disadvantages of each data source.

- Describe the need to collect data, interpret it (e.g., "What does it mean? How can it be used to improve instruction?"), and identify instructional implications. Provide teachers with a sample data set that they can use to practice their interpretation skills, perhaps using a specific data analysis protocol (several are suggested in chapter 8, activity 3). Using a data set from your school provides more meaningful data for teachers to analyze.

Follow-Up Questions for the Grade-Level or Academic Team

Although we value the use of multiple measures for making decisions about individual students and instruction, we suggest that literacy leaders begin by working with teachers on a single source of data (e.g., a specific decoding test, student writing samples, reading-response journals, results of a student assignment) as a means of introducing teachers to data analysis procedures and possibilities. Select a source for analysis by taking into consideration these questions: What is a data source valued by your school or district? Which do you want teachers to become especially competent in using? By beginning with a single source, teachers can see the value of analyzing results for individuals and groups of students.

Ask participants to review the data collaboratively, addressing each of the following questions:

- What do these results indicate in terms of student strengths? Needs?

- What do the data mean? Is there a need for additional instruction or a change in instruction? What questions do the data raise?

- Based on analysis, what recommendations for instruction might be useful?

Implementation

Ask teachers to follow the recommendations raised in the data analysis process and be prepared to share results of their implementation efforts at the following meeting (perhaps in a month). As a literacy leader, indicate your availability for helping with implementation efforts or to answer questions.

Individual Support and Feedback

Be prepared to work with individuals who may need modeling or additional support in their implementation efforts.

Developing a Comprehensive Reading Plan: Questions to Consider

Curriculum Questions

- Does the school have a vision and mission for its reading program? Has the school established goals and standards (prekindergarten through twelfth grade)? Has it considered the amount of time for reading instruction at the primary and intermediate levels? The relationship between reading and the other language arts? The role of content-area teachers at all levels but especially at the middle school and high school levels in helping students handle the literacy demands of their classrooms?

- Do standards address the need for a developmental continuum that considers the reader at all stages: emergent, beginning, transitional, intermediate, and skilled reading and writing? Do they recognize the needs of learners at the middle school and secondary levels?

- Are the standards based on what is known about effective reading instruction and assessment? That is, are they evidence-based?

- Do they address the essential elements of effective reading instruction?

- Have materials, print and nonprint, been selected that enable teachers to address the goals? Do these materials address the needs of all learners (e.g., struggling readers, ELs, and so on)? Do they provide for the varying reading levels of students? Is a variety of materials available (e.g., narrative, informational, poetry, and so on)? Do they provide students with opportunities to understand their own backgrounds and that of others?

- Is there a written framework or guide that makes the curriculum visible and usable?

Instruction Questions

- Has consideration been given to how reading instruction will be organized, including allocation of time to reading at different levels? How the differing needs of students will be met? Grouping options? Materials? Additional time? Additional support of specialized professionals?

- Is there coordination and coherence among all the reading programs in the school (e.g., the core, the programs for struggling readers, ELs, and so on)?

- Are teachers given opportunities to gain knowledge and understanding of the current research and literature about effective reading instruction? Is there coherence between the written curriculum of the school and actual classroom practices?

Assessment Questions

- Is there an assessment system (prekindergarten through twelfth grade) that is coordinated across the grades? Is there provision for outcome measures? Screening measures? Diagnostic measures? Progress-monitoring measures?

- Is there alignment between the standards of the district and the assessment system (i.e., is the assessment system measuring what is being taught)?

- Do the assessment measures address high level cognitive thinking?

- Do the classroom assessment measures assist teachers in instructional decision making? Do they assist teachers in identifying the needs of the struggling readers, ELs, and high achievers?

Process-for-Change Questions

- Is the committee or group assigned the task of developing the comprehensive reading plan a representative one? That is, does it include constituents at all levels? To what extent are teachers involved in the curriculum-development process? Have they had opportunities to discuss their beliefs and understandings and learn more about how reading can be taught effectively?

- Is there leadership support for the development of the comprehensive reading plan? Is time provided for meeting, and are the necessary resources available to members of the group? Do leaders encourage and support the work of the members of the group?

- Is there a process for sharing the plan with all those in the school and for obtaining feedback from those not directly involved in the development of the plan?

- Have teachers been provided with the professional development they need to implement the program effectively? Does this professional development include opportunities for support and feedback (e.g., literacy coaching)?

- Does the professional development provide teachers with opportunities to learn from each other and collaborate? In other words, are teachers working together, so that change can occur at the school level?

- Are administrators supportive and involved in the change effort? Do they understand what is required of their teachers, so that they can provide the necessary support?

Source: Reprinted by permission of the publisher. From Shelley B. Wepner, Dorothy S. Strickland, and Diana J. Quatroche, eds., The Administration and Supervision of Reading Programs, 5th Ed. *New York: Teachers College Press. Copyright © 2014 by Teachers College, Columbia University. All rights reserved.*

Action-Planning Guide

Literacy leaders might use the following matrix as a planning guide, supporting their collaborative identification of change goals, action steps, timelines, initiative leaders, resources, and evidence of change.

Element	Priority (What is the goal?)	Action Steps (Who will do what? How?)	Timeline	Lead Person	Resources Needed	Evidence of Implementation and Impact
Standards and Goals						
Curriculum and Instruction						

Element	Priority (What is the goal?)	Action Steps (Who will do what? How?)	Timeline	Lead Person	Resources Needed	Evidence of Implementation and Impact
Assessment						
Professional Learning for Teachers						

continued →

Element	Priority (What is the goal?)	Action Steps (Who will do what? How?)	Timeline	Lead Person	Resources Needed	Evidence of Implementation and Impact
Community Involvement						
Other						

*Visit **www.learningsciences.com/bookresources** to download a reproducible version of this figure.*

An Adapted Data-Driven Dialogue Protocol From Hudson High School

This protocol was used by the Hudson High School Literacy Action Team to analyze the results of the CALS (available for free online at http://adlitpd.org/category/assess/). The protocol was adapted from the Data Driven Dialogue protocol designed by School Reform Initiative Affiliates (http://schoolreforminitiative.org/doc/data_driven_dialogue.pdf) and reprinted here with permission from Hudson teachers and leaders.

Our objective for examining the data from the teacher survey is to understand our colleagues' perceptions, practices, and professional development needs regarding literacy. Along with the student survey, it will guide our literacy action plan. To keep us focused on the task and on the data, we will use the following protocol to examine the survey. Adapted from a School Reform Initiative protocol, the three-part process aims to "replace hunches and feelings with data-based facts . . . and generate 'root-cause' discussions that move from identifying symptoms to possible causes."

Phase I: Predictions—5 Minutes—On Your Own

Before examining the survey, reflect privately and record several of your preliminary thoughts about the data. During this time, you activate prior knowledge, surface assumptions, and make predictions, thus creating readiness to examine and discuss the data. You hear and honor all assumptions and ideas as "building blocks for new learning." One or more of the following thought-starters may be helpful:

- "I predict . . . "
- "I wonder . . . "

- "My questions/expectations are influenced by . . . "
- "I hope to find out . . . "

Phase II: Observations—15 Minutes—On Your Own

Study the data privately and record several of your observations:

- "I observe . . . "
- "Some patterns I notice . . . "
- "I can count . . . "
- "I am surprised to see . . . "

Phase III: Sharing Observations—15 Minutes— In Small Groups

Note only the facts that you can observe in the data. Conjectures, explanations, conclusions, and inferences are off-limits. You may make statements about quantities (e.g., "Over half the teachers . . . ") and the presence of certain specific information or numerical relationships between ideas (e.g., "Over 90 percent of the teachers feel that . . . ")

Phase IV: Inferences Dialogue—15 Minutes—In Small Groups

Now, you can:

- Generate multiple explanations for your Phase III observations
- Propose solutions and responses

Phase V: Whole-Team Inference Dialogue—20 Minutes—As a Whole Team

Finally, we'll share our discussions with the whole team. While keeping the conversation grounded in the data, we'll discuss the following questions:

- What general patterns are we observing?

- What areas of need are we identifying, and how might we meet these needs?

- What will be our goals when looking at the survey data by subject area?

- What else do we need to know, and how can we find it out?

- How might we share the data and our findings with teachers?

References

Afflerbach, P. (2014, May). *What's new in literacy teaching?: Assessment.* Paper presented at the annual meeting of the International Reading Association, New Orleans, LA.

Afflerbach, P., Kim, J., Crassas, M. E., & Cho, B. (2011). Best practices in literacy assessment. In L. M. Morrow & L. B. Gambrell (Eds.), *Best practices in literacy instruction* (4th ed., pp. 319–340). New York, NY: Guilford Press.

Alexander, K. L., Entwisle, D. R., & Olson, L. S. (2001). Schools, achievement, and inequality: A seasonal perspective. *Educational Evaluation and Policy Analysis, 23*(2), 171–191.

Allen, D., & Blythe, T. (2004). *The facilitator's book of questions: Tools for looking together at student and teacher work* (2nd ed.). New York, NY: Teachers College Press.

Allen, D., & Blythe, T. (2015). *Facilitating for learning: Tools for teacher groups of all kinds.* New York, NY: Teachers College Press.

American Education Research Association. (2005). Research points. *Teaching teachers: Professional development to improve student achievement, 3*(1) [Brochure]. Washington, DC: Author.

American Statistical Association. (2014). *ASA statement on using value-added models for educational assessment.* Retrieved from American Statistical Association website: https://www.amstat.org/policy/pdfs/ASA_VAM_Statement.pdf

Argyris, C., & Schön, D. A. (1974). *Theory in practice: Increasing professional effectiveness.* San Francisco, CA: Jossey-Bass.

Argyris, C., & Schön, D. A. (1996). *Organizational learning II: Theory, method and practice.* Reading, MA: Addison-Wesley.

Barton, P. E., & Coley, R. J. (2010). *The black-white achievement gap: When progress stopped.* Retrieved from Educational Testing Service website: https://www.ets.org/Media/Research/pdf/PICBWGAP.pdf

Bean, R. M. (2014). Developing a comprehensive reading plan (preK–grade 12). In S. B. Wepner, D. S. Strickland, & D. Quatroche (Eds.), *The administration and supervision of reading programs* (5th ed., pp. 11–29). New York: Teachers College Press.

Bean, R. M. (2015). *The reading specialist: Leadership and coaching for the classroom, school, and community* (3rd ed.). New York, NY: Guilford Press.

Bean, R. M., Dole, J. A., Nelson, K. L., Belcastro, E., & Zigmond, N. (2015). The sustainability of a national reading reform initiative in two states. *Reading and Writing Quarterly: Overcoming Learning Difficulties, 31*(1), 30–55.

Bean, R. M., Draper, J. A., Hall, V., Vandermolen, J., & Zigmond, N. (2010). Coaches and coaching in Reading First schools. *Elementary School Journal, 111*(1), 87–114.

Bean, R. M., Kern, D., Goatley, V., Ortlieb, E., Shettel, J., Calo, K., et al. (2015). Specialized literacy professionals as literacy leaders: Results of a national survey. *Literacy Research and Instruction, 54*(2), 83–114.

Bean, R., & Lillenstein, J. (2012). Response to intervention and the changing roles of schoolwide personnel. *The Reading Teacher, 65*(7), 491–501.

Bean, R. M., & Swan Dagen, A. (Eds.) (2012). *Best practices of literacy leaders: Keys to school improvement.* New York, NY: Guilford Press.

Bean, R. M., Turner, G. H., & Belski, K. (2002). Implementing a successful America Reads Challenge tutoring program: Lessons learned. In P. E. Linder, M. B. Sampson, J. Dugan, & B. Brancato (Eds.), *24th yearbook of the College Reading Association* (pp. 169–187). Easton, PA: College Reading Association.

Beck, I. L., & Beck, M. (2013). *Making sense of phonics: The hows and whys* (2nd edition). New York: Guilford Press.

Beck, I. L., McKeown, M. G., & Kucan, L. (2002). *Bringing words to life: Robust vocabulary instruction.* New York, NY: Guilford Press.

Bennis, W. (2009). *On becoming a leader* (4th ed.). Philadelphia, PA: Basic Books.

Berebitsky, D., Goddard, R. D., & Carlisle, J. F. (2014). An examination of teachers' perceptions of principal support for teacher change and teachers' collaboration and communication around literacy in Reading First schools. *Teachers College Record, 116*(4), 1–28.

Beresik, D. L., & Bean, R. M. (2002). Teacher practices and the Pennsylvania system of school assessment. *Pennsylvania Reads: Journal of the Keystone State Reading Association, 111*(11), 16–29.

Bernhardt, V. L. (2013). *Data analysis for continuous school improvement* (3rd edition). New York, NY: Routledge.

Biancarosa, G., Bryk, A. B., & Dexter, E. (2010). Assessing the value-added effects of Literacy Collaborative professional development on student learning. *Elementary School Journal, 111*(1), 7–34.

Biancarosa, G., & Snow, C. E. (2006). *Reading next—A vision for action and research in middle and high school literacy: A report to Carnegie Corporation of New York* (2nd ed.). Washington, DC: Alliance for Excellent Education. Retrieved from Carnegie Corporation of New York website: www.carnegie .org/media/filer_public/b7/5f/b75fba81-16cb-422d-ab59-373a6a07eb74 /ccny_report_2004_reading.pdf

Black, P. J., & Wiliam, D. (1998). Assessment and classroom learning. *Assessment in Education: Principles, Policies, and Practice, 5*(1), 7–73.

Bond, N. (2015). *The power of teacher leaders: Their roles, influence, and impact.* New York, NY: Routledge.

Boudett, K. P., & City, E. A. (2014). *Meeting wise: Making the most of collaborative time for educators.* Cambridge, MA: Harvard Education Press.

Boutte, G. S., & Johnson, G. L. (2014). Community and family involvement in urban schools. In H. R. Milner & K. Lomotey (Eds.), *Handbook of Urban Education* (pp. 167–187). New York, NY: Routledge.

Bradford, D. L., & Cohen, A. R. (1997). *Managing for excellence: The guide to developing high performance in contemporary organizations.* New York: John Wiley & Sons.

Bradford, D. L., & Cohen, A. R. (1998). *Power up: Transforming organizations through shared leadership.* New York: John Wiley & Sons.

Breidenstein, A., Fahey, K., Glickman, C., & Hensley, F. (2012). *Leading for powerful learning: A guide for instructional leaders.* New York, NY: Teachers College Press.

Brock, C. H., Goatley, V. J., Raphael, T. E., Trost-Shahata, E., & Weber, C. M. (2014). *Engaging students in disciplinary literacy, K-6: Reading, writing, and teaching tools for the classroom.* New York, NY: Teachers College Press.

Bryk, A. S. (2015). 2014 AERA distinguished lecture: Accelerating how we learn to improve. *Educational Researcher, 44*(9), 467–477.

Bryk, A. S., Sebring, P. B., Allensworth, F. E., Luppescu, S., & Easton, J. A. (2010). *Organizing schools for improvement: Lessons from Chicago.* Chicago, IL: University of Chicago Press.

Buly, M., & Valencia, S. (2002). Below the bar: Profiles of students who fail state reading assessments. *Educational Evaluation and Policy Analysis, 24*(3), 219–239.

Burton, E. (2013, January 8). Parent involvement in early literacy [Web log post]. Retrieved from www.edutopia.org/blog/parent-involvement-in-early -literacy-erika-burton

Carnegie Council on Advancing Adolescent Literacy. (2010). *Time to act: An agenda for advancing adolescent literacy for college and career success.* New York, NY: Carnegie Corporation of New York.

Carroll, K. (2007). *Conversations with coaches: Their roles in Pennsylvania Reading First schools* (Unpublished doctoral dissertation). University of Pittsburgh, Pittsburgh, PA.

Castek, J., & Gwin, C. B. (2012). Technology in the literacy program. In R. M. Bean & A. S. Dagen (Eds.) *Best practices of literacy leaders: Keys to school improvement.* New York: Guilford Press.

Chapin, S. H., O'Connor, C., & Anderson, N. C. (2013). *Classroom discussions in math: A teacher's guide for using talk moves to support the Common Core and more, grades K–6: A multimedia professional learning resource* (3rd ed.). Sausalito, CA: Math Solutions.

City, E. A. (2007). Is coaching the best use of resources? For some schools, other investments should come first. *Harvard Education Letter, 23*(5), 6–7.

Coburn, C. E., & Woulfin, S. L. (2012). Reading coaches and the relationship between policy and practice. *Reading Research Quarterly, 47*(1), pp. 5–30.

Cochran-Smith, M., & Lytle, S. L. (2009). *Inquiry as stance: Practitioner research for the next generation.* New York, NY: Teachers College Press.

Coiro, J. (2009). Promising practices for supporting adolescents' online literacy development. In K. D. Wood & W. E. Blanton (Eds.), *Promoting literacy with adolescent learners: Research-based instruction* (pp. 442–471). New York, NY: Guilford Press.

Coiro, J. (2015). The magic of wondering: Building understanding through online inquiry. *The Reading Teacher, 69*(2), 189–193.

Coleman, A. L., Negron, F. M., & Lipper, K. (2011). *Achieving educational excellence for all: A guide to diversity-related policy strategies for school districts.* Retrieved from www.nsba.org/educationexcellenceforall

Coles, G. (2003). *Reading the naked truth: Literacy, legislation, and lies.* Portsmouth, NH: Heinemann.

Collins, J. (2001). *Good to great.* New York, NY: HarperCollins.

Constantino, S. M. (2008). *101 ways to create real family engagement.* Galax, VA: ENGAGE! Press.

Costa, A., & Garmston, R. (2002). *Cognitive coaching: A foundation for renaissance schools* (2nd ed.). Norwood, MA: Christopher-Gordon.

Danielson, C. (2006). *Teacher leadership that strengthens professional practice.* Alexandria, VA: ASCD.

Darling-Hammond, L. (2010). *The flat world and education: How America's commitment to equity will determine our future.* New York: Teachers College Press.

Deussen, T., Coskie, T., Robinson, L., & Autio, E. (2007). *"Coach" can mean many things: Five categories of literacy coaches in Reading First* (Issues & Answers Report, REL 2007-No. 005). Washington, DC: US Department of Education, Institute of Education Sciences, National Center for Education Evaluation and Regional Assistance, Regional Educational Laboratory Northwest. Retrieved from http://ies.ed.gov/ncee/edlabs/regions/northwest/pdf/rel_2007005.pdf

Dewitz, P., Leahy, S. B., Jones, J., & Sullivan, P. M. (2010). *The essential guide to selecting and using core reading programs.* Newark, DE: International Reading Association.

Dobbs, C. L. (2013). Vocabulary in practice: Creating word-curious classrooms. In J. Ippolito, J. F. Lawrence, & C. Zaller (Eds.), *Adolescent literacy in the era of the Common Core: From research into practice* (pp. 73–83). Cambridge, MA: Harvard Education Press.

Dole, J. (2004). The changing role of the reading specialist in school reform. *The Reading Teacher, 57*(5), 462–471.

Donaldson, M. L., Johnson, S. M., Kirkpatrick, C. L., Marinell, W. H., Steele, J. L., & Szczesiul, S. A. (2008). Angling for access, bartering for change: How second-stage teachers experience differentiated roles in schools. *Teachers College Record, 110*(5), 1088–1114.

Drago-Severson, E. (2009). *Leading adult learning: Supporting adult development in our schools.* Thousand Oaks, CA: Corwin Press.

DuFour, R. (2004). What is a "professional learning community"? *Educational Leadership, 61*(8), 6–11.

Dumay, X. (2009). Origins and consequences of schools' organizational culture for student achievement. *Educational Administration Quarterly, 45*(4), 523–555.

Duncan, M. (2006). *Literacy coaching: Developing effective teachers through instructional dialogue.* Katonah, NY: Richard C. Owen Publishers.

Edwards, P. A., Paratore, J. R., & Sweeney, J. S. (2014). Working with parents and the community. In S. B. Wepner, D. S. Strickland, & D. J. Quatroche (Eds.), *The administration and supervision of reading programs* (5th ed., pp. 214–222). New York: Teachers College Press.

Elish-Piper, L., & L'Allier, S. (2011). Examining the relationship between literacy coaching and student reading gains in grades K–3. *Elementary School Journal, 112*(1), 83–106.

Elmore, R. F. (2004). *School reform from the inside out: Policy, practice, and performance.* Cambridge, MA: Harvard Education Press.

Epstein, J., Sanders, M. G., Sheldon, S., Simon, B. S., Salinas, K. C., Jansorn, N. R., . . . Williams, K. J. (2009). *School, family, and community partnerships: Your handbook for action* (3rd ed.). Thousand Oaks, CA: Corwin Press.

Evans, R. (2007). The authentic leader. In *The Jossey-Bass Reader on Educational Leadership* (2nd ed.). San Francisco, CA: Jossey-Bass.

Fahey, K., & Ippolito, J. (2015). *Towards a general theory of SRI's intentional learning communities.* Retrieved from School Reform Initiative website: http://www.schoolreforminitiative.org/wp-content/uploads/2014/02/SRI _General_Theory_ILC_print.pdf

Fixsen, D. L., Naoom, S. F., Blasé, K. A., Friedman, R. M., & Wallace, F. (2006). *Implementation research: A synthesis of the literature* (FMHI Publication No. 231). Tampa, FL: University of South Florida Louis de al Parte Florida Mental Health Institute: National Implementation Research Network.

Frost, S., & Bean, R. M. (2006). *Qualifications for literacy coaches: Achieving the gold standard.* Retrieved from www.literacycoachingonline.org/briefs /literacycoaching.pdf

Fullan, M. (1993). *Change forces: Probing the depths of educational reform.* Levittown, PA: The Falmer Press, Taylor & Francis.

Fullan, M. (2001). *The new meaning of educational change* (3rd ed.). New York: Teachers College Press.

Garmston, R. (2005). *The presenter's handbook: A practical guide* (2nd ed.). Norwood, MA: Christopher-Gordon.

Gawande, A. (2011, October 3). Personal best. *The New Yorker.*

Genest, M. T. (2014). Reading is a BLAST! Inside an innovative literacy collaboration between public schools and the public library. *Reading Horizons, 53*(1), 4.

Genest, M. T., & Bean, R. M. (2007). *Bringing libraries and schools together (BLAST): A collaborative program between Carnegie Library of Pittsburgh and the Pittsburgh Public School District (year 5)* (Unpublished technical report).

Gladwell, M. (2000). *The tipping point: How little things can make a big difference.* New York, NY: Little, Brown.

Goldstein, J. (2009). Designing transparent teacher evaluation: The role of oversight panels for professional accountability. *The Teachers College Record, 111*(4), 893–933.

Graham, S., & Perin, D. (2007). *Writing next: Effective strategies to improve writing of adolescents in middle and high schools—a report to Carnegie Corporation of New York.* Washington, DC: Alliance for Excellent Education. Retrieved from www.carnegie.org/media/filer_public/3c/f5/3cf58727-34f4-4140-a014 -723a00ac56f7/ccny_report_2007_writing.pdf

Grierson, A. (2011, April). *Walking the talk: Supporting teachers' growth with differentiated professional learning.* Paper presented at the annual conference of the American Educational Research Association. New Orleans, LA.

Guskey, T. R., & Yoon, K. S. (2009). What works in professional development? *Phi Delta Kappan, 90*(7), 495–500.

Hamilton, L., Halverson, R., Jackson, S., Mandinach, E., Supovitz, J., & Wayman, J. (2009). *Using student achievement data to support instructional decision making* (NCEE 2009-4067). Washington, DC: National Center for Education Evaluation and Regional Assistance, Institute of Education Sciences, Department of Education. Retrieved from http://ies.ed.gov/ncee /wwc/pdf/practice_guides/dddm_pg_092909.pdf

Hamilton, R. L. (1993). *Chapter I: Reading instruction: Exemplary reading specialists in an in-class model* (Unpublished doctoral dissertation). University of Pittsburgh, Pittsburgh, PA.

Heifetz, R., Grashow, A., & Linsky, M. (2009). *The practice of adaptive leadership: Tools and tactics for changing your organization and the world.* Cambridge, MA: Harvard Business Press.

Hemphill, F. C., & Venneman, A. (2011). *Achievement gaps: How Hispanic and white students in public schools perform in mathematics and reading on the national assessment of educational progress* (NCES 2011-459). Washington, DC: National Center for Education Statistics, Institute of Education Sciences, US Department of Education.

Henderson, A., & Mapp, K. (2002). *A new wave of evidence: The impact of school, family, and community connections on student achievement* (Annual Synthesis). Austin, TX: National Center for Family and Community Connections with Schools, Southwest Educational Development Laboratory.

Hersey, P., & Blanchard, K. (1977). *Management of organizational behavior: Utilizing human resources* (3rd ed.). Englewood Cliffs, NJ: Prentice-Hall.

Hirsch, E. D. (2006). *The knowledge deficit: Closing the shocking education gap for American children.* New York: Houghton Mifflin.

Hynd-Shanahan, C., Holschuh, J., & Hubbard, B. (2004). Thinking like a historian: College students' reading of multiple historical documents. *Journal of Literacy Research, 36*(2), 141–176.

IDEO LLC. (2012). *Design thinking for educators* (2nd ed.). Retrieved from www.designthinkingforeducators.com

International Literacy Association. (2015). *Multiple roles of specialized literacy professionals: Position statement.* Newark, DE: Author.

International Reading Association. (2000). *Making a difference means making it different: Honoring children's rights to excellent reading instruction.* Newark, DE: Author.

International Reading Association. (2004). *The role and qualifications of the reading coach in the United States: A position statement of the International Reading Association.* Newark, DE: Author. Retrieved from www.literacyworldwide. org/docs/default-source/where-we-stand/reading-coach-position-statement .pdf?sfvrsn=6

International Reading Association. (2006). *Standards for middle school and high school literacy coaches.* Newark, DE: Author. Retrieved from www .literacyworldwide.org/get-resources/standards/standards-for-literacy-coaches

International Reading Association. (2012a). *Adolescent literacy: A position statement of the International Reading Association.* Newark, DE: Author. Retrieved from www.literacyworldwide.org/docs/default-source/where-we-stand/adolescent -literacy-position-statement.pdf?sfvrsn=8

International Reading Association. (2012b). *Literacy implementation guidance for the ELA Common Core State Standards.* Newark, DE: Author. Retrieved from http://literacyworldwide.org/docs/default-source/where-we-stand/ela -common-core-state-standards-guidance.pdf?sfvrsn=8

International Reading Association. (2013). *Formative assessment: A position statement of the International Reading Association.* Newark, DE: Author.

International Reading Association. (2014). *Using high-stakes assessments for grade retention and graduation decisions: A position statement of the International Reading Association.* Newark, DE: Author.

International Society for Technology in Education (2007). ISTE Standards for students. Retrieved from www.iste.org/standards/ISTE-standards/standards-for-students

Ippolito, J. (2009). Principals as partners with literacy coaches: Striking a balance between neglect and interference. *Literacy Coaching Clearinghouse.* Retrieved from http://www.literacycoachingonline.org/briefs/Principals_as_Partners.pdf

Ippolito, J. (2010). Three ways that literacy coaches balance responsive and directive relationships with teachers. *The Elementary School Journal, 111*(1), 164–190.

Ippolito, J. (2012). As literacy coach positions disappear "coaching" doesn't have to. *New England Reading Association Newsletter, 3*(2), 5–7.

Ippolito, J. (2013). Professional learning as the key to linking content and literacy instruction. In J. Ippolito, J. F. Lawrence, & C. Zaller (Eds.), *Adolescent literacy in the era of the Common Core: From research into practice* (pp. 235–249). Cambridge, MA: Harvard Education Press.

Ippolito, J., Lawrence, J. F., & Zaller, C. (Eds.) (2013). *Adolescent literacy in the era of the Common Core.* Cambridge, MA: Harvard Education Press.

Ippolito, J., & Lieberman, J. (2012). Reading specialists and literacy coaches in secondary schools. In R. M. Bean & A. S. Dagen (Eds.), *Best practices of literacy leaders: Keys to school improvement* (pp. 63–85). New York, NY: Guilford Press.

Ippolito, J., & Pomerantz, F. (2013–2014). Protocols as essential tools for literacy professional learning communities in the common core era. *Massachusetts Reading Association Primer, 42*(2), 44–55. Retrieved from School Reform Initiative website: http://www.schoolreforminitiative.org/wp-content/uploads/2014/02/IppolitoPomerantzMRAFinal_to_Ruth.pdf

Jerald, C. (2005). *The implementation trap: Helping schools overcome barriers to change* (policy brief). Washington, DC: The Center for Comprehensive School Reform and Improvement.

Johnson, D. W., & Johnson, F. P. (2003). *Joining together: Group theory and group skills* (8th ed.). Boston, MA: Allyn-Bacon.

Kaner, S. (2014). *The facilitator's guide to participatory decision-making* (3rd ed.). San Francisco: Jossey-Bass.

Kaner, S., & Berger, D. (n.d.). The role of the facilitator. Retreived from http://enrapkscurriculum.pbworks.com/f/Role+of+Facilitator+-+Sam+Kaner.pdf

Kapinus, B. (2014). Assessing students' reading achievement. In S. B. Wepner, D. S. Strickland, & D. J. Quatroche (Eds.), *The administration and supervision of reading programs* (pp. 135–144). New York, NY: Teachers College Press.

Kegan, R. (1998). *In over our heads: The mental demands of modern life.* Cambridge, MA: Harvard University Press.

Kinnucan-Welsch, K., Rosemary, C. A., & Grogan, P. R. (2006). Accountability by design in literacy professional development. *The Reading Teacher, 59*(5), 426–435.

Klein, A. (2015, November 30). ESEA reauthorization: The every student succeeds act explained [Web log post]. Retrieved from http://blogs.edweek.org/edweek/campaign-k-12/2015/11/esea_reauthorization_the_every.html

Leana, C. R. (2011). The missing link in school reform. *Stanford Social Innovation Review, 9*(4), 30–35.

Leana, C. R., & Pil, F. K. (2006). Social capital and organizational performance: Evidence from urban public schools. *Organization Science, 17*(3), 353–366.

Learning Forward. (2010). Key points in Learning Forward's definition of professional development. *Journal of Staff Development, 31*(6), 16–17.

Learning Forward. (n.d.). *Standards for professional learning: Quick reference guide.* Retrieved from http://learningforward.org/docs/pdf/standardsreferenceguide.pdf

Leithwood, K., & Jantzi, D. (2008). Linking leadership to student learning: The contributions of leader efficacy. *Educational Administration Quarterly, 44*(4), 496–528.

Leithwood, K., & Mascall, B. (2008). Collective leadership effects on student achievement. *Educational Administration Quarterly, 44*(4), 529–561.

Lewis-Spector, J., & Jay, B. (2011). *Leadership for literacy in the 21st century.* Association of Literacy Educators and Researchers. Retrieved from http://c.ymcdn.com/sites/www.aleronline.org/resource/resmgr/files/aler_white_paper_on_literacy.pdf

Lieberman, A., & Miller, L. (2004). *Teacher leadership.* San Francisco, CA: Jossey-Bass.

Lortie, D. C. (1975). *Schoolteacher: A sociological study* (2nd ed.). Chicago: University of Chicago Press.

Louis, K. S., Leithwood, K., Wahlstrom, K. L., & Anderson, S. E. (2010). *Investigating the links to improved student learning: Final report of research findings* (Unpublished document). Duluth, MN: University of Minnesota.

MacDonald, E. (2011). When nice won't suffice: Honest discussion is key to shaping school culture. *Journal of Staff Development, 32*(3), 45–51.

Mangin, M. M., & Dunsmore, K. (2015). How the framing of instructional coaching as a lever for systemic or individual reform influences the enactment of coaching. *Educational Administration Quarterly, 51*(2), 179–213.

Mangin, M. M., & Stoelinga, S. R. (Eds.). (2008). *Effective teacher leadership: Using research to inform and reform.* New York: Teachers College Press.

Marzano, R. J. (2003). *What works in schools: Translating research into action.* Alexandria, VA: Association for Supervision and Curriculum Development.

Matsumura, L. C., Garnier, H. E., Correnti, R., Junker, B., & Bickel, D. D. (2010). Investigating the effectiveness of a comprehensive literacy coaching program in schools with high teacher mobility. *The Elementary School Journal, 111*(1), 35–62.

Matsumura, L. C., Garnier, H. E., & Spybrook, J. (2013). Literacy coaching to improve student reading achievement: A multi-level mediation model. *Learning and Instruction, 25*, 35–48.

Matsumura, L. C., Sartoris, M., Bickel, D. D., & Garnier, H. (2009). Leadership for literacy coaching: The principal's role in launching a new coaching program. *Educational Administration Quarterly, 45*(5), 655–693.

McDonald, J. P. (2014). *American school reform: What works, what fails, and why.* Chicago: University of Chicago Press.

McDonald, J. P., Mohr, N., Dichter, A., & McDonald, E. C. (2013). *The power of protocols: An educator's guide to better practice* (3rd ed.). New York: Teachers College Press.

McGill-Franzen, A., Lanford, C., & Adams, E. (2002). Learning to be literate: A comparison of five urban early childhood programs. *Journal of Educational Psychology, 94*(3), 443–464.

McKenna, M. C., & Walpole, S. (2008). *The literacy coaching challenge: Models and methods for grades K–8.* New York: Guilford Press.

McLaughlin, M. W. (1990). The RAND change agent study revisited: Macro perspectives and micro realities. *Educational Researcher, 19*(9), 11–16.

McTighe, J., & Wiggins, G. (2012). *From Common Core standards to curriculum: Five big ideas.* Retrieved from: https://grantwiggins.files.wordpress .com/2012/09/mctighe_wiggins_final_common_core_standards.pdf

Meltzer, J., & Jackson, D. (2010). *Guidelines for developing an effective district literacy action plan* (version 1.1). Malden, MA: Massachusetts Department of Elementary and Secondary Education and Public Consulting Group. Retrieved from Massachusetts Department of Elementary and Secondary Education website: http://www.doe.mass.edu/literacy/presentations /LiteracyGuidelines.pdf

Messina, L. (2013). Disciplinary literacy in practice: The disciplinary literacy network as vehicle for strengthening instruction across content areas. In J. Ippolito, J. F. Lawrence, & C. Zaller (Eds.), *Adolescent literacy in the era of the Common Core: From research into practice* (pp. 37–60). Cambridge, MA: Harvard Education Press.

Mezirow, J. (2000). *Learning as transformation: Critical perspectives on a theory in progress.* San Francisco, CA: Jossey-Bass.

Michener, C. J., & Ford-Connors, E. (2013). Research in discussion: Effective support for literacy, content, and academic achievement. In J. Ippolito, J. F. Lawrence, & C. Zaller (Eds.), *Adolescent literacy in the era of the Common Core* (pp. 85–102). Cambridge, MA: Harvard Education Press.

Moje, E. B. (2015). Doing and teaching disciplinary literacy with adolescent learners: A social and cultural enterprise. *Harvard Educational Review, 85*(2), 254–278.

Moll, L. (2000). The diversity of schooling: A cultural-historical approach. In M. Reyes & J. Halcon (Eds.), *The best for our children: Critical perspectives on literacy for Latino students* (pp. 29–47). New York, NY: Teachers College Press.

Moran, M. C. (2007). *Differentiated literacy coaching: Scaffolding for student and teacher success.* Alexandria, VA: ASCD.

Nater, S., & Gallimore, R. (2006). *You haven't taught until they have learned: John Wooden's teaching principles and practices.* West Virginia: Fitness Information Technology.

National Assessment of Educational Progress. (2015). *Nation's Report Card in reading and math.* Retrieved from www.nationsreportcard.gov/reading _math_2015/#reading?grade=4

National Center for Literacy Education. (2014). *Remodeling literacy learning together: Paths to standards implementation.* Urbana, Illinois: National Council of Teachers of English. Retrieved from www.literacyinlearning exchange.org/remodeling-together

National Council of Teachers of English (2013). *Framework for 21st century curriculum and assessment.* Washington, DC: Author. Retrieved from www.ncte.org/positions/statements/21stcentframework

National Education Association. (n.d.). *Wraparound services: An NEA policy brief.* Washington, DC: Author.

National Governors Association Center for Best Practices & Council of Chief State School Officers (2010). *Common Core State Standards.* Washington, DC: Authors.

National Institute of Child Health and Human Development. (2000). *Teaching children to read: An evidence-based assessment of the scientific research literature on reading and its implications for reading instruction* (NIH Publication No. 00-4769). Washington, DC: US Government Printing Office. Retrieved from www.nichd.nih.gov/publications/pubs/nrp/documents/report.pdf

Nielson, D. C., Barry, A. L., & Staab, P. T. (2008). Teachers' reflections on professional change during a literacy-reform initiative. *Teaching and Teacher Education, 24*(5), 1288–1303.

Paratore, J. R., Steiner, L. M., & Dougherty, S. (2014). Developing effective home-school literacy partnerships. In R. M. Bean & A. S. Dagen (Eds.), *Best practices of literacy leaders: Keys to school improvement* (pp. 317–336). New York, NY: Guilford Press.

Pennsylvania Department of Education. (2012). *The comprehensive literacy plan: Keystones to opportunity.* Retrieved from http://static.pdesas.org/content /documents/PA%20Comprehensive%20Literacy%20Plan.pdf

Perkins, D. (2014). *Future wise: Educating our children for a changing world.* San Francisco, CA: Jossey-Bass.

Peterson, D. S., Taylor, B. M., Burnham, B., & Schock, R. (2009). Reflective coaching conversations: A missing piece. *The Reading Teacher, 62*(6), 500–509.

Phillips Galloway, E., Lawrence, J. F., & Moje, E. B. (2013). Research in disciplinary literacy: Challenges and instructional Opportunities in teaching disciplinary texts. In J. Ippolito, J. F. Lawrence & C. Zaller (Eds.), *Adolescent literacy in the era of the Common Core* (pp. 13-36). Cambridge, MA: Harvard Education Press.

Printy, S. (2008). Leadership for teacher learning: A community of practice perspective. *Educational Administration Quarterly, 44*(2), 187–226.

PTA. (2008). *National standards, goals, and indicators for family-school partnerships.* Retrieved from PTA website: https://www.pta.org/files/National_Standards _2.pdf

Pushor, D., & Ruitenberg, C. (2005) *Parent engagement and leadership.* Saskatoon, SK: Dr. Stirling McDowell Foundation for Research into Teaching Inc. Retrieved from www.mcdowellfoundation.ca/main_mcdowell/projects /research_rep/134_parent_engagement.pdf

Quatroche, D. J., Bean, R. M., & Hamilton, R. L. (2001). The role of the reading specialist: A review of research. *The Reading Teacher, 55*(3), 282–294.

Rainville, K. N., & Jones, S. (2008). Situated identities: Power and positioning in the work of a literacy coach. *The Reading Teacher, 61*(6), 440–448.

Reed, M. (2015). To find solutions, look inward. *Educational Leadership.* Retrieved from www.ascd.org/publications/educational-leadership/jun15/vol72 /num09/To-Find-Solutions,-Look-Inward.aspx

Reeves, D. B. (2009). *Leading change in your school: How to conquer myths, build commitment, and get results.* Alexandria, VA: Association for Supervision and Curriculum Development.

Risko, V. J., & Vogt, M. E. (2016). *Professional learning in action: Inquiry for teachers of literacy.* New York, NY: Teachers College Press.

Scharmer, C. O. (2009). *Theory U: Learning from the future as it emerges.* San Francisco, CA: Berrett-Koehler.

Schein, E. H. (2010). *Organizational culture and leadership* (4th ed.). San Francisco, CA: Jossey-Bass.

Schmoker, M. (2011). *Elevating the essentials to radically improve student learning.* Alexandria, VA: Association for Supervision and Curriculum Development.

Schön, D. A., & Rein, M. (1994). *Frame reflection: Toward the resolution of intractable policy controversies.* New York, NY: Basic Books.

Shanahan, T., & Shanahan, C. (2008). Teaching disciplinary literacy to adolescents: Rethinking content-area literacy. *Harvard Educational Review, 78*(1), 40–59.

Shanahan, T., & Shanahan, C. (2012). What is disciplinary literacy and why does it matter? *Topics in Language Disorders, 32*(1), 7–18.

Shanahan, C., & Shanahan, T. (2014). Does disciplinary literacy have a place in elementary school? *The Reading Teacher, 67*(8), 636–639.

Shanahan, C., Shanahan, T., & Misischia, C. (2011). Analysis of expert readers in three disciplines: History, mathematics, and chemistry. *Journal of Literacy Research*, *43*(4), 393–429.

Smith, A. T. (2007). The middle school literacy coach: Considering roles in context. In D. W. Rowe et al. (Eds.), *56th yearbook of the national reading conference* (pp. 53–67). Oak Creek, WI: National Reading Conference.

Smith, A. T. (2009). Considering literacy coaching responsibilities in terms of teacher change. *Literacy Coaching Clearinghouse*. Retrieved from http://www.literacycoachingonline.org/briefs/coaching_trajectory_a_smith.pdf

Stiggins, R. J. (2014). Improve assessment literacy outside of schools too. *Phi Delta Kappan*, 96(2), 67–72.

Stiggins, R., & Chappuis, J. (2005). Using student-involved classroom assessment to close achievement gaps, *Theory into Practice*, *44*(1), 11–18.

Stigler, J. W., & Hiebert, J. (1999). *The teaching gap: Best ideas from the world's teachers for improving education in the classroom*. New York, NY: Free Press.

Supovitz, J., Sirinides, P., & May, H. (2010). How principals and peers influence teaching and learning. *Educational Administration Quarterly*, *46*(1), 31–56.

Swan Dagen, A., & Bean, R. M. (2014). High-quality, research-based professional development: An essential for enhancing high-quality teaching. In L. E. Martin, S. Kragler, D. J. Quatroche, & K. L. Bauserman (Eds.). *Handbook of professional development in education: Successful models and practices, preK–12* (pp. 42–63). New York: Guilford Press.

Taylor, B. (2011). *Catching schools: An action guide to school wide reading improvement*. Portsmouth, NH: Heinemann.

Taylor, B. M., Raphael, T. E., & Au, K. H. (2011). Reading and school reform. In M. L. Kamil, P. D. Pearson, E. B. Moje, & P. Afflerbach (Eds.), *Handbook of reading research* (Vol. 4, pp. 594–628). New York: Routledge.

Timperley, H. (2008). Teacher professional learning and development. Brussels, Belgium: International Academy of Education. Retrieved from www.ibe.unesco.org/fileadmin/user_upload/Publications/Educational_Practices/EdPractices_18.pdf

Timperley, H. (n.d.). *Using evidence in the classroom for professional learning*. Paper presented to the Ontario Education Research Symposium. Retrieved from https://cdn.auckland.ac.nz/assets/education/about/schools/tchldv/docs/Using%20Evidence%20in%20the%20Classroom%20for%20Professional%20Learning.pdf

Toll, C. A. (2006). Separating coaching from supervising. *Teachers Teaching Teachers, 2*(4), 1–4.

Torgeson, J. K., & Miller, D. H. (2009). *Assessments to guide adolescent literacy instruction.* Portsmouth, NH: RMC Research Corporation, Center on Instruction.

U.S. Department of Education. (2011). *Teachers' ability to use data to inform instruction: Challenges and supports.* Washington, DC: Author.

Vanderburg, M., & Stephens, D. (2010). The impact of literacy coaches: What teachers value and how teachers change. *The Elementary School Journal, 111*(1), 141–163.

Vescio, V., Ross, D., & Adams, A. (2008). A review of research on the impact of professional learning communities on teaching practice and student learning. *Teaching and Teacher Education, 24,* 80–91.

Vogt, M. E., & Shearer, B. A. (2010). *Reading specialists and literacy coaches in the real world* (3rd ed.). Boston, MA: Pearson.

Walpole, S., & Beauchat, K. A. (2008). *Facilitating teacher study groups.* Denver, CO: Literacy Coaching Clearinghouse. Retrieved from www.literacycoaching online.org/briefs/StudyGroupsBrief.pdf

Walpole, S., & McKenna, M. C. (2009). Everything you wanted to know about literacy coaching but were afraid to ask: A review of policy and research. In K. M. Leander, D. W. Rowe, D. K. Dickinson, R. T. Jimenez, M. K. Hundley, & V. J. Risko (Eds.), *Fifty-ninth yearbook of the National Reading Conference* (pp. 23–33). Milwaukee, WI: National Reading Conference.

Warren, M. R. (2005). Communities and schools: A new view of urban education reform. *Harvard Educational Review, 75*(2), 133–173.

Wasley, P. A., Hampel, R. L., & Clark, R. W. (1997) *Kids and school reform.* San Francisco: Jossey-Bass.

Welch, S. (2010). *10-10-10: A fast and powerful way to get unstuck in love, at work, and with your family.* New York: Scribner.

Wigfield, A., & Guthrie, J. T. (2000). Engagement and motivation in reading. *Handbook of Reading Research, 3,* 403–422.

Zigmond, N., Bean, R. M., Kloo, A., & Brydon, M. (2011) Policy, research, and reading first. In A. McGill-Franzen & R. L. Allington (Eds.), *Handbook of reading disability research* (pp. 464–476). New York, NY: Routledge.

Zwiers, J., & Crawford, M. (2011). *Academic conversations: Classroom talk that fosters critical thinking and content understandings.* Portland, ME: Stenhouse.

Index

A

active listening, 76
assessment
    cycle, 143
    definition of, 136
    high stakes, 138–141
    large-scale, 138–141
    literate in, 138
    purpose of, 136–137
ATLAS protocol, 146

B

Bill of Assessment Rights, 146, 147
book club, 129
bubble children, 140

C

capital
    human, 59–61, 64–66
    matrix, 61
    social, 59–61
coaching
    as activity rather than role, 2
    assumptions about, 13–17
    basic beliefs about, 2–3
    the case for, 1–18
    case studies, 207–224
    culture conducive to, 13
    definition of, 5
    develop teacher capacity, 14
    developing relationships, 83–89
    differentiating experiences, 9–12
    directive, 104
    effective, 2, 5, 6, 9, 29, 66,76, 85, 203, 211, 222
    gaining momentum, 2
    goal of, 5
    large group, 126–128
    mindsets and roles, 8–9
    nonevaluative, 13–14
    pathways into, 4–5
    and the principal, 67–70
    responsive, 104
    small group, 119–121
    stances, 107–109
    thinking about individuals and systems, 7
coaching mindsets, 19–36
    thinking like an advocate, 19, 31–35
    thinking like a designer, 19, 29–31
    thinking like a facilitator, 19, 26–29
    thinking like a leader, 19, 20–26
Coalition for Community Schools, 181
Common Core State Standards (CCSS), 3, 16, 39, 40, 41, 45, 48, 51, 53, 140, 168, 169, 197, 218
communication, 76–79
    with families, 178–181
Consultancy protocol, 80

Content Area Literacy Survey (CALS), 160–161, 218–220

Content-area Reading Initiative (CRI), 213–217

Continuum, 82

co-teaching, 95–97

culture, 6, 57–74
    artifacts, 58
    assessment, 148, 150
    espoused values, 58
    importance of, 59–61
    toxic, 115
    underlying assumptions, 59

D

data
    analysis, 162
    collection tools, 160–161
    for decision making, 64, 142
    to improve instruction, 141–146
    to improve school and district, 147–150
    meetings, 130, 144, 145
    sources of, 137

DiMartino, Linda, 13, 22, 23, 83, 84, 125

disciplinary literacy, 3, 5, 16, 42, 45, 46–50, 88, 97, 119, 155, 193, 194, 197, 202, 212–217

discussion-based protocols, 79–82

discussion questions, 158, 253–255

diversity, 64–66

double-loop learning, 8, 22

Dynamic Indicators of Basic Early Literacy Skills (DIBELS), 209–210

E

Eisenberg, Ellen, 140, 220

Elementary and Secondary Education Act (ESEA), 138

English learner(s), 17, 66

Evans, Robert, 21, 22, 191

Every Student Succeeds Act (ESSA), 138–139

F

Framework for Thinking and Working Like a Coach, 2, 5, 6–13, 17, 19, 58, 225–230

G

Gawande, Atul, 2, 12

grant writing, 184–185

H

Hardisty, Fran, 49, 175, 177

heroic leadership, 189

Hudson High School, 160–161

I

implementation, 164–167
    roadblocks, 165
    solutions, 165

International Literacy Association, 4, 11, 27, 139, 169, 188, 194, 196

K

Kegan, Robert, 23, 24, 25, 191

knowledge domains, 190–194

L

leadership, 20–26, 63
    authentic, 21
    balancing commitments, 22
    managing versus leading, 20–22
    stance, 25–26, 27, 28

learning walks, 130–131

Levels of Intensity, 6, 9, 10–11, 12, 26, 82, 92, 102

literacy leader(s)
    as advocates, 31–36, 141, 168, 173, 189, 199, 204
    as experts, 188–190
    Melinda, xvi, 1–2, 19, 37, 57, 75, 91, 93, 113, 135–136, 153, 173, 187
    observing teachers, 97–111
    supporting the principal, 69–70

using standards, 38–40

working with communities, 174, 175–177, 181–184

working with families, 174, 176, 178–181

working with groups, 113–133

working with specialized professionals, 71–72

working with teachers, 75–90, 91–112

literacy leadership team, 156–157

literacy plan, 162–164

   dual focus, 170–171

   materials, 168–170

M

Magee, Shauna, 3, 82, 129

Mead, Margaret, 154

modeling, 93–95

N

National Alliance for Excellent Education, 197

National Center for Literacy Education, 14, 17

National Core Arts Standards, 47

National Council for the Social Studies, 47

National Council of Teachers of English, 47, 196, 201

National Council of Teachers of Mathematics, 47

National Implementation Research Network, 164

National Science Teachers Association, 47

needs assessment process, 154, 159–162

nonverbal communication, 76

norms, 116–117, 122

O

observation, 97–111

   analysis of, 103–105

   cycle, 99

   post-observation conversation, 105–111

   pre-observation conversation, 100

   strategies for, 101–103

P

Parent Academy, 179

Partnership for Assessing Readiness for College and Careers, 140

Pennsylvania Institute for Instructional Coaching (PIIC), 203, 220–224

professional learning, 9–12

professional learning community (PLC), 128–129

professional organizations, literacy-focused, 195–196

Put Into Practice, xvi, 32, 61, 71, 87, 95, 97, 119, 122, 147, 148, 165, 175

Q

questioning techniques, 76–79

R

Reading First, 27, 62, 95, 166, 167, 209, 210, 211

Reflect, xvi, 12, 26, 41, 44, 50, 73, 150

S

self-assessment, 146–147

   rubric, 197–200

   tools, 201–203

shifts in literacy instruction, 40–44

single-loop learning, 8, 20

Smarter Balanced Assessment Consortium, 140

Steinbacher-Reed, Christina, 66, 167, 195, 208

study group, 129

sustainability, 166–167

T

technology, 51–54

   helping teachers learn, 53

   strategies to support students, 52

tenet 1, 7

tenet 2, 8–9

tenet 3, 9–12

tenet 4, 13

Toothman, Tracy, 49, 175, 177

Turner, Marsha, 32, 93, 114, 123, 190

V

Vietmeier, Annette, 49, 175, 177

vignette, xvii

Voices From the Field, 3, 13, 23, 32, 49,
      66, 82, 84, 93, 114, 125, 129, 140,
      167, 175, 177, 190, 195

W

ways of knowing, 24–26, 106, 107, 126,
      198

   instrumental, 24–26, 106, 107, 109,
      110, 126, 198

   self-authoring, 24–26, 106, 108, 111,
      198

   socializing, 24–26, 106, 107, 108, 111,
      126, 198

Welch, Suzy, 124

Winter Meeting, 196

Wooden, John, 135